Vigilante Feminists and Agents of Destiny

Children and Youth in Popular Culture

Series Editor: Debbie Olson, Missouri Valley College

Children and Youth in Popular Culture features works that interrogate the various representations of children and youth in popular culture, as well as the reception of these representations. The series is international in scope, recognizing the transnational discourses about children and youth that have helped shape modern and post-modern childhoods and adolescence. The scope of the series ranges from such subjects as gender, race, class, and economic conditions and their global intersections with issues relevant to children and youth and their representation in global popular culture: children and youth at play, geographies and spaces (including World Wide Web), material cultures, adultification, sexuality, children of/in war, religion, children of diaspora, youth and the law, and more.

Advisory Board

LuElla D'Amico, Whitworth University; Markus P. J. Bohlmann, Seneca College; Vibiana Bowman Cvetkovic, Rutgers University; Adrian Schober, Australian Catholic University, Melbourne

Vigilante Feminists and Agents of Destiny

Violence, Empowerment, and the Teenage Super/heroine

Laura Mattoon D'Amore

LEXINGTON BOOKS
Lanham • Boulder • New York • London

Published by Lexington Books
An imprint of The Rowman & Littlefield Publishing Group, Inc.
4501 Forbes Boulevard, Suite 200, Lanham, Maryland 20706
www.rowman.com

6 Tinworth Street, London SE11 5AL, United Kingdom

British Library Cataloguing in Publication Information Available

Library of Congress Cataloging-in-Publication Data

Names: D'Amore, Laura Mattoon, author.
Title: Vigilante feminists and agents of destiny : violence, empowerment, and the teenage super/heroine / Laura Mattoon D'Amore.
Description: Lanham : Lexington, 2021. | Series: Children and youth in popular culture | Includes bibliographical references and index. | Summary: "This book tracks the vigilante feminist teenage super/heroine in comics and YA literature, a character who acts as a vigilante on behalf of the protection of girls and women. It traces the trajectory of super/heroines who experience violent trauma and are subsequently empowered by use of violence to reclaim control over their lives and bodies"-- Provided by publisher.
Identifiers: LCCN 2020058593 (print) | LCCN 2020058594 (ebook) | ISBN 9781793630605 (cloth) | ISBN 9781793630612 (epub) | 9781793630629 (pbk)
Subjects: LCSH: Women superheroes in literature. | Young adult fiction, American--History and criticism. | Comic books, strips, etc.--United States--History and criticism. | Vigilantes in literature. | Teenage girls in literature. | Women in literature. | Violence in literature.
Classification: LCC PN1009.5.S77 D36 2021 (print) | LCC PN1009.5.S77 (ebook) | DDC 741.5/3522--dc23
LC record available at https://lccn.loc.gov/2020058593
LC ebook record available at https://lccn.loc.gov/2020058594

To Sophie and Lola, for whom the world must become a better place.

Table of Contents

Acknowledgments

The research and development of the arguments in this book took me on a long journey. I began presenting conference papers on violence and empowerment in fairy tale revisions and comics in 2012, and slowly over time began to home in on this thread of the vigilante feminist super/heroine. For their valuable feedback along the way, I am grateful to the national conferences organized by the National Women's Studies Association, Film and History, Popular Culture/American Culture Association, and Berkshire Conference on Histories of Women, Genders, and Sexualities. Exposure to each of these conferences deepened and enriched my thinking on various pieces of the book project, because interdisciplinary as it is, it was important for me to get it in front of audiences and panelists who had adjacent expertise in various facets of the project. In particular, I want to thank Area Chair manager Cindy Miller at Film and History for always being supportive of my ideas and helping me find a home to explore them at the conference. As well, Nicole Freim, Area Chair for Comic Art and Comics, and Robin Gray Nicks, past Area Co-Chair for Fairy Tales, for giving me the opportunity over the past years to present my papers in front of the vast array of experts that each of their areas draws. I also want to thank Cristina Bacchilega and Anne Duggan, editors of *Marvels and Tales: Journal of Fairy-Tale Studies*, and Pauline Greenhill, for their invaluable feedback on the article that inspired this book, "Vigilante Feminism: Revising Trauma, Abduction, and Assault in American Fairy-Tale Revisions." Knowing that the central argument held up to their scrutiny was the push I needed to expand the project.

I was fortunate to receive funding for my sabbatical archive research, and valuable course releases, from the Foundation to Promote Scholarship and Teaching at Roger Williams University. With that funding, I was able to travel to the Ray & Pat Browne Library for Popular Culture Studies at Bowling Greene State University in August 2017 to access their phenomenal comics archive. The staff there, Dr. Nancy Down and Steve Ammidown, made it so easy to be a researcher, pulling anything I needed and having it ready when I arrived. The library itself was a cozy and inspirational space to get inspired to really get writing. Though I had conference papers prepared since 2012, it was Fall 2017, during my sabbatical, that clarity on the organization of the book and commencement of the writing began in earnest.

This book has also been developed and honed with my students at Roger Williams University in mind. I created four courses from my research on this project over the years, including "Fairy Tales and Feminism," "Super/heroines in American Popular Culture," "Vigilante Women," and "Me Too." Each and every semester that I have the good fortune to teach one of those classes, I am always inspired by the ways that my students interact with the material. They have helped clarify focal points by the kinds of questions they had, and by the kinds of conversations that emerged in those spaces. This book is, after all, about girls, and having the opportunity to engage with college age women not far out of girlhood themselves keeps this material present and relevant for me.

I am also grateful to Judith Lakamper, Associate Acquisitions Editor at Lexington Books, for her early and persistent interest in publishing this project. As well, Shelby Russell, Assistant Editor at Lexington Books, who helped fine tune so many of the details along the way. Publishing with Lexington Books has been a truly gratifying and enjoyable experience. It was an honor, too, to be invited by Debbie Olsen to be part of the *Children and Youth in Popular Culture* book series, which will mean that my book will be part of a community of scholars doing really interesting, innovative, and cutting edge interdisciplinary work.

Last, I thank my family for their support throughout the research and writing process. They were troopers when they agreed to make Ohio our August vacation destination the year that I did archival research, so that I could spend the time I needed in the archives and still be able to spend some valuable summer time with them. My two daughters were the catalyst for my writing a book that centers on girls and theorizes about the ways that scholars can take the perspectives of girls seriously. They are young feminists, share my love of heroines who kick-butt, and are inspired by stories of agency. Their optimism and resilience in a world that is hostile to girls and women is powerful, and they are an inspiration to me and to the work that I am doing.

Introduction

I am a fan of girls and women who kick ass, in life as well as in popular culture. I am a mother whose daughters feel an affinity to girls who fight in young adult literature, comics, film, and television. I am also a teacher who has watched young women have the same reaction to kick-ass girls and women when I teach them in class. I have never been satisfied with feminist analyses of the relationship between violence, agency, and empowerment in super/heroine narratives (in this book, "super/heroine" refers to representations that are based on comic book superheroines, as well as those that are based on heroines from YA fantasy literature), because so often the critique is that, for something to be *truly* feminist, it must be peaceful, collective, and/or make systemic changes to oppressive structures. Much feminist theorizing about popular culture has gotten caught up in analysis of the "male gaze," the sexualization of the super/heroine body, and the ways in which they read superheroines as reinforcing, rather than dismantling, patriarchy. There are important issues laid bare by such critiques, such as the lack of women writers, directors, producers, and editors, that reinforces a male-centered landscape of cultural production. But when we are thinking about representation, in particular representations that are *about* teenage girls, and which are predominantly *consumed* by girls and young women, we should not hold the subject, nor the audience, to an idealized version of feminist theory that is unattainable to them. By theorizing from that standpoint, scholars essentially erase the agency and voice of the audience, which consumes these characters through a feminist lens that is contemporary and mainstream, not historically centered and obscure. Studying the girl subject compels scholars to take a different approach, one that more closely aligns with the lives and values of girls and young women. Doing so provides us with a resistive, oppositional framework through which to read the super/heroine, one which recognizes

1

agency and empowerment in the representations of girls and young women that are usually overpowered by the interpretation of more dominant voices.

This book examines the ways in which the use of violence is experienced as agency and empowerment for the characters of girls and young women who are victims of trauma, abduction, assault, and sexual violence in comics and young adult fantasy literature. The teenage super/heroines examined in this book are characters who have the ability—through super power, or supernatural and magical ability—to fight back against those who seek to cause them harm. We like strong heroines in this cultural moment. We seek them, feel empowered by them. We are attracted to stories of strength, of overcoming, of triumph in the face of tragedy, of evil, of trauma. As Jeffrey A. Brown describes in *Beyond Bombshells*, "audiences in this new millennium have demonstrated that they want to see women kick ass, and they are willing to pay to enjoy the heroic exploits of female characters . . . but, as with any wide-ranging trend in popular culture, [the heroine] also needs to be considered as more than just a harbinger of evolving gender politics" (J. A. Brown 2015, 6). This book explores what is at stake when violence is used as a mechanism for growth and character-development, in the face of sexual violence, abduction, and trauma; when the systems that purport to protect girls and women fail, and the only satisfactory response is a violence that feels cathartic, like relief. This investment in fantasy violence can feel restorative, healing, fulfilling, and we know that it strikes a chord because of the immense popularity of these characters, the ones who embrace, rather than reject, their violent gifts.

This book takes seriously this notion of empowerment as agentic, especially in its relationship to young adults. In critical feminist discourse, "empowerment" often raises critiques about its personal, and short-lived nature. To feel empowered by something is, perhaps, not the same as empowerment, especially when examining the difference between how one girl, or even a group of girls, feels compared to real, measurable, actionable social change. To empower, or to be empowered, is not the same as to feel empowerment. However, "[e]merging research in the areas of psychology and neuroscience points to the importance of stories in everyday life, how stories shape personality, develop empathy, create community, change minds, and alter consciousness" (J. M. Del Negro 2017, ix). The feeling of empowerment that girls get from interacting with stories has positive effects on the way they conceptualize their real lives, like they can take on the world with a little more courage and confidence as a result of this material. Furthermore, "viewing television shows with storylines about sexual violence can lead to a better understanding of consent, lessen victim-blaming, and increase bystander intervention" (Cruger 2017, 127). We can also gauge this by listening to fans, or by experiencing the emotional connection to fantasy material ourselves.

Sujin Huggins explores a variety of reasons why stories are important to the lives of young adults, including "emotional responses ('individual contemplation,' 'the creation of bonds,' 'encourages emotional release'), psychological advantages ('aids in the search for identity,' 'aids in developing value systems'), and intellectual development ('aids in developing the imagination, listening skills, language skills, and discrimination/critical thinking'), as well as sociocultural awareness ('establishing a sense of belonging,' and 'preserving traditions and cultures')" (Huggins 2017, 1). These feelings connect audiences and readers to the texts they consume and provide a sense of belonging. Jessica Kokesh and Miglena Sternadori found that young readers "often identify with and form parasocial relationships with characters in the novels, idolize their favorite characters, but some (especially those in their early teens) also believe the majority of events described in the novels to be true to life" (Kokesh and Sternadori 2015, 139). The girls interviewed in their study show that readers see themselves in "characters experiencing situations, thoughts, and feelings highly similar to their own," become strongly emotionally attached to characters in books, and feel as though they are active "participants in the books and in the characters' lives" (Kokesh and Sternadori 2015, 151–152). They learned that girls find that "books 'help you' in becoming socially adept because readers can 'kind of learn from' a character's mistakes" (Kokesh and Sternadori 2015, 154). And, in scholarship about young adult development, stories have a substantial impact on the ways that young adults interpret and interact with real life stressors. The literature also demonstrates that young adults can parse out the difference between real life and fantasy, and that they are savvy about the differences in what is acceptable behavior in the realm of fantasy versus their real world. The feeling of empowerment provided by these vigilante characters in popular literature and culture matters.

There is a major gap between scholarship about girls and young women, and that scholarship's relevance to the lives of actual girls and young women. When we are talking about massively produced, widely-read characterizations, scholars must find a way to come into conversation with the ways in which readers and audiences conceptualize their own feminist lenses. Furthermore, the characters explored in this book are dealing directly with violence against girls and women. They are fantasy variations of real life problems of sexual violence, abduction, assault, and trauma, and as such it is critically important to explore the ways in which the characters themselves navigate that terrain. Katherine Cruger explains that "[a] distinguishing characteristic of the YA genre is hope. Narratives about individuals who are survivors of sexual violence do have the potential to provide hope for readers that they can recover too" and that "researchers have found that narratives surrounding victims of sexual violence can have a positive impact" (Cruger 2017, 126–127). Mere criticism of these cultural productions as neo-liberal, postfeminist, or worse, anti- or counter-feminist does not take into account the relevance of these characters, in this particular cultural moment, to girls and women who find them cathartic or personally fulfilling in other ways. As Kokesh and Sternadori explain, "Identification is one of the main mechanisms through which people develop their social attitudes and construct their identities," and such identification often comes from imagining oneself as the character in a narrative, taking on their "thoughts, emotions, behaviors, goals and traits as if they were one's own" (Kokesh and Sternadori 2015, 142). This book reads superheroines for what they *do* for girls and young women, not what they fail to do.

To do this work, I have conceptualized a characterization that is particular and unique to the super/heroine genre: the vigilante feminist. The characters are all, themselves, vigilante girls and young women. They exist in violent spaces where girls and young women are assaulted and abducted, and they take on the role of protectors against that violence. They are forced to do so outside the parameters of law and society (as vigilantes), because the institutions that are supposed to protect them against violence—and bring justice to aggressors—have systemically failed them. As well, this feminism performs as a sort of vigilante or outlaw, because it exists at the edge of what is considered acceptably (dogmatically, theoretically) feminist. For example, it is nearly always violent, but not for the sake of dominating or taking power. It is violence against violence—a corrective action taken against those who harm girls and women.

We are living in a rape culture. This is a reality of American culture and society in the twenty-first century. Despite centuries of feminist movement, women and girls[1] continue to feel unsafe, living by a "rape schedule" which forces them to alter their daily lives in order to limit their chances of sexual assault (Valenti 2007). Whether it is carrying our keys in our hands when we walk home so that we have a makeshift weapon in case we are attacked; or locking the doors of our cars as soon as we get inside in case someone has followed us; or choosing clothing that might let us remain inconspicuous so that we are not harassed or catcalled on the street, women and girls live their lives against the backdrop of fear. This fear is so normalized, so culturally ingrained, that it might not even be something we consciously recognize. Popular culture reflects historical moments, as well as their attendant cultural anxieties, and so the proliferation and popularity of strong female characters in film, television, comics, and literature who can fight their attackers is unsurprising in this context. Of this phenomenon in film, Tiina Vares writes in "Action Heroines and Female Viewers: What Women Have to Say," that "women employ physical feats usually reserved for male heroes, they get even in the face of victimization and oppression, and act autonomously on their own and other women's behalf. Violent action and physical display, although offensive to some female viewers, appear to tap into others' fantasies of power" (Vares 2001, 219). One space to examine this representation is through the super/heroine who battles villains who threaten abduction or assault. Claiming agency over their own lives and bodies, these young women seek alternative paths to justice that fall outside of law and policy, taking on the position of a violent vigilante—traditionally the purview of righteous men—to deeply unsettle the structures of power implicit in patriarchy. Their existence as vigilante feminist super/heroines serves as a fantasy corrective to the powerlessness experienced by those who feel like passive participants in their own disempowerment.

An especially thought-provoking barometer of the popularity of this characterization is through the examination of teenage super/heroines who have been envisioned for twenty-first century audiences. When the creation of a super/heroine happens during a cultural moment like our present, the vigilante feminist super/heroine's battle becomes an ideological one, on behalf of girls and women, fighting against the social and political forces that desire to possess and contain them. This book examines teenage vigilante feminist super/heroine characters that are found across television, film, young adult literature, and comics; it is, in fact, the ubiquity of the character type across genres that makes it especially relevant to feminism and popular culture. Brown articulates that "the marked increase in adolescent heroines is also an indication of a younger generation's acceptance and desire for strong female characters . . . the [young heroine] still grapples with discrimination, sexism, and gender expectations, but she presents a fantasy of overcoming all these factors that try to limit her" (J. A. Brown 2015, 11). Specifically, this book explores the stories of Feyre Archeron, from *A Court of Thorns and Roses*, a YA fantasy novel series by Sarah J. Maas; Scarlett March and Gretchen Kassel, from the Retold Fairytales YA fantasy novel series by Jackson Pearce; Laura Kinney/X-23, a Marvel teenage superheroine who has been part of the Avengers, the X-Men, and the X-Force, as well as the lead in her own comic titles; and Jules and Ophelia from *Sweet/Vicious*, an MTV television series, in which two young women in college take on the role of vigilantes to fight back against men who get away with sexual assault on their campus. Reading these characters as vigilantes working to protect girls and young women from brutality and violence situates them as agents of what I am naming "vigilante feminism," at the intersection of the justice-seeking vigilante with the equality-seeking feminist.

This book considers girls and women in comics, YA literature, film, and television who use violence in a world in which superpowers and/or magic exist. These characters could be defined, especially in comics, as superheroines, who are heroic characters who possess extraordinary or superhuman powers. Though the area can sometimes be murky, superheroines are generally set apart from supervillains by their tendency to do "good," instead of "evil." Similarly, this text considers heroines in fairy tale revisions and YA fantasy literature who embody superheroine-like characteristics. For example, Feyre Archeron, in the *Court of Thorns and Roses* series of books (which loosely retells the fairy tale "Beauty and the Beast"), possesses great skill and cunning with which she saves the Faerie Realm while a mere human. When circumstances coalesce to turn Feyre into a Faerie, she develops a wide range of superpowers such as manipulation of the elements of water, air, and fire; teleportation of herself and others; shapeshifting; and flying. She uses her power and her position to save both the human and faerie realms from destruction by extraordinary magical forces. A character such as Feyre fits into this book because it explores girls and women in popular culture and popular literature who use their extraordinary and/or superhuman abilities in ways that are violent, but which also serve to protect others. Furthermore, in a world in which hundreds of thousands of rape kits go untested by American police precincts, pop culture vigilantes like Jules and Ophelia in MTV's *Sweet/Vicious* find other (often violent) mechanisms of ensuring that rapists no longer rape (Staff 2016).

VIGILANTE FEMINIST

I use "vigilante feminist" in this book to describe the characters that I am writing about who take on the role of the vigilante for feminist ends. This is complicated terrain, because vigilantism by definition utilizes threat, force, and violence, and historically many feminists have named those as weapons of the patriarchy. When women have tried to claim those acts as empowering, they have been labeled postfeminist, or have been accused of misunderstanding feminist principles. As Alison Graham-Bertolini writes in *Vigilante Women*, "Perhaps most prominent in feminist studies are active proponents of passive resistance . . . [who] believe that violence should never be an option, and that to engage in violence is to adopt the erroneous behavior of the oppressor" (Graham-Bertolini 2011, 164–165). There is a lot of discomfort in talking about the ways that violence functions proactively in the lives of girls and women, and it can lead to rather dogmatic, blanket statements that violence is never "the way." This book problematizes that tendency, in order to come into conversation with the girls and young women who are drawn to texts about vigilante feminist characters, and who feel vicarious catharsis in their violent acts.

In *Full Frontal Feminism* (2007), Jessica Valenti describes the "rape schedule" by which all women live. It is, as she describes,

> a constant fear of rape (conscious or not), [when] women do things throughout the day to protect themselves. Whether it's carrying our keys in our hands as we walk home, locking our car doors as soon as we get in, or not walking down certain streets, we take precautions. . . . It's essentially like living in a

prison—all the time. We can't assume we're safe anywhere: not on the streets, not in our homes. And we're so used to feeling unsafe that we don't even see that there's something seriously fucked up about it. (Valenti 2007, 63)

Today's girls and young women have grown up in a world in which feminism has successfully broken down many barriers, but in which they continue to feel unsafe. There is potential to consider the vigilante feminist teenage super/heroines of today as emblematic of a specific kind of physically powerful feminism in which girls and young women can take care of themselves in ways, often violent, that allow them to protect themselves from the danger that lurks around every corner.

In her groundbreaking 1984 text, *Feminist Theory from Margin to Center*, bell hooks defines feminism simply: "Feminism is the struggle to end sexist oppression." Her text warns against the oversimplification of feminism as an "'anything goes' approach to the definition of the word [that] has rendered it practically meaningless. What is meant by 'anything goes' is usually that any woman who wants social equality with men regardless of her political perspective . . . can label herself feminist" (hooks 1984, 25). hooks reiterates these ideas in *Writing Beyond Race* (hooks 2013), and in her dialogue with Laverne Cox, hosted at The New School, in 2015 (hooks 2015). hooks' main critique of a feminism that focuses on the social equality of women with men is that it fails to recognize the interconnected ways that "race and class . . . in conjunction with sexism, determine the extent to which an individual will be discriminated against, exploited or oppressed" (hooks 1984, 25). hooks recognizes that oppressions are interwoven, and that an end to oppression for one must be an end to oppression for all. In *Feminism is for Everybody* (2000), hooks directly connects violence to both cultural domination and patriarchal thinking (hooks 2000, 113).[2]

In their popular cultural representations, vigilante feminist super/heroines respond to patriarchal violence that is directly related to the violent world in which they—and their audiences—exist. Feminist critiques have tended to villainize choices like these, which reform, rather than dismantle, the conditions of oppression that girls and women struggle against. Thinking about the vigilante as a sort of "militarized" characterization of the super/heroine, we can think about the ways that feminist theorists have imagined women's relationship to the military. For example, Ilene Rose Feinman explores the theoretical and practical disparity between feminist antimilitarists and feminist egalitarian militarists in her text, *Citizenship Rites*, which examines gender equality through women's access to military combat. North American feminist antimilitarists argue that "masculinist militarism depend[s] on the oppression of women," and that militarism is opposite to women's culture and feminist goals and an impediment to "justice and peace" (Feinman 2000, 1). In contrast, feminist egalitarian militarists "insist that it is women's right and even responsibility to perform martial service, because the military is the *sine qua non* of full citizenship, and thus, equality" (Feinman 2000, 1). I argue that this latter argument can be applied more broadly to conceptualizations of equality in culture as bestowed upon those who have access to the arbitration of truth and justice. The vigilante feminist super/heroine represents one who takes on truth and justice, becoming a capable fighter and an agent of her own rescue. This can serve as a fantasy corrective to the feelings of powerlessness that girls and women may experience growing up in a patriarchy.

The vigilante feminist super/heroine's practice, as the performance of violence against violence, does not neatly fit within the context of feminism's historic anti-violence stance. Individually, a vigilante feminist might be criticized for using the "master's tools," which, as Audre Lorde wrote, "will never dismantle the master's house. They may allow us temporarily to beat him at his own game, but they will never enable us to bring about genuine change" (Lorde 2007, 332). Furthermore, Cynthia Enloe, in theorizing linkages between militarization and patriarchy, cautions that "Patriarchy is the system that links militarized femininities to militarized masculinities in a way that sustains the domination of certain brands of masculinity while keeping women in their assigned places" (Cockburn and Enloe 2012, 4). For Enloe, militarized women reinscribe gender roles and norms that maintain male hegemony, because rather than changing the game they are joining it. However, in the case of the vigilante feminist super/heroine, the difference is that their violent actions are disrupting dominance, because they are a response to a pervasive rape culture of violence against girls and women against which they are unprotected. By protecting themselves and others and seeking justice where justice is absent, they interrupt patriarchal dominance by revising the rules about who gets to wield violence, and for what ends.

In writing about feminism and film violence through analysis of the film *Kill Bill*, Lisa Coulthard notes that "[w]ith the advent of third-wave and postfeminism, the concerns of violence, gender, and representation have shifted in favor of the latter critical framework as a new emphasis on 'post-victim' feminism has transferred attention toward debates about the presence of violent women in cinema and popular culture and away from women as victimized subjects to violence" (Coulthard 2007, 154). This is an important intervention in thinking through the potential linkages between violence and feminism, that we read girls and women as agents of their stories rather than victims of their circumstances. Coulthard also explains that "[i]nterrogations of violence and gender have always been a significant part of film, feminist theory, and film criticism. As a limit and excess that emphasizes the social, political, and ethical dimensions of film reception and representation, violence provides a particularly loaded entry point for questioning shifts, trends, or tropes of gender representation or transgression" (Coulthard 2007, 156).

However, as she teases apart her argument a bit more, she acknowledges the reductive ways that feminist analysis usually approaches the subject of violence. Explaining that violence in film is always questionable or suspect, and framed by ethical and social responsibilities, she writes: "the presence of graphic violence is thus frequently thrown into a discourse of justification or condemnation based on its perceived relation to actual violence, audience identification, and response to character, narration, and style" (Coulthard 2007, 157). The rationale for condemning such violence usually relates to arguments examined earlier, about peaceful resistance or the linkage between militarization and patriarchy. And though I believe that audience identification is a valid reason to be drawn to vigilante feminist violence, the arguments presented in this book do not use audience identification or response as justification for violent acts. The violent action heroine investigated in Coulthard's article does not have the same motivations as the heroines examined in this book. Those heroines are violent for "apolitical, individualistic, and capitalistic celebration," where "the violent action heroine offers the image of innovative or even revolutionary change while disavowing any action engagement with violence and its relation to feminism and female solidarity, collectivity, or political action" (Coulthard 2007, 173). However, the violence wielded by girls in this book is often explicitly related to feminism and female solidarity, it is deeply politicized, and it is wielded toward a greater collective good.

Graham-Bertolini also locates feminist positions that take more proactive stances on women's violent response to violence. Kathleen Martindale, for example, notes "that in some instances passive resistance is not effective in warding off predators or predatory behavior," such as in combating rape and rapists (Graham-Bertolini 2011, 165). Jeffner Allen theorizes that "nonviolence is a patriarchal construct that has been assigned to women because it is ineffective and self-destructive," and that it, in effect, keeps women powerless (Graham-Bertolini 2011, 165). The highly gendered assumption that women should be nonviolent is, itself, a product of the patriarchy, fully intended to "burden women with nonviolence as a defining characteristic because it keeps women in a persistent state of subservience" (Graham-Bertolini 2011, 165). Furthermore, "there are feminists who believe that the laws in place to protect women are not adequate, and that the definition of self-defense needs to be expanded, so that it includes instances of violence used to protect oneself or ones loved ones" (Graham-Bertolini 2011, 165). Graham-Bertolini's book foregrounds the work of women writers who "formulate new relations between [women's] bodies and language, casting women as active subjects and overturning false representations that depict women as being unable to inflict conscious violence" (Graham-Bertolini 2011, 167). Like those in my book, the characters that Graham-Bertolini writes about do not exist in peaceful worlds, and they have been victims of extensive violence themselves. Her analysis is incredibly powerful when she argues that "their violent responses to such treatment free them from the shackles of violent men and/or other violent and damaging patriarchal constraints" (Graham-Bertolini 2011, 168). Her reframing of the relationship between violence, equality, and empowerment speaks to the historical and social contexts in which women make their choices to wield it.

In *Fight Like a Girl*, Megan Seely writes that one reason why women are afraid to fight back is because they are taught that they should not fight back, or even that they are not worth fighting for (Seely 2007, 187). Seely argues that scenes of victimized women in media and popular culture are ubiquitous, creating a culture of fear for women, and desensitizing men to violence against women:

> Why don't we ever hear stories about women who fight back? Instead of this ever-so typical garage scene where the woman runs and falls and becomes a victim, why don't we see her turn around and yell, "Get the fuck away from me!" Why aren't there more movies about girls who kick ass? Why aren't we our own superheroes? Why don't we hear more real life stories of women who defend themselves . . . ? Why don't we hear more stories of the countless women who fight back in the streets, on our campuses, and in our homes? . . . Why don't we learn the history of women warriors? Perhaps if they knew these stories, more girls and women would know their strength, believe in their worth, and not internalize fear-based assumptions about their ability and safety. And maybe more men would learn to appreciate and respect women's strength. A reach? Perhaps. But this vision requires us to imagine a society that does not yet exist. (Seely 2007, 185–186)

Seely reminds us that "women have always been warriors—from Greek and Roman times to the modern day, across the globe and in every culture," but that this part of our history is hidden from girls. She asks, "What would it be like for little girls if they grew up knowing their history as fighters? I wonder how this knowledge would have impacted our self-esteem when it came time to defend ourselves—physically, but also emotionally. We need to reclaim our history as warriors, respect the fight within us, at the same time we seek peaceful resolution. We need to recognize and respect that women fight everyday for safety, self-determination, and freedom" (Seely 2007, 186). In other words, women are not inherently peaceful, and they never have been. It is a mechanism of gendered control, to erase the history of women warriors and replace that with peaceful women. To insist otherwise is to cause harm to the emotional and physical well-being of girls and women who could otherwise be prepared to defend themselves and others against the epidemic of violence that pervades every corner of our consciousness.

The critique that women's use of violence against violence cannot be feminist is outdated, deeply reliant on gender norms that normalize the supposed (and culturally constructed) passivity and compliance of women, and does not take into account the context in which these narratives are being claimed. As Roxana Baldrich explains, "[d]iscourses that describe women as non-violent, peaceful, or pacifying, amongst others, are based on the assumption that there are fundamental differences between what women and what men can do and how they should behave," and that "when women perpetrate violence, their actions are portrayed in ways that emphasize their singularity and deny their agency in their own violence (Baldrich 2014, 6–7). Since 2004, groups of vigilante women have sprung up in countries like India and Mexico, part of a new "global trend of outcries against violence against women, especially against rape, which has been accompanied by the forming of more and more all-female self-defense and vigilante groups" (Baldrich 2014, 12). As Baldrich explains, "vigilantism is a shifting concept that articulates to ever-changing social realities" (Baldrich 2014, 14), but "the motivational factors of the vigilante groups . . . range from abstract values (law, justice, equality, etc.) to much more concrete and determinable reasons (abusive spouses, rapists, harassers, corrupt officials, thieves, etc.) and . . . the women . . . reach beyond prescribed social roles to take action, sometimes for their own protection, sometimes for the protection of others (their children, family, community, etc.), sometimes for a moral ideal" (Baldrich 2014, 18). In other words, it is not only the purview of fiction worlds where girls and women are finding ways to interrupt violence against women with vigilante tactics that take justice into their own hands. These are examples of direct disruptions to violence against women and girls in communities where authorities like law enforcement and government officials leave them unprotected, and unheard.

Writing about Sampat Pal, the founder of the Gulabi (Pink) Gang in Upper Pradesh, India, in 2012, Amana Fontanella-Khan describes the conditions under which a grassroots group of vigilante women can rise to fill a void of justice in the poorest region of the country:

> There is no doubt that a strong Pink Gang is needed now more than ever. The challenge criminal politicians pose is a national problem. . . . This may be why life in India is steadily worsening for women, who suffer the most when the police and judiciary systems are corrupted. Rape is now the fastest growing crime in the country. In the past four decades, the number of reported rapes shot up by 782 percent. Conviction rates, however, are dropping. A similar story is found in domestic violence, which has climbed by 30 percent in the same time period. Across the board, crimes against women have been increasing. . . .
> The scale of the problem, which seems insurmountable, has made Sampat even more bent on social justice . . . "If the problem is big, we must become even bigger than it. In unity there is a lot of power, that is why politicians fear us," she says. (Fontanella-Khan 2013, 264)

The story of Sampat Pal shows that when women organize and collectively get in the way of political machines, they can be heard. Their tactics range from shouting and shaming, to threats of violence and aggressive physical conduct that sometimes leads to violence. And importantly, the Gulabi Gang has the support of their communities, who know that they are helpless against deeply corrupt officials from local to national levels.

Aaronette White and Shagun Rastogi explore the Gulabi Gang and the Mahila Aghadi in "Justice by Any Means Necessary: Vigilantism Among Indian Women," in order to develop a feminist theory of female vigilantism in India. They explain that "the chances of vigilante group activity arise when: (a) overwhelming structural conditions of injustice exist; (b) individual experiences of criminal victimization are experienced collectively; and (c) an atmosphere of everyday violence pervades society" (White and Rastogi 2009, 314). They "adopt a feminist definition of violence to distinguish ethical practices of violence—that involve proportionate punishment in the context of failed or grossly compromised judiciaries that deny due process—from unethical practices of violence that involve murder. . . . We also adopt a feminist definition of justice that includes retributive and restorative components. We argue what is deemed ethical and unethical violence must be judged on a case-by-case basis" (White and Rastogi 2009, 315). Furthermore, "Our feminist definition stresses the ethical legitimacy of violence in the pursuit of collective political ends, when imbalances of power exist between men and women in the context of ineffective and otherwise unresponsive local judiciaries. . . . Postcolonial feminist ethics recognize both the ethical value of specific cultural and social contexts and the importance of the self-determination of feminist goals within those contexts" (White and Rastogi 2009, 315). Their theorization of a feminist definition of violence, including the legitimization of violence toward collective political ends, resonates deeply with the kinds of stories taken up in this book. The girls and women who use violence in this text, who I am calling vigilante feminists, are taking action against pervasive violence in their communities with the hope that they can end that violence for all girls and women. Violence serves as both a personally fulfilling act, where they regain a sense of control over their lives and bodies, and a community act, where their acts intentionally center the quest for the safety of others.

In addition to the Gulabi Gang and the Mahila Aghadi, in recent years other groups have formed to meet this need as well. The Red Brigade in Northern India form groups who protect girls and women from sexual assault (Interesting 2015). In Nigeria, an all-female sector of the Civilian Joint Task Force (CJTF) hunt Boko Haram criminals who have kidnapped and raped girls and women from their villages; the CJTF is known to be more effective in combatting Boko Haram than the Army (Okeowo 2015). In Mexico, female vigilantes have trained themselves to combat femicide, such as "Diana,

The Bus Driver Hunter," in Ciudad Juarez "who avenged the 800 girls and women who had been killed or gone missing at the hands of the city's bus drivers" (Interesting 2015). It is important to note that this book does not intend to characterize violence as inherently preferable to peace in its adoption of the descriptor of the vigilante feminist. Rather, this book starts from the position that women and girls are not living in a peaceful world to begin with, and that the violence of growing up as a girl or woman is an intensely experienced reality for many. Furthermore, the texts examined in this book, where the marker of the vigilante feminist is applied, contain violent spaces, and those spaces have ripped away any sense of agency and control the girls in the stories might otherwise have had. In writing about Indian women, White and Rastogi explain: "Women presented here live under violent circumstances whether they fight back or not; multiple patriarchies inadvertently and repeatedly condone men's violence against women. As a result, some women disrupt this power dynamic by relearning their propensity for violence. Although women reclaiming the ability and right to use force will not by itself end patriarchy, it may be a useful form of empowerment and protection in the short term when accompanied by long-term liberatory vision" (White and Rastogi 2009, 317). They hypothesize the potential for redefining the way that women may reclaim agency over their own lives and communities, which is a mechanism by which to survive the patriarchy—not overthrow it. If we grant as feminist only that which dismantles patriarchy, we fail our girls and young women with definitions that are unreachable and untenable, and which do not include these vigilantes who are deeply empowering, and fighting for them.

This project recognizes and respects feminist positions that coalesce around the critique of patriarchy and sexist oppression, and their concern that young feminists have shifted the focus to individual—rather than systemic—empowerment as feminism's end goal. However, in the quest to understand the popularity of the contemporary vigilante super/heroine in popular culture and literature within the context of the lives of girls and young women today, space must be made to venture into a dialogue with their interpretation of feminism. Recently, there has been a feminist resurgence unlike anything seen among young people in decades, and much of their feminism is being learned through media and journalism, rather than through classic feminist texts. Influenced by writers like Jessica Valenti and Chimamanda Ngozi Adichie, and celebrities who have chosen to use their influential platforms for a social equality-based feminism, such as Beyoncé and Emma Watson, their encounters with feminist rhetoric are deeply intertwined with one's relationship to the personal. For example, Valenti tells young women that they "are hard core feminists, I swear," in her introduction to *Full Frontal Feminism*, and "[o]ne of the best things about feminism is that you don't have to be a professional feminist to take part in the movement. And feminism is something you can be involved with without dedicating your life to it" (Valenti 2007, 238). Adichie dubs herself a "Happy African Feminist Who Does Not Hate Men And Who Likes To Wear Lipgloss And High Heels For Herself And Not For Men" (Adichie 2014). In *We Should All Be Feminists*, Adichie expresses her love of femininity, wielding it as empowering: "I have chosen to no longer be apologetic for my femininity. And I want to be respected in all my femaleness. Because I deserve to be. I like politics and history and am happiest when having a good argument about ideas. I am girly. I am happily girly. I like high heels and trying on lipsticks" (Adichie 2015). Beyoncé says plainly: "I've always considered myself a feminist, although I was always afraid of that word because people put so much on it. . . . When honestly, it's very simple. It's just a person that believes in equality for men and women" (Hare 2014). As the UN Ambassador for the HeForShe campaign to end gender inequality, Emma Watson urged others to "take action against all forms of violence and discrimination faced by women and girls" (Herman 2014). Importantly, Watson's brand of feminism invites men to the table, a subject that younger generations have argued was lacking among their feminist foremothers for more than 175 years.[3] The HeForShe website homepage articulates that "The movement for gender equality was originally conceived as a struggle led only by women for women. In recent years men have begun to stand-up in addressing inequalities and discrimination faced by women and girls" (HeForShe.org 2014). In these contexts, young feminists believe that women have the potential to exist on a level playing field with men, and they believe that a clear path to that equality is through the powerful choices they make as individual women.[4]

These representations of feminism encourage girls and women to believe that they can be whoever they want, that their actions are unlimited, and that their possibilities are endless. Vigilante feminism, as used here, applies specifically to the performance of vigilantism by girls and women who have undertaken their own protection, and the protection of others, against violence—such as sexual assault, abduction, abuse, and trauma—because they have been otherwise failed in that manner. These characters make the choice to be strong on behalf of others, and they actively seek paths of justice that deeply unsettle the structures of power implicit in patriarchy.[5]

Vigilante feminism, as a theory, is reflexive, indicating a version of feminism that itself performs as an outlaw, outside the boundaries of a feminist praxis that has historically been rooted in peace and the eradication of systems of power and dominance. Vigilante feminists aspire to social equality between men and women by taking on the tactics of a traditionally violent masculinity, exploding the gendered assumptions about who appropriately wields violence. As a fantasy characterization it can feel satisfying. Maud Lavin explains that "In my world as a writer and a professor, the existence of cultural representations of aggressive women is part of the support I feel in a self-aware effort to deploy my own aggression effectively" (Lavin 2012, 239). Other women channel this aggression in more physical ways, through martial arts and self-defense. In an essay exploring her feminist awakening through learning karate and empowering herself to "take down" an attacker, Whitney Walker writes that "Equal rights means women should be equal to (not the same as, but equal to) men in all ways—including equal fighters" (Walker 2001, 159). Furthermore, in an article titled "The Importance of Self-Defense Training for Sexual Violence Prevention," Jocelyn A. Hollander explains that martial arts empowers women, and acts as a practical tool in the fight against sexual assault. She writes: "empowerment-based self-defense training helps to change the root conditions that allow violence against women to flourish" (Hollander 2016). Examining the vigilante feminist super/heroines in popular culture connects to a sensibility that some violence can be empowering, and that the empowerment of girls and women is an act of feminist rebellion.

Facing the question of "whose feminism is the right feminism," I have found myself working through feminism's often "contradictory objects and aims." In this, I find clarity in Teresa de Lauretis' theory of "beyond reconciliation," which:

> refuses to be pulled to either side of an opposition. . . . It proceeds . . . [by] upping the "anti": by analyzing the undecidability, conceptual as well as pragmatic, of the alternative as *given*, such critical works release its terms from the fixity of meaning into which polarization has locked them, and reintroduce them into a larger contextual and conceptual frame of reference; the tension of positivity and negativity that marks feminist discourse in its engagement with the social can then displace the impasses of mere "internal" opposition to a more complex level of analysis. (de Lauretis 1993, 319)

Through this way of reading, I resist the temptation to merely label something as feminist/anti-feminist by reading it in the context of its social function. The vigilante feminist super/heroine may not be perfectly feminist; however, the actions of vigilante feminist super/heroines, in the super/heroine re/visions explored in this book, are a response to violence against women, a corrective to a massive imbalance in power, and—for the purposes of the stories—a literal life or death matter. In its social context, it can be read an act of feminist rebellion.

VIOLENCE, AGENCY, AND EMPOWERMENT

In this book I have identified particular characters in fiction who fit the parameters of a teenage vigilante feminist super/heroine, in order to develop a way to talk about all of those identity markers in relation to one another.

The construction as teenage means that this book falls under the parameter of childhood studies, interrogating the identities of children, and in the case of this book specifically, girls and young women. Of those, super/heroine is perhaps the least controversial of the labels, because children—especially teens—have always occupied the space of the hero in fiction (thinking of Shakespeare and Greek mythology, for example, as spaces where young folks have always occupied starring roles). However, to think of children as vigilantes means that we must make space for children to be recognized as having agency. Vigilantism relies on a particular set of choices; it is the act of intentionally seeking justice for wrongdoing where no justice is found. Even moreso, to label a child's actions as feminist presumes an intellectual capacity to recognize what they are doing as part of a larger, collective vindication on behalf of other girls and women. Not only do the characters that I explore in this book have agency and the intellectual capacity to do the work of the vigilante with purpose, and for the end-goal of making the world safer for other girls and women, but they are empowered to do so through violence. Asking readers to imagine violence as empowering, and as agentic, is central to this book.

Kokesh and Sternadori identify agency as a sort of self-identification or self-direction "that disrupts oppressive social practices, transcends individual autonomy, and recognizes the interrelatedness of women's lives. Women's agency is usually discussed as synonymous with power and control over one's life" (Kokesh and Sternadori 2015, 141). Furthermore, they articulate that establishing agency in young adult fiction often requires rebellion. This experience of agency in the characterization of the heroines in this study matter to readers because they "identify with certain characters to a great degree. They usually 'saw' themselves in characters experiencing situations, thoughts, and feelings highly similar to their own" (Kokesh and Sternadori 2015, 151). Readers experience "narrative transportation," experiencing "vivid mental images" and impacting their sense of identification with a character in a novel (Kokesh and Sternadori 2015, 143). It is critical to study what is at stake in young adult novels if young readers are experiencing this sort of embodied and affective response, for the effects that they might have on girls' developing sense of identity.

Another approach to understanding embodied agency is produced by Claire Maxwell and Peter Aggleton, in their article, "Bodies and Agentic Practice in Young Women's Sexual and Intimate Relationships." Maxwell and Aggleton study how young women (ages 16–18) describe and understand their bodies, in particular the ways in which their bodies are "imbued with power," that "appear to lead and be integral to practices which are agentic" (Maxwell and Aggleton 2012, 306–307). When young women believe that their bodies are powerful, they are more likely to exhibit agency over their bodies, lives, and choices in measurable and sustained ways. In this study, Maxwell and Aggleton are looking specifically at sexual and intimate relationships, noting that "a crucial step to being agentic within sexual and intimate relationships is for young women to feel connected to their bodies and to pursue sexual pleasure. Feeling and/or articulating sexual desire is argued to be a measure of power as it indicates 'whose pleasure is prioritized in social relationships'" (Maxwell and Aggleton 2012, 308). In this book, the stories of Feyre, X-23, Scarlett, Gretchen, Jules, and Ophelia all coalesce around negative bodily experiences which left them feeling disconnected from their bodies, their lives, and their agency. Violence provides them with a connection to their embodied selves, which is a way to shift that power inequity and connect their bodies to their sense of purpose, and which in turn empowers them to reclaim their power and to be agentic.

Maxwell and Aggleton argue that this knowledge of one's own bodily power can influence other agentic practices, such as "assertive, refusing, proactive, and interrogative strategies . . . the grammar of a more inclusive theory of agency that goes beyond the inadequacies of framing practice as affirmation and/or resistance" (Maxwell and Aggleton 2012, 319). This is one example of how empowerment becomes embodied, and is actively transformed into agency. In writing about the ways that people heal from trauma, Debra Jackson explains that "[r]ecovering one's subjectivity requires, then, the reestablishment of one's embodied agency, including the ability to authoritatively tell one's own story" (Jackson 2016, 211). Embodied agency, as Maxwell and Aggleton describe it, is something that arises out of positive bodily experiences. It is also, as Jackson explains it, something that comes from being able to claim one's own voice and narrative through healing. Both of these are crucial to the stories of the characters explored in this book.

Ingrid E. Castro and Jessica Clark describe that children assert agency when they enact "an ethic of care" and note that care relationships can "reflect (intra) independent and empowering social relationships between children and others close to them" (Castro and Clark 2019, 8–9). The intentional defense of other girls and young women from violence, of the kind that is explored in this book, could be interpreted as an ethic of care. Thinking more about the role that care takes in the forging of agency in the lives of children, by analyzing Katniss Everdeen from *The Hunger Games* series Megan McDonough notes that "[i]n choosing to be Mockingjay, Katniss claims agency and helps fight for those she cares about. Throughout the series, Katniss makes critical decisions and then takes action in her agency; it is agency, through which she changes the world around her, that makes her a strong, empowered female protagonist" (McDonough 2019, 131). Katniss, like the super/heroines explored in this book, does not shy away from violence as a mechanism to achieve a more just society. And as Kelly Oliver notes in *Hunting Girls*: "we can embrace the ways in which these strong role models for young girls bond together with their sisters to stand up against violence toward them. While they may fight violence with more violence, they successfully ward off the worst violence in order to survive. . . . Whatever else they are, they are survivors. And rather than just focus on their violence, we should emphasize the ways in which girl power in these films is also the result of girls and women bonding together to nurture and protect each other" (Oliver 2013). All of these examples speak to the ways that girls and young women are empowered to become agents in their own right, and who can use that agency in ways that are violent. The teenage super/heroine subjects in my book all develop a sense of self that derives from understandings of power imbalances in their relationships, and from mostly negative bodily experiences, offering them the space to develop and embody sustained agentic practice in the wake of their traumas.

Furthermore, in feminist analyses of agency in literature, particularly in texts read by children, it is "crucial for the protagonist to find her voice in order to claim agency and power within her own life. She must then work to keep her voice and continue claiming agency and power for herself" (McDonough 2019, 134). As McDonough writes about agency in the *Hunger Games* series, "literature serves as a platform for children to see their own importance in society . . . [and] allows for the exploration of the inner self. Not only do we get to see the actions a person takes, we also get to explore the protagonist's inner thoughts and motivations, adding to the layered complexity of voice and agency within literary texts" (McDonough 2019, 134). The vigilante feminist subjects explored in this book experience trauma, but are able to find ways to work through it, and ultimately to make the world better for others.

VIOLENCE AND TRAUMA

Literature plays a crucial role in helping young adults shape their identities and worldviews. For example, Katherine Cruger writes that "[t]eenaged girls identify heavily with characters in the YA books that they read. In some cases, teenaged readers sometimes look to these characters as a model of how to handle real life situations" (Cruger 2017, 116). Furthermore, Janice Del Negro notes that "the young adult is measuring the world every day, seeking the right disguise, the right armor, the right path, the right energy that will protect and propel them through life. If the stories we tell create our reality, the importance of providing a strong narrative voice to young adults cannot be underestimated. . . . Stories that depict heroes and heroines overcoming extraordinary odds are critical to the emotional health of all listeners, but to no one more so than adolescents who are tentative and uncertain of their own emotional survival" (J. M. Del Negro 2017, 95–97). Sarah Hentges, too explains that "the texts that girls consume, as well as the texts that we consume about girls, are important for an understanding of the roles that girls play in life and in our imaginations" (Hentges 2018, 54).

In her conclusion to *Hunting Girls*, Kelly Oliver notes that "[w]e live in a culture of wounded, traumatized subjects, reminiscent of the Young Adult dystopias presented in recent literature and films" (Oliver 2013). She is making a correlation between the real world and the world of fantasy, in terms of the pervasiveness of sexual violence in both spaces. Furthermore, Cruger argues that "YA franchises do cultural work, meaning that they are both constructive of and constituted by our larger cultural and social ideas about gender, romance, sexuality, heroism, and ideology" (Cruger 2017, 115). Importantly, theorizing about the vigilante feminist in popular culture does not posit violence as preferable to peace. Were the world a peaceful place, girls and women would not need to act as vigilantes on behalf of the protection of themselves and others against those who cause harm. Lavin differentiates between accepting representations of violence versus being a violent person. She writes: "my focus is on something more basic and internal: the acceptance of the possibility of violence, namely, excessive aggression generated by the self. For U.S. women, this acceptance, this acknowledgement, has not historically been culturally condoned, and I think this has been a psychic disadvantage. Now with female action heroines in mass culture like Xena, Warrior Princess, Lara Croft, and Beatrix Kiddo, visualization of feminine violence (in an idealized, stylized way) is growing more common" (Lavin 2012, 121–122). The vigilante feminist super/heroine is being theorized in a world that is not only *not* peaceful, but also a world that actively rejects the rights of girls and women to autonomy over their own bodies, including the right to imagine themselves as aggressive or violent subjects.

The pervasive devaluation of girls and women stems from an organized system, which Kate Manne identifies as misogyny. It serves to: "uphold patriarchal order, understood as one strand among various systems of domination (including racisms, xenophobia, classism, ageism, ableism, homophobia, transphobia, and so on). Misogyny does this by visiting hostile or adverse social consequences on a certain (more or less circumscribed) class of girls or women to enforce and police social norms that are gendered either in theory (i.e., content) or in practice (i.e., norm enforcement mechanisms)" (Manne 2018, 13). Manne describes the social function of misogyny as women encountering hostility through the enforcement and policing of patriarchal norms and expectations if they violate patriarchal law and order (Manne 2018, 19). Misogyny is a form of social control, and it is so deeply embedded in culture (Manne talks specifically about the U.S., Great Britain, and Australia) that we often do not see it for what it is or how it functions. Manne differentiates between "sexism" and "misogyny" by noting that sexism justifies and rationalizes patriarchal social order, while misogyny is the system that polices and enforces patriarchy's norms and expectations. She argues that "sexism is scientific; misogyny is moralistic. And a patriarchal order has a hegemonic quality" (Manne 2018, 20). It is critically important to have this vocabulary when examining the function of the vigilante feminist super/ heroine in comics, literature, and television because it answers the underlying question of why the world devalues girls and women so systematically, at least insofar as it identifies the function that it holds: to uphold patriarchal order, and keep women in line. Specifically, Manne argues that misogyny is a political phenomenon that "operates within a patriarchal social order to police and enforce women's subordination and to uphold male dominance" (Manne 2018, 33).

To demonstrate the political phenomenon of misogyny in the United States, we need look no further than May 2020, when the U.S. Secretary of the Department of Education, Betsy DeVos, announced sweeping changes to guidelines for schools about handling sexual assault cases; especially important is that she asserted that Title IX, as it relates to sexual misconduct cases, needs to weigh equally the stories of rapists and victims, and severely narrowed the scope of complaints that colleges are required to investigate: "[i]n other words, according to the federal government, Title IX covers only sexual harassment that meets its new definition: 'unwelcome conduct' that is 'so severe, pervasive, and objectively offensive that it effectively denies a person equal access to education'" (S. Brown 2020). The Department of Education's press release on May 6, 2020, explains: "this new Title IX regulation reflects Secretary DeVos' commitment to ensuring that every survivor's claim of sexual misconduct is taken seriously, and every person accused knows that guilt is not predetermined" (Office 2020). The main thrust of the new regulations is to ensure that both accused and accusing students are equally protected. For example, it:

> will secure due process rights for students who report sexual misconduct and for those accused of it by requiring colleges to provide live hearings and allowing students' advisers to cross-examine parties and witnesses involved. Under the new rules, institutions must presume that those accused of sexual misconduct are innocent prior to the investigative and decision-making process. . . . The new evidence and cross-examination standards have been points of contention for advocates for survivors of campus sexual assault, who say live questioning could retraumatize and prevent victims from coming forward to report sexual misconduct. Statements made by parties and not cross-examined as part of a Title IX investigation may not be used as evidence." (Anderson 2020)

Advocates for survivors note that the new regulations make it "harder for survivors to report sexual violence, reduces schools' liability for ignoring or covering up sexual harassment, and creates a biased reporting process that favors respondents and schools over survivors' access to education" (Anderson 2020). Importantly, these new regulations remove trauma-informed investigation procedures, "that take into account the psychological impact sexual misconduct can have on survivors' memory and interpretation of events." Furthermore, the cross-examination and live hearing process "could also make survivors subject to 'being interrogated' by anyone the opposing party chooses to represent them, including a friend, parent or 'vicious' attorney" (Anderson 2020). These new regulations do not put survivors, the vast majority of whom are girls and women, first. Manne notes that misogynistic social forces "often target girls and women (in the relevant class) for action, perceived, or representative challenges to or violations of applicable patriarchal norms and expectations" (Manne 2018, 63). Title IX and the drawing attention to the epidemic of sexual violence in schools is undoubtedly perceived as a way that girls and women are trying to push back against oppressive forces, and new regulations like those by DeVos are a reactionary backlash to push them back in line.

As well, unprecedented restrictions on abortion access during the Trump administration severely curtailed the rights of girls and women to make reproductive decisions that are safe for their own bodies and lives. Furthermore, a 2015 study by the Centers for Disease Control and Prevention found that every two and a half minutes someone is sexually assaulted in the United States, that one in five women has been raped in her lifetime, that for young women the numbers are even worse, that 80 percent of rape victims are under 34 years old and that 30 percent are under 18 years old (Black, et al. 2011). Violence is being done in the "real world." Vigilante feminists—who are fictitious characters—offer a vicarious escape from a terrifying reality. Not only that, but they represent the taking on of roles that have historically been coded as male, and viewed as acceptable behavior for men, which offers a radical way of imagining the power of girls and women.

This project is situated within the context of a variety of real-world social movements, including It's On Us, Me Too, Time's Up, and Why I Didn't Report. It is deepened further still by the #GirlsToo movement, launched in 2019 by Girls, Inc., a national organization that inspires girls to be "strong, smart and bold, through direct service and advocacy." With the slogan "Respect Starts Young," and an invitation to "Join the Movement," Girls, Inc. describes #GirlsToo as "a national campaign to shift the deeply entrenched norms that lead to sexual harassment and violence in our society, and to create a culture where all girls and young people grow up safe, respected, and valued." With a "Did You Know?" series of slides, the website informs that one in four girls experience sexual abuse or sexual assault by the age of eighteen; and that seven in ten girls are sexually harassed at some point in high school. They explain: "Sexual harassment and violence is an epidemic and it starts at a young age. Still, as a society we perpetuate attitudes and behaviors that harm girls and follow them into adulthood. #MeToo brought the issue mainstream. Together, we can build a more equitable society that values and promotes the dignity of all people" (Girls, Inc. 2020). Violence against girls is a constant condition of life as a girl in the U.S.; it is inescapable. As such, it is critically important to engage with the fantasies that they consume, and to understand how their heroines fight against this epidemic.

Some popular culture utilizes violence gratuitously, in that it creates a story in which violence is perpetrated without logic or reason. However, the super/heroines addressed in this book are not using violence to those ends. These girls and women use violence as a means to combat injustice in a world that does not protect them, often meeting violence with violence in self-defense. For example, YA heroine Scarlett March—in *Sisters Red*, by Jackson Pearce—survived the wolf's attack in this retelling of "Little Red Riding Hood." Having fought the wolf to protect her younger sister, she is badly scarred; she lost an eye, and carries the scars of the encounter all over her body. But her survival—and the knowledge that she carries that monsters really do lurk in the darkness—has hardened her into a fierce wolf hunter.

In addition to reading these teenage super/heroines as vigilante feminists, this book also recognizes that in representing deeply traumatized subjects, these texts contribute to a cultural discourse about trauma, including secondary trauma, that permeates the lives of girls and women. The field of critical trauma studies examines "catastrophes such as war, genocide, forced migration, and 9/11," as well as the "everyday experiences of violence, loss, and injury . . . [recognizing tensions] between the everyday and the extreme, between individual identity and collective experience, between history and the present, between experience and representation, between facts and memory, and between the 'clinical' and the 'cultural'" (Casper and Wertheimer 2016, 4). This is important for two main reasons; first, these narratives of trauma connect readers with real lives to the experiences of fiction subjects, in a sense bearing witness to the traumas of characters in comics, film, television, and young adult novels. And second, audiences are also experiencing vicarious, or secondary, trauma in multiple ways. As girls and young women living in a society where 25 percent of their peers will be sexually assaulted in their lifetime—a number that is significantly higher if they are queer or trans—they are saturated with media reports and personal accounts of sexual violence. To work through these fears, Sarah Hentges notes that "[w]hat we find in the characters of books not only helps us to see ourselves more clearly, these stories also help us escape into another world where we can see other women fight similar battles" (Hentges 2018, 76). Furthermore, Kristina Deffenbacher explains that fantasy "engage[s] issues of sexual violence and female agency in a space that is at once like and safely beyond their world" (Deffenbacher 2014, 924). As well, "stories of women warriors suggest the possibility of women not just facing and surviving rape but also facing down and successfully fighting rapists, and rape culture itself" (Deffenbacher 2014, 932).

Superhero comics and heroine-based YA novels examined in this book demonstrate that violence is a reality of the fiction worlds of girls and women, but these are characters that can take care of themselves. Far from the damsel in distress, their physical and mental strengths are valued (within their universes) for their contributions to balancing the scales. The vigilante feminist super/heroine, as used in this book, refers specifically to vigilantism by girls and women who have undertaken their own protection, and the protection of others, against violence—such as sexual assault, abduction, abuse, and trauma—because they have been otherwise failed in that manner. Furthermore, female vigilantes respond to the critique that "girl power" feminism plagues many contemporary stories, which "emphasize individual strength and independence," but "do not challenge systemic sexism [and] fail to make social criticisms" (Williams 2010, 109). Rather, these characters are strong on behalf of others, and they actively seek paths of justice that deeply unsettle the structures of power implicit in patriarchy.

CHAPTER OUTLINE

Chapter One: Finding Agency after Trauma: Crafting a Community of Consent in Sarah J. Maas' YA Series A Court of Thorns and Roses considers the characterization of Feyre Archeron, the super/heroine of the *A Court of Thorns and Roses* young adult fantasy novel series by Sarah J. Maas. Initially a retelling of *Beauty and the Beast*, Feyre's story rewrites the narrative to make Beauty the one who saves the Beast. However, beneath the surface of the story, Feyre's life is filled with realities that she did not choose, and over which she feels as though she has no control. She is kidnapped, imprisoned, forced to become Fae, and suffers in an abusive relationship when her overprotective lover (Tamlin, the Beast) uses his overwhelming love for her as an excuse to hold her hostage for her own protection. The series is a slow unraveling of Feyre coming to terms with the conditions of her life, and her struggle to change them. Feyre suffers from PTSD, has low self-esteem, and trouble trusting others, and has never had the freedom to explore her own desires. Her life has always been so intricately intertwined with the needs to others, that she has little self-awareness other than self-loathing. When she escapes from Tamlin and finds herself in a new Court that values freedom and autonomy of its people, Feyre begins to learn who she is. She is magically powerful—the most powerful, perhaps, in the world—she is artistic, she is kind and empathetic, and she grows into a sexually curious selfhood. She learns to control her powers and to fight. She channels her energy into forging her body into one that can never be overpowered or exploited again. She feeds her artistic and intellectual interests so that she can learn about herself in the world. She forges herself into a powerful weapon of defense of her loved ones, and offense to those who would rip agency and autonomy from others. Her whole being becomes one that is invested in leaving the world a better place than she found it. This chapter is about the ways in which Feyre empowers herself to choose agency over her own life, to fight for the right to make choices freely and to give others that same right, and about life after torture and domestic abuse. Scholarship shows that storytelling offers adolescents space to work through the personal, and even secondary, trauma of violence against girls and women. Characters like Feyre represent a fantasy reckoning for the powerlessness felt by girls and women, which is cast aside when she takes on the powerful role as a body of vengeance and an agent of rescue.

Chapter Two: "Choice is Your Weapon"[6]: *Violence, Empowerment, and X-23's Journey Toward Consent and Agency"* explores the journey of teenage Marvel superheroine, X-23/Laura Kinney, from 2003 to today, which is largely about developing her understanding of choice, and what constitutes autonomy and freedom of choice in her own life. She is a clone of Wolverine, and was created to be a weapon—with her strength, skill, mutant claws, and healing factor, she is nearly invincible. However, being created as a weapon in a lab, she was raised, from birth, as a soldier, trained to obey orders, to live for directives. She was tortured all through childhood in order to make this conditioning stick, to obey without hesitation, to suppress empathy or identification with others, and to see herself—her body and her mind—as a weapon. When she begins to develop an instinctual resistance to orders to kill, especially children, the scientists develop a trigger scent to overpower her higher senses and send her into a killing rage over which she has no control. Because of this manipulation, X-23 has no control over her life or her body as a child. In a cultural moment during which we are talking about the nature of consent, X-23 is a particularly interesting subject of analysis, because her right to choice is never developed, and when she attempts to exercise it, the trigger scent rips away her ability to voluntarily consent. This chapter explores the ways in which X-23 reclaims violence as a tool of empowerment, and uses it in the service of others who need her protection. I've theorized her as a vigilante feminist super/heroine, because her empowerment is discovered through violence, and though it is not a radical destruction of patriarchal structures, it does radically interrupt a cycle of violence that leaves girls and women powerless in a violent world. X-23's pathway is dark, but when she escapes from the Facility that held her as a child she fights against her history of mindless violence to try to use her abilities for justice. This chapter delves deeply into the power of choice and consent as agentic factors that shift X-23's narrative to one of empowerment.

Chapter Three: Hunting Wolves: Violence, Agency, and Empowerment in Jackson Pearce's Retold Fairytales Young Adult Fantasy Series considers two of Jackson Pearce's young adult novels from the Retold Fairytales series. *Sisters Red*, a retelling of Little Red Riding Hood, is told from the perspective of teenaged sisters Scarlett and Rosie March, who survived the wolf's attack in their grandmother's cottage when they were children. Scarlett, having fought the wolf to protect her sister, is badly scarred; she won the battle and killed the wolf, but she lost an eye, and carries the memory of her encounter all over her body. Their survival—and the knowledge that they carry now that they know that monsters really do lurk in the darkness—has hardened them into fierce wolf hunters. *Sweetly*, a retelling of Hansel and Gretel, is told from the perspective of Gretchen, an eighteen-year-old girl who finds herself a guest at the home of a candy shop owner. Twelve years ago, she and her brother Ansel survived an attack by a witch in the woods, but her twin sister was lost, and never heard from again. When she meets a handsome woodsman in her new town, she begins to unravel the reality of the community she is visiting, which has a terrifying history of the annual disappearance of eighteen-year-old girls. Both the *Sisters Red* and *Sweetly* books in the Retold Fairytales series of young adult novels by Jackson Pearce have at their core the existence of werewolves called Fenris. [7] Fenris can transform anytime—day or night, full moon or no moon—and they hunt girls and women. In their human form, they are imperceptible as wolves—except to the eyes of a trained hunter—and wear the bodies of very good-looking, sweet-talking, suave men. [8] The Fenris prey on girls in a sexualized way. In all four of the Retold Fairytales novels the Fenris charm young women, woo them, attract them, and then they eat them. [9] They are strengthened and titillated by fear, and so they are well practiced in luring girls into spaces where they are cut off from safety, and terrifying them at the moment of their transformation. They transform into werewolves for the sole purpose of eating their prey, and on the rare occasion that they are interrupted in that process—usually by a hunter—they are weakened and ravenous until they are able to feast. The longer they go without feeding, the wilder they become, and the more victims they devour. I argue that the Fenris is a metaphor for the rapist, whose hunting grounds are areas where young girls and women reside. The girls in this series overcome their powerlessness and train to become fierce, capable, and powerful hunters to fight against the creatures cloaked as men that wish them harm. They train themselves as weapons focused entirely on the eradication of this threat, and they protect other girls in doing so. The girls, always sisters in these stories, take on the burden of knowledge about the Fenris, and commit themselves to destroying them. This chapter reads these novels alongside cultural conversations about victim blaming, "boys will be boys" rape culture, and activist movements like Slut-Walk.

Chapter Four: "I Know How to Do Things Most People Don't:" Rape and Vigilante Justice on a College Campus in MTV's Sweet/Vicious, explores the MTV show *Sweet/Vicious*. Here, Jules and Ophelia, who were dubbed by the media as the "vigilante superheroes for the millennial generation," are college students who team up to avenge rape survivors by attacking their assaulters. Learning about the epidemic of sexual assault on their college campus, and the repeated, systematic failure of the campus police, Title IX Office, and District Attorney's office to take the cases seriously, Jules and Ophelia take justice into their own hands. As the "Darlington Vigilante," they instill fear in rapists by turning the tables on them to make them feel powerless, threatening them if they assault again, and then leaving them injured—broken bones, knife wounds, bruised faces. As a survivor, Jules' own experience with the system after being raped by a star athlete inspired her to take up martial arts and become a ninja-by-night who hunts and attacks the assaulters. When Ophelia discovers Jules' secret, they team up, and Ophelia shares the burden of their justice-seeking. The show used great intentionality in showing what it is like to be a sexual assault survivor on a college campus that fails them at every level, demonstrating the ways that it affects academics, friendships, and weakens the community. Jules has PTSD, and takes on this role for her own healing, and also to take action to make rapists stop attacking other women. She is a vigilante on behalf of other girls and women, and she invents her violent system of vengeance as a response to the violent culture she is forced to exist within. Starting as a TV series in 2016–2017, the story of Jules and Ophelia is about empowering women as a mechanism of healing after trauma, refusing to accept systems that fail to serve justice, and is a vicarious fantasy corrective to the realities of the epidemic of sexual violence on college campuses—right at a time when the U.S. Department of Education is proposing to further weaken the responsibilities of colleges and universities to act on behalf of students victimized on their campuses. Darlington University is a #MeToo campus, where everyone knows someone who has been sexually assaulted; Jules and Ophelia act as vigilantes on behalf of those victims.

Finally, the *Conclusion* ties together the book as a whole. By tracing the main themes of trauma, agency, empowerment, and violence through the introduction and four chapters, the conclusion reiterates the ways the character journeys in the texts explored can be interpreted through these stages. The conclusion also explores the ways that feminism is interwoven throughout the analysis, connecting feminism to violence in a way that is unusual in feminist scholarship.

NOTES

1. Women and girls are not the only people who feel fear in a rape culture. Folks who are LGBQ and trans, and men and boys who do not live up to expectations of masculine ideals also face these fears. For the purposes of this project, I am concentrating on people who live their lives as women and girls.

2. Significant portions of this section of my introduction have been excerpted from my article, "Vigilante Feminism: Revising Trauma, Abduction, and Assault in American Fairy Tale Revisions," published in *Marvels and Tales* in Winter 2017. It is excerpted here with permission from Wayne State University Press.

3. An assertion that many feminist scholars have disagreed with, but as Watson represents young feminism, her position here is critical to foreground.

4. The HeForShe campaign mythologizes a feminist past that relies less on historical accuracy, and more on popular opinion about that history. However, as a globally influential feminist platform, the interpretation is critical to this analysis of a contemporary vigilante feminist sensibility.

5. Though not explored in this chapter, it may be possible to tease a queer reading out of these tales, as well. Ravenna, Gretel, and Scarlett all eschew heterosexual romance in order to devote total focus to the project of vigilantism in protection of girls and women. As Kay Turner and Pauline Greenhill note, "Certain tales present a choice to turn away from heteronormativity" (Turner and Greenhill 2012, 9) opening up space for a transgressive analysis.

6. Liu, *The Killing Dream* #3, 63.

7. The other three texts are: *Sweetly* written in 2011 (a retelling of Hansel and Gretel); *Fathomless* written in 2012 (a retelling of The Little Mermaid); and *Cold Spell* written in 2013 (a retelling of The Ice Queen).

8. In *Sisters Red*, there is reference to a boy as young as 14, and men closer to 50 with gray hair. The age of the Fenris depends upon the age in which they are located and turned. They are described as "frat boys," "rock stars," "chiseled," "charming," "attractive," and "disarming."

9. Similarly, in the section titled "Moral" in Charles Perrault's *Little Red Riding Hood* (1697), he wrote of wolves that: "Some are perfectly charming, not loud, brutal, or angry, but tame, pleasant, and gentle."

Chapter One

Finding Agency after Trauma

Crafting a Community of Consent in Sarah J. Maas'
Young Adult Series A Court of Thorns and Roses

Feyre Archeron's story is one of repeated trauma. First, she experiences trauma as a child when her mother dies and she must grow up much too quickly to take care of her family.[1] Then she is kidnapped and kept prisoner by Tamlin, and brainwashed into believing she loves him. She believes, at first, that their sexual relationship is consensual, because she does not yet have the language and perspective to describe the sexual coercion that she endures. Later, she is tortured and killed by the Queen Under the Mountain. Finally, she is forcibly brought back to life and, again without her consent, transformed into an immortal High Fae. This deep consideration of consent and healthy relationships in the *A Court of Thorns and Roses*, a popular YA fantasy book series, parallels the world of its young readers. Feyre's story will be familiar and recognizable to many who have lost loved ones, or found themselves in unhealthy relationships. Importantly, Feyre persists, and this chapter traces her pathway as she reclaims her agency after finding space for healing. As an agentic heroine, Feyre embraces her role as the most powerful being in her world, which means also embracing her capacity to be violent in protection of others, especially innocents, and survivors of assault. And ultimately it is as protector of her people that she is able to create a community where consent and choice are foregrounded as the most important aspects of their society.

We like strong heroines in this cultural moment. We seek them, feel empowered by them. We are attracted to stories of strength, of overcoming, of triumph in the face of tragedy, evil, and trauma. I am interested in what is at stake when violence is used as a mechanism for empowerment in the face of sexual violence, abduction, and trauma; when the systems that purport to protect girls and women fail, and the only satisfactory response is a vigilante violence that feels cathartic, that feels like relief. As Clare R. Johnson and Jean M. Campbell articulate, stories carry "a universal power," which "draws on a deep, collective imagery and passes messages through metaphor . . . story can be used as a healing art" (Johnson and Campbell 2016, 34). There is evidence that demonstrates that fantasy violence can "bolster confidence" and present an "empowering challenge to overcome" (Gackenbach, et al. 2016, 92–93). This happens for readers of literature, players of video games, and audiences of television. For young adults, this can be especially impactful, since, as Johnson and Campbell note, they are "looking for ways to grow into adulthood," and see the worlds of fantasy as a space to resolve their anxieties (Johnson and Campbell 2016, 34). Janice M. Del Negro and Melanie A. Kimball write that emerging research in psychology and neuroscience demonstrates that "stories shape personality, develop empathy, create community, change minds, and alter consciousness" (Del Negro and Kimball 2017, ix). Del Negro also argues that "[s]tories that depict . . . heroines overcoming extraordinary odds are critical to the emotional health of all listeners, but to no one more so than adolescents who are tentative and uncertain of their own emotional survival" (Del Negro 2017, 97). And specifically, Kristina Deffenbacher articulates the importance of texts in combatting rape culture, noting: "stories of women warriors suggest the possibility of women not just facing and surviving rape but also facing down and successfully fighting rapists, and rape culture itself" (Deffenbacher 2014, 932). It is my curiosity about the role of violence-wielding heroines in young adult fantasy literature and superheroine comics that brought me to this book.

Thinking about the representation of girls in young adult literature in *Girls on Fire*, Sara Hentges theorizes about the "girls on fire" protagonist who is "complex, intelligent, brave and a triumphant survivor of impossible situations. . . . As a genre of Girls on Fire, these girls speak to an important cultural moment and an optimism that shapes the future" (Hentges 2018, 5). I, too, am defining a category of girls and young women, in my analysis of the "teenage vigilante feminist super/heroine." The girls in the stories Hentges analyzes have similar drives and motivations to each other, just as the girls in the sources I examine share the desire to protect girls and young women from violence. Hentges notes that the U.S. "shares many dystopic qualities with the fictional settings imagined by writers and devoured by readers" (Hentges 2018, 5). This can be extrapolated to the sources I am examining in this book, because the U.S. also shares many of the qualities found in the super/heroine stories, primarily in the devaluation of girls and women and the failure of systems that protect them, such that a vigilante protector is needed. Hentges notes that "these books speak back to the institutions and structures that continue to limit girls' roles and opportunities," in much the same way that the stories of super/heroines call out the mechanisms of power that continue to enable harm to girls and young women (Hentges 2018, 10). Hentges notes that, because of their "power to unsettle dominant discourses" and "afford the potential for subversion," "the texts that girls consume, as well as the texts that we consume about girls, are important for an understanding of the roles that girls play in life and in our imaginations" (Hentges 2018, 54). She acknowledges the power of characters and books, especially as fans, noting "what we find in the characters of books not only helps us to see ourselves more clearly, these stories also help us escape into another world where we can see other women fight similar battles" (Hentges 2018, 76). This is the central importance of this chapter's analysis, as it not only follows a character who experiences trauma, but it also traces her pathway as she reclaims her agency and finds healing.

The set of texts at the center of this chapter's analysis is the *A Court of Thorns and Roses* (*ACOTAR*) young adult book series by Sarah J. Maas, the first of which was published in 2015. At its core, this is an extended universe sparked by a fairy-tale retelling of "Beauty and the Beast," and as a mechanism for that it centers the Beast as a manipulative, coercive High Fae High Lord of the Spring Court, and Feyre—the "beauty"—as his eventual, ultimate demise. The series is best-selling, with a committed fan base. It is displayed as a "Can't Miss Book" with an eye-catching display at the bookstore. *A Court of Wings and Ruin*, the third book in the series published in 2017, sold more than 100,000 copies that year. That the text is so popular deems it fodder for analysis, to interrogate what young adult readers are encountering. But moreover, it does so with a story that challenges gender norms, centers sexual agency and pleasure, engages discussions about agency and consent, and explores healing in the wake of trauma—all in the age of #MeToo and #WhyIDidntReport. This chapter is a close reading of the first three books in the *ACOTAR* series (*A Court of Thorns and Roses*, *A Court of Wings and Ruin*, and *A Court of Mist and Fury*), tracing key moments in Feyre's trajectory that contextualize her traumas, and then follow her as she finds healing, empowerment, and ultimately, agency. The close reading is interspersed with analysis of the novels through the lens of childhood studies, young adult literature studies, trauma studies, and agency theory.

In "Myth (Un)Making: The Adolescent Female Body in Mythopoeic YA Fantasy," Leah Beth Phillips explains the critical influence that YA fantasy can have on readers. She argues "where popular and media culture offers illusions of choice, impossible ideals and silences, [fantasy] offers bodies that possess multiplicity and difference, thereby offering frameworks for living and being a body that challenge the dominant, hegemonic fantasy of adolescence" (Phillips 2016, 27). And talking specifically about the topic of sexual consent and fairy-tale revisions, Del Negro explains that "[t]een listeners are drawn to these tales and to reinterpretations of these tales, deeply engaged by their exposure to them in contemporary media. Their willingness to step into the fantastical as limned by these supernatural, romantic, and tragic tales allows them to interact with powerful emotional moments in the safety of a narrative frame. The discussion of sexual consent triggered by the early versions of Sleeping Beauty was a vociferous and productive one" (Del Negro 2017, 99). Despite facing seemingly overwhelming physical and emotional obstacles, the heroine of Sarah J. Maas' series, Feyre Archeron, reclaims agency and power and then works to forge a community of consent, freedom, healing, equality, pleasure, and wellness. Thus, YA fantasy, like the *A Court of Thorns and Roses* series of novels, offers a space for girls to work things out, to find role models, and to understand the complexities of the experiences of their fiction heroines.

At the outset of *A Court of Thorns and Roses*, Feyre (pronounced fay-RUH) Archeron has been kidnapped by Tamlin, the High Fae High Lord of the Spring Court. He takes advantage of her childhood of poverty and hardship, seduces her with promises of a better future, and convinces her to give up her entire world for him—which is no small thing, given that it means never returning to her family. Deluded, believing that what she feels for Tamlin is love, Feyre risks her human life to save him. She overcomes extraordinary obstacles and tests to free him from an evil Fae queen. She is actually killed in the process, but is saved and reborn as High Fae, having been given a drop of lifeforce from the High Lords of each Court in Prythian. Tamlin "demonstrates" his gratitude and love for her by imprisoning her within the confines of his manor for her own protection. He is irrationally terrified that she will be taken from him, though he positions himself as justified in his fear, and he makes her believe that it is true. However, as time passes, Feyre begins to notice that she never freely consented to her relationship or her life with Tamlin; she was always the object of his whim and desire. She did not freely consent to becoming High Fae; the life force that brought her back from death was bestowed upon her and meant that she literally lost her humanity. Her life with Tamlin, the Beast, is not her own.

The vigilante feminist character is one who takes on the role of avenger and protector of girls and young women who are threatened by violence because those who are supposed to protect them (families, law enforcement, High Lords) fail to do so. In the stories that I am analyzing, the vigilante feminist is a teenage super/heroine who has herself experienced violence, trauma, and a loss of agency in the aftermath. The reclamation of her body, and her agency, through the quest to protect others, is empowering and healing for her. Feyre Archeron's story begins when she forfeits her life for a debt owed to Tamlin after killing one of his soldiers. Feyre's backstory is that, as a child, her family was wealthy, and her life was easy. When she was ten years old her mother grew very ill, and upon her deathbed, perhaps knowing that Feyre—though the youngest of her daughters—was the strongest, she made Feyre promise to take care of her sisters. After her mother dies, her merchant father loses his fortune when ships carrying goods he was trading overseas are lost, and the financiers backing the journey take everything they own to pay for the failed voyage. They also beat her father horribly, and one of his legs never fully recovers. Lost to grief and depression, he psychologically abandons Feyre and her sisters, unable to find work, with no way to pay bills. At age twelve, Feyre realizes that her father is too weak and selfish to find a way to feed her family. They were out of food, and so recognizing the reality of her circumstances and seeing the hunger and desperation on the faces of her sisters who she has sworn to protect, Feyre picks up a bow and arrow and goes hunting. With no one to teach her how to hunt, fish, swim, and survive, she trains herself by spying on others, and learning by trial and error. As she describes it, "When I missed, we didn't eat. So learning how to aim was the first thing I figured out" (Maas 2016, 110). By the time the story begins, Feyre is nineteen years old, and has grown into a skilled huntress with the ability to not only find food for her family, but also to kill enough extra that she can sell it in town and make just barely enough money for her family to live on. They almost never have anything extra—their boots are worn, and their coats are thin—but she manages, because no one else does.

This is an interesting origin to this revision of "Beauty and the Beast." In the various fairy tale iterations developed over time, Beauty often has some type of virtue or talent. In the 2017 film adaptation of the story, Belle is an inventor with a kind heart and a desire to see the world. Her father is a bit bumbling and forgetful, and Belle patiently assists him with his tinkering while also ensuring that they eat proper meals. But it is often Beauty's love for her father that enters into these tales as the reason for her eventual imprisonment by the Beast. In many of the popular retellings for children, her father takes a rose from the Beast's rose garden to give to Beauty upon his return from a long journey, and in his rage over the supposed theft, the Beast demands repayment with life in prison in his castle dungeon. Panicked, Beauty goes looking for her father, and finding him weak, cold, and jailed, she begs the Beast to allow her to trade places with him. He agrees, and offers her a lovely bedroom rather than a dungeon cell. The core of this connection is the love between a father and a daughter.

Feyre receives no such fatherly love. In *A Court of Thorns and Roses*, there are rumors of faeries crossing the magical barrier between Prythian and the mortal lands, and raiding and pillaging villages along the border. Feyre should not be hunting in the woods near nightfall, nor should she venture too far away from her cottage which lay a mere two day's journey from the immortal border. She had taken a great risk coming so far into the forest, but her family does not stop her. They are too preoccupied with themselves, never offering kindness or assistance to the youngest of the family. And so, when she finds her family in the all-too-common position of running out of food, she enters the woods in search of a kill, and, as luck would have it, happens upon a doe "not yet too scrawny from winter," who could feed her family for a week or more (Maas 2016, 4). However, in this moment she realizes she is not alone in the forest; another beast, an enormous golden-eyed, silver-haired wolf, the size of a pony, is hunting the deer as well. Worse than his size, she notes, is his "unnatural stealth: even as he inched closer in the brush, he remained unheard, unspotted by the doe. No animal that massive could be so quiet" (Maas 2016, 4). She worries, momentarily, that the wolf might in fact be of faerie origin. Feyre, having never faced a wolf before, relies on her instincts because if she allows the wolf to kill the doe he will ruin precious amounts of hide and fat. She trusts her eight years of hunting skill, and sinks an arrow deep into the wolf's side as the wolf pounces for the deer's neck. Barking in pain, the wolf turns to Feyre and growls, but merely looks at her "with an awareness and surprise that made me fire the second [ash] arrow. Just in case—just in case that intelligence was of the immortal, wicked sort" (Maas 2016, 7). The wolf collapses, and Feyre waits until it stops breathing. She cannot carry both the doe and the wolf, and she needs the doe for meat, so she skins the wolf before hoisting the pelt and the deer across her shoulders and trudging home several miles, in the snow, to her cottage.

That night, as Feyre sits with her sisters and her father dozes in front of the fire, a deafening roar is followed by the breaking of the front door, as "an enormous, growling shape appeared in the doorway" (Maas 2016, 32). In a moment Feyre is holding her hunting knife and facing a gigantic beast with golden fur, as she moves in front of her shrieking sisters and her terror-stricken father. She notes that the beast is the size of a horse, with a feline body and a "distinctly wolfish" head with curled, elk-like horns protruding from it, with "black, daggerlike claws and yellow fangs" (Maas 2016, 33). In this moment of chaos, Feyre has only her family in mind, explaining "I didn't have room for terror, wouldn't give it an inch of space, despite my heart's wild pounding in my ears. Somehow, I wound up in front of my sisters, even as the creature reared onto its hind legs and bellowed through a maw full of fangs 'MURDERERS!'" (Maas 2016, 33). Noting the pathway to her bow and arrow was across the room, behind the beast, Feyre bravely grasps her hunting knife and a dinner knife as she snaps "Get out, and begone" (Maas 2016, 34). She hurls her hunting knife at his neck as it lets out a roar, but he smacks it out of the way and snaps for her face with his teeth.

The way that Feyre reacts to this terrifying intrusion demonstrates her skill at survival. The wolf has followed the scent of his murdered comrade to Feyre's doorstep, and she learns that her suspicions were accurate—she had killed a Fae who had shape-shifted into a wolf. The beast in her doorway demands to know who did it, and when she takes responsibility he disbelieves her, thinking that she must be protecting her father or her older sisters. Feyre assures him that it is her fault and asks to know what the punishment is. In various iterations of the Beauty and the Beast story, Beauty purportedly "willingly chooses" imprisonment to pay the debt owed by her father, who trespasses or steals from the Beast, but it is actually always the Beast's cunning manipulation of a situation related to an unpaid debt that lures Beauty to his castle. And beneath that, there is also always the fact that he has been cursed and needs a woman to break the spell. In this version, the manipulation is a supposed Treaty. When the wall was built between the human lands and the Fae, a Treaty of Peace was signed ensuring that both stayed on their own sides. When Feyre asks what the price is, she is told that her life has become forfeit, and the beast offers her a choice: he can kill her now, or she can come to live on his estate, where he would grant her protection. Her father urges her to go to the estate so that she may live. She chooses to go, despite knowing she may never see her family again. She intends to find a way to escape and return home, if for no other reason than knowing that her family would starve without her. Feyre trusts herself as a weapon and believes she can outwit the Beast. Despite the enormous odds against her she is courageous, and though she intends to fight to the death to stay alive, she is entirely willing to sacrifice herself for her family. "I loosened my grip on the hilt of my remaining dagger and stared into those green eyes for a long, silent while before I said, 'When do we go?' . . . I could smell my doom on his breath as he said, 'Now'" (Maas 2016, 39).

Arriving at the Beast's (in this story, the Beast is named Tamlin) manor in the Spring Court shows Feyre that he is nobility. It is oddly quiet, practically empty save for Lucien, who is Tamlin's best friend and Captain, and Alis, who serves as Feyre's servant while at the manor. When she asks why the manor is empty, Tamlin tells her that his needs are few. The strangeness of Tamlin's court mimics the strangeness of the Beast's castle in *Beauty and the Beast*, where some enchantment has taken over its residents and servants. What few people Feyre meets in Tamlin's manor wear masks that they never remove. Tamlin's is a beast with horns, Lucien's is a fox, Alis's is a bird. The masks are the remnants of a curse cast by an evil faerie queen. Similar to how the Disney version of *Beauty and the Beast* has servants and guards who have been cursed to live as household objects, these have been cursed to wear the masks they were wearing when the spell was cast, which happened to be during a costume ball. Tamlin, we learn quickly, has shape shifting powers (like the wolf who broke down Feyre's door), so the "beast" lurks beneath his surface at all times.

It is clearly evident at this moment in the book that Feyre is in great danger at all times. Tamlin's Beast-under-the-surface is part of that, but it is also true that Feyre, as a human, is not safe in Prythian. This is a reality that Tamlin holds over Feyre. For example, on her first night in Prythian, Tamlin demands Feyre's presence at dinner in the dining room. Alis attempts to put her in a dress, but Feyre refuses to change out of her own clothes. Tamlin tells Feyre to eat, but—though she is nearly starving—she refuses that, as well. When she attempts to rise from her chair to leave the dinner table, Tamlin uses his magic to restrain her, securing her to the wood so tightly that it makes her back ache, and tells her that if she does not want to stay she is "free" to leave, and live out the rest of her sentence fearing for her life in Prythian. Feyre does not stand much chance of survival in Prythian; Tamlin's manor is the "safest" place for her, though safety seems subjective. Tamlin promises Feyre that he will protect her life, but as a mere human she is always endangered. The intricacy of Tamlin's coercion is wrapped up in the façade of safety and protection from the start.

He is also coercive and manipulative in how he holds her family's security over her head. Tamlin assures her that her family are alive and well cared for: "You think so low of faeries that you believe I'd take their only source of income and nourishment and not replace it'" (Maas 2016, 62)? He also reminds her that if she tries to escape and return to the moral realm lands, her family would no longer be afforded that luxury. She feels trapped, because she and her sisters would have no place to go.

This is illustrative of her first days in the Spring Court. Tamlin is loud, angry, violent, and intrusive. Whenever she explores, he appears. She scopes out the castle for ways she might escape. Used to starving, the sumptuous food is tantalizing for Feyre and so she eats with him, though she resists his formal civility. As with the fairy tale, Feyre's refusal to put on a lovely dress and engage in polite conversation enrages the Beast, who cannot help but show his claws in anger. Eventually, he shows her his study which is filled with more books and maps than Feyre has ever seen, let alone read. Education was one of the things lost after they became destitute from her father's lost fortune, and her sisters never bothered to teach her themselves. When she finds herself intrigued by the various comforts of the manor, she feels guilty, like a glutton who is enjoying this new luxurious lifestyle, and she dislikes herself for it. Tamlin learns that she loves art and painting. He buys her paints and dedicates a room as her studio. Having lived a life of poverty, her world was gray. Afforded the time for rest, she begins seeing things in color for the first time. Tamlin basks in Feyre's happiness, soaking it up and opening up in ways that he never has before. "'Has anyone ever taken care of you?' he asked quietly. 'No.' I'd long since stopped feeling sorry for myself about it" (Maas 2016, 110). He begins taking care of her as no one has ever done for her in the past. He reminds her that since her family is well and cared for, she does not need to continue to worry about her duty to them. Feyre begins to have an internal crisis; she hates her captivity, and she wants to return home, but she realizes that at home she has never been taken care of, and never had the freedom to be a child. She begins to feel like her captivity with Tamlin is liberating because she does not have to worry about food, her family is well off, and for the first time in her life she can spend her time as she wishes. Her satisfaction yields to a sense of welcome, which becomes a notion of belonging, and then longing, until she finds herself having feelings for Tamlin.

One feminist challenge to the Beauty and the Beast story is that Beauty falls in love with her captor. He wears her down. In the original 1783 story, by Jeanne-Marie LePrince de Beaumont, the Beast asks Beauty to marry him on her first night in his castle. "You alone are mistress here . . . everything here is yours, and I should be very uneasy, if you were not happy." Beauty, terrified of angering the monster, answers no, and he responded with a "hiss so frightful that the whole palace echoed." Thereafter the Beast asks for her hand in marriage every night for three months, to which Beauty replies: "Beast, you make me very uneasy. I wish I could consent to marry you, but I am too sincere to make you believe that will ever happen; I shall always esteem you as a friend, endeavor to be satisfied with this." He is not. Unable to have her hand in marriage, he coerces her to promise "never to leave" him (de Beaumont 1783). The lesson here suggests girls should be content to be held captive by a beast. No never really means no. In the 1991 Disney animated version, the Beast is grumpy, arrogant, and violent, and yet Beauty begins to see the beauty in the Beast. She sees him as a victim, she sees his desperation, and though at first it causes pity, eventually it leads to love. In the fairy tale, Beauty's love, as demonstrated through a kiss, turns the beast into a handsome prince.

It is equally unsettling when Feyre falls for her captor in this retelling of the story. She worries about him when he is on patrol, and she watches for him when he is expected to return. She enjoys his company at dinner, and, as he begins to loosen up, he woos her with flowers, picnics, horseback rides, dancing, and music. Free from worry, and unaccustomed to such decadent attention, her affection grows, as does her attraction to Tamlin. The Calanmai celebration of spring approaches, during which ritual debauchery replenishes magic for the coming year. Feyre is not invited to the party; in fact, Tamlin told her specifically to stay in her room, and even warns her to set a snare. But Feyre finds herself drawn to the party. Not liking to be told what to do, and not liking to be locked away bored and waiting while others live their lives freely, she does not heed his warning. This is a recurring theme through the series, that Tamlin tells Feyre to do something, and she bristles against the limitation. She ignores Tamlin's orders to stay locked away for the night and goes to the party. Calanmai celebrates a "Great Rite," the details of which Feyre does not know. But the reality of her position as a human on faerie lands becomes precariously real, because when she refuses Tamlin's order to stay in her room and follows the faeries to the party she is nearly raped. She is pulled into the forest by three faeries: "One of them ran a hand down my side, its bony fingers digging into my ribs, my hips. I jerked back, only to slam into the third one, who wove his long fingers through my hair and pressed close. No one looked; no one even noticed . . . I pushed and thrashed against them; they only hissed" (Maas 2016, 185). She is fortunately rescued by a handsome and powerful stranger, and she runs back to the manor, confused and terrified.

Feyre is also nearly raped that night by Tamlin, her protector, the man who she is beginning to have feelings for. During the spring ritual, it was Tamlin's job as High Lord of the Spring Court to copulate in order to replenish the magic back into the earth. It is described that he is taken over by a spirit, and his body becomes the vessel through which the blessing of the earth happens. Prior to the evening's ritual he told Feyre to stay in her room because he did not want himself to smell her, and want her, while he was overtaken. When she went to the ritual against orders anyway, he was almost unable to control himself. After being closed up in her room all night, she finds Tamlin blocking her path as she walks through the hallway on her way to get a snack:

> I was about to pass him when he grabbed me, so fast that I didn't see anything until he had me pinned against the wall . . . he grasped my wrists. "I smelled you," he breathed, his painted chest rising and falling so close to mine. "I searched for you, and you weren't there." "Let go," I said as evenly as I could, but his claws punched out, imbedding in the wood above my hands . . . "You drove me mad," he growled . . . I cried out as his teeth clamped onto the tender spot where my neck met my shoulder. . . . He didn't pierce my flesh, but rather bit to keep me pinned. . . . "Don't ever disobey me again," he said, his voice a deep purr that ricoched through me, awaking everything and lulling it into complicity (Maas 2016, 195–197).

Though she finds herself turned on by his actions, she does not like to be told to obey, and so she slaps him: "'Don't tell me what to do,' I breathed, my palm stinging. 'And don't bite me like some enraged beast.'. . . He growled once, low and frustrated and vicious, before prowling away" (Maas 2016, 197). The sexual violence lurking under the surface of this interaction is unsettling. He bites her, traps her, and growls at her. There is a part of Feyre that responds to the sensation of his body, and which clouds her senses, but when she realizes what he is asking of her, she slaps him. The next night, Tamlin apologizes with a bouquet of white roses. For the first time in a long while, Feyre sleeps peacefully. And the next day, for the first time since she arrived at the Spring Court, Feyre wears a dress to dinner.

Kristina Deffenbacher describes this phenomenon in contemporary fiction, noting that "the paranormal serves to renaturalize rape as part of men's biological makeup: the supernatural male is driven by the 'nature' of his species to lay sexual claim to his instinctively recognized mate. In the logic of such texts, the singular, supernatural bond that the hero shares with his mate ensures that although she might initially resist, it is not rape; it is a biologically driven sex act determined by (supernatural) genetics, as opposed to a socially driven act of violence influenced by constructions of assaultive masculinity" (Deffenbacher 2014, 926). In the *ACOTAR* universe, this notion of fae males seeking out their mates does occur; it is the fairy-tale subtext of the true and magical bond that is the most desirable form of relationship in the series. In this specific case, Tamlin believes Feyre is his mate, and in believing it himself he makes Feyre believe it too. As is evidenced by this example of his violent claiming of her in the hallway, and her subsequent capitulation to his advances indicated by her wearing a gown to dinner, she forgives his tactics when she realizes it is all part of a larger plot of true love.

Tamlin tells Feyre that he wants her to remain at his manor where he can look after her, to be able to come home and know she is there, "painting and safe" (Maas 2016, 206). He is unashamed to relegate her to the domestic realm in his fantasies about their future. Feyre loses sight of herself within his flattery. He tells her that while he has had many lovers, none have under-stood him like Feyre does, knowing "what it is like, for me to care for my people, my lands. What scars are still there, what the bad days feel like" (Maas 2016, 207). Having both been left unexpectedly responsible for their family's well-being, Tamlin believes that he finds in Feyre a kindred spirit. This series of events shifts the course of the novel from one where Feyre is fighting her plight as a prisoner of Prythian to one in which she succumbs to the pleasures of Prythian, including her relationship with Tamlin which rap-idly grows romantic. After a night of drinking, dancing, and kissing at the summer solstice, Feyre feels happy. Happier than she ever believed possible. She tells Tamlin: "My father once told me that I should let my sisters ima-gine a better life—a better world. And I told him that there was no such thing . . . I never understood—because I couldn't . . . couldn't believe that it was even possible. . . . Until now" (Maas 2016, 230). This is a cycle that Tamlin and Feyre have begun, one in which Tamlin feels protective of her as a mortal and as his lover, and Feyre is drawn to him for the safety he provides and the bliss that she experiences in those moments where she lives without struggle. That Feyre is, in fact, a prisoner of Prythian and a mortal who is "safest" on Tamlin's estate is forgotten. Feyre sees herself as the agent of her own fate, as autonomous in her pleasure. This is the trickery of the Beauty and the Beast tale, as well, as Belle sees the good beneath the beast's exterior and falls in love. So Feyre chooses to see Tamlin's kindness, chivalry, and sexual generosity over the rougher parts of her reality.

Feyre learns the next day that it is the dark magic of an evil Faerie Queen that threatens Prythian, and cursed Tamlin's court. The Queen demonstrates her power by killing two dozen of the Winter Court's children. The next day, Feyre learns that "the blight" has killed two dozen children in the Winter

Court. What Feyre does not know is that Tamlin had repeatedly refused Amarantha's advances, and so she cast a spell upon the members of the Spring Court, permanently affixing the masks to their faces and keeping them from being able to access their full powers. She agreed to lift the curse if Tamlin would become her lover, and when he refused Amarantha turned his heart to stone and gave him forty-nine years to find a mortal who would freely confess her love for him. That mortal must originally harbor a deep mistrust and hatred for the Faeries, going as far as to slay one of them in cold blood. If he did not manage to complete this task, she would claim him and all of his subjects as slaves and imprison them in Under the Mountain. The curse does not allow them to tell any of this to Feyre. However, it is revealed to readers that Feyre was that mortal, and Tamlin had found her in the final year. The demonstration of power which killed the children of the Winter Court was confirmation that time was running out.

When Tamlin goes to her bed that night he apologizes and tells her that he is sending her home. He tells her that he has taken on her life debt to the Treaty and that he will take responsibility for his comrade's death. When Feyre originally begged Tamlin for a way to end the Treaty she was told there was no possible way to get around it. She sought answers and found no mercy. However, once Tamlin has fallen in love with Feyre his fear that she will be taken from him propels him to find a way out of the bond. Tamlin believes that he is merciful, and that he is selfless in sending Feyre away, but he is selfish in only finding solutions when it is him who stands to lose something. He is selfish in having kept Feyre at his manor, just in case it was possible for her to fall in love with him. And now this is not what Feyre wants. She has grown accustomed to Prythian and the ease of life in the Spring Court, returning to the human realm seems harsh. She has found comfort, safety, and affection in Prythian, and she begs Tamlin to let her stay. He refuses and tells her she will leave in the morning.

They spend their last night entangled, in all the ways that they have not allowed themselves to be until then. Sex, for Feyre and Tamlin, is an inter-play of enthusiastic consent and female sexual pleasure. Tamlin waits for Feyre's cues before he proceeds, moving slowly. When she sucks in a breath at his touch, he hesitates and pulls back, pausing at each step to make sure Feyre is with him. "Don't stop," she tells him. Even so, he asks again— warning her that "If we keep going, I don't be able to stop at all" (Maas 2016, 246). She looks him directly in the eye as she removes her clothes, and verbally consents, "Give me everything." And though the description of their coupling is heavily focused on "a beast freed of its tether," he also makes sure she is pleasured first, giving her an orgasm before he even begins. And again, he waits for her to have an orgasm again before he finishes his. He stays all night, cuddling, nestling, stroking her hair. Feyre is saddened: "Just when this place had become more than a sanctuary . . . and Tamlin far, far more than a savior or friend, I was leaving. It could be years until I saw this house again, years until I smelled his rose garden, until I saw those gold-flecked eyes. Home—this was home. 'I love you,' he whispered, and kissed my brow. 'Thorns and all'" (Maas 2016, 248). Their last night is a perfect night, which seems to erase Feyre's memories of the months she spent in the castle in captivity.

Just as with the traditional Beauty and the Beast tale, Feyre misses Tamlin when she returns to the human realm. She knows that he is in danger, because when the curse was left unbroken the Spring Court was ordered to move Under the Mountain, which is the royal court of Queen Amarantha. So, Feyre journeys for days to find her way back, and finds the house empty save for Alis, who is packing to return to her home in the Summer Court. Alis tells Feyre how she can get to Under the Mountain through a secret passageway, but warns her that she will only find pain and devastation. Determined to beg the Queen to save Tamlin's life, Feyre journeys on. What she finds is a palace filled with extraordinary torture, abuse, manipulation, coercion, and trickery. The Fae are known in the human world to be cruel, and to enjoy the pain and suffering of others, but Feyre learns that this is only the truth for some. That tendency, however, when it is present, is extreme, because the Fae are powerful, they possess magic, and they are immortal. The sadistic creativity Amarantha imagines in order to control her kingdom bears no match, and even with every High Lord imprisoned in the same place, they still are unable to outmaneuver her. She is supported by dark magic from an object long believed to have been forgotten, called "the cauldron." With her power amplified by objects from the cauldron, she is unstoppable. For one man who jilted his lover, who happened to be Amarantha's sister, she imprisons his soul in a glass eyeball which she wears around her neck, so that he will have to witness her reign for eternity. For Rhysand, the High Lord of the Night Court, who was instrumental in killing one of Amarantha's closest allies, Tamlin's father, she coercively takes him as her lover, controlling him through both magic and manipulation to serve her every sexual whim. She also forces him to serve as her Second, which puts him in the position of having to kill for her, betray for her, gather secrets for her. For a spy whose disloyalty was uncovered in the Winter Court, Amarantha killed twenty children. And for Tamlin, who spurred Amarantha as a lover for decades, she forces him to sit in a throne by her side as she tortures the human girl she believes is his love.

Amarantha is furious when Feyre arrives Under the Mountain, because she thought she had already been captured, tortured, and killed. Amarantha mistakenly had kidnapped another girl from her home village. She had been pinned to the wall, stripped naked, brutalized, and flayed, her face in death still relaying the pain she endured before she died. Amarantha makes a deal with Feyre that if she can live through three tests and solve a riddle, she will set everyone, Tamlin included, free. While Tamlin remains still as a stone, unmoving, and unemotional, Feyre accepts, knowing that she will die either way; at least having accepted the challenge, she can go out fighting.

Feyre's time Under the Mountain foregrounds her incredible bravery and skill, and also highlights the tortures and torments that will haunt her nightmares for years to come. In the first trial, Feyre faces the Middengard Wyrm in an underground maze of tunnels. The wyrm is an enormous wormlike monster with a front end made up of ring after ring of razor sharp teeth. If Feyre faces it head on she will die; but it happens to be blind for having been raised underground. She outsmarts it by setting a trap for it by crafting a pillory of bones of previous victims, but she is badly wounded and thrown back into her prison cell. She makes a bargain with Rhysand, who is Amarantha's Second, to heal her. Otherwise, she will not survive her infection. Her bargain is that she will spend one week per month for the rest of her life in the Night Court. For her second trial she is placed in a pit with a large fence across the middle, with Lucien chained on the other side. There are three levers on the wall; if Feyre pulls the right one, they will be freed. If she pulls the wrong one they will be impaled by spikes on the ceiling. Despairing and certain she will die, she notices a tingling sensation on her hand each time she moves it near a lever. She realizes that this is Rhysand telling her which one to pull; since he healed her in her cell, she chooses to trust him, and she lives. The third, and final, trial requires Feyre to kill three innocent faeries by stabbing them in the heart. The first is a boy who pleads for his life, the second is a girl who says a prayer and then asks Feyre to kill her, and the third is Tamlin. She stabs Tamlin in the heart not knowing that he had been cursed with a heart of stone, and he survives. As everyone clamors to be freed by Feyre's success Queen Amarantha discloses her trickery, that she had only said they would be freed, not when, and that Feyre has still not solved the riddle. Also, she never made a promise to allow Feyre to live, so she breaks every bone in Feyre's body. Right before she dies, Feyre realizes the answer to the riddle is "love," and she breathes it out with her dying breath. Her actions break the spell instantly. The masks are dropped, everyone's powers are restored, and with the surge of power and anger Tamlin immediately kills Amarantha. For her bravery, and for having saved them all, each High Fae High Lord approaches Feyre's dead body and releases a small cloud of particles over her, which are absorbed into her body. It is a drop of lifeforce, and with the lifeforce of all seven High Lords at once she is reborn, made immortal, and turned to High Fae.

At the start of book two, *A Court of Mist and Fury*, Feyre is settling in at the Spring Court, and gets engaged to Tamlin. After having been tortured, killed, and reborn as High Fae, Feyre is traumatized. She is having nightmares, dreams where she cannot decipher between waking and dreaming, during which she is locked in a dark cell. She awakens panicked: "This was real. I had survived; I'd made it out . . . I wished my human heart had been changed with the rest of me, made into immortal marble. Instead of the shredded bit of blackness that it now was. . . . And I didn't think even eternity would be long enough to fix me" (Maas 2017, 6). She is depressed, and having difficulty adjusting to her new life, and her new reality. Whole nights pass in a trancelike state where she does not recognize the passing of time, sometimes vomiting through the night. Her reaction is normal within the context of trauma, the symptoms of which can "include repetition of the event, flashbacks, nightmares, hypersensitivity, hyperarousal, unprovoked violent outbursts, evasion of certain situations or sensations, irrational anger, emotional and psychological numbing, and a disrupted sense of personal time" (Earle 2017, 31). But Tamlin does not see this. He does not awaken when she gets out of bed, or when she is violently ill all night long. During his waking hours he is possessive, but at night he is emotionally distant.

Having nearly lost Feyre, Tamlin is more protective of her than ever. She wants to explore their kingdom, help with the rebuilding efforts, but he will not allow it, telling her it is not safe for her, claiming: "I can't do what I need to do if I'm worrying about whether you're safe" (Maas 2017, 11). As she heals, she begins to realize that when the High Lords saved her life with a drop of their lifeblood, she inherited a bit of each of their powers. This makes her potentially the most powerful being who has ever existed, able to wield the powers of all the High Lords at once. Rhysand of the Night Court is believed to be the most powerful High Lord alive, but Feyre has the potential to be much stronger. When Tamlin learns about this he insists that she keep it a secret and stay out of sight: "You don't need to train. I can guard you from whatever comes our way" (Maas 2017, 86). And she justifies his control over her by telling herself: "He was High Lord—my High Lord. He was the shield and defender of his people. Of me. And keeping me safe meant that his people could continue to hope, to build a new life, that he could do the same . . . I could bow to him on this one thing. I could do it." But Rhysand's words, spoken to her at one of her bargained visits to the Night Court, echo in the back of her mind: "You are no one's subject . . . It's your choice to make—no one else's" (Maas 2017, 74). Feyre chafes at the limits Tamlin has placed on her movements, and on her body, but she excuses his actions by believing that this is how he shows her his love.

Feyre's trauma has left her claustrophobic, and so when she senses that Tamlin's repeated limitations mean that she is not allowed to leave the manor, it causes her to panic. One afternoon she dares to confront Tamlin about it, telling him that living under guard day and night feels like suffocation: "'I'm drowning,' I managed to say. 'I am drowning. And the more you do this, the more guards. . . . You might as well be shoving my head under the water'" (Maas 2017, 99). When Feyre says this to Tamlin, he lashes out violently, "his power blasted through the room. The windows shattered. The furniture splintered . . . paints and brushes and paper . . . exploded into dust and glass and wood. One breath, the study was intact. The next, it was shards of nothing, a shell of a room" (Maas 2017, 100–101). When Tamlin realizes what he has done, he feels devastation, pain, fear, and grief. He apologizes and promises to give her more freedom.

Up until this point in the series, Feyre believes that she is independent, that her relationship with Tamlin is a consenting one, and that her choice to rescue him (and ultimately save Prythian) is one made freely. But in reality, as noted at the start of this chapter, Feyre's story is one of repeated trauma, especially in relation to Tamlin. Feyre's well-being is deeply, though perhaps unconsciously, affected by her narrative of "ambiguous sexual trauma," which is an "event that included a romantic partner, events that started with some degree of consent, or an internalized belief that they should 'go along with' the sexual coercion" (Fahs 2016, 69). Women who experience ambiguous sexual trauma often perceive "themselves as complicit in the encounter, as if they did something to inspire sexual violence," and often blame themselves because they felt "pressured to allow coercion to occur [suggesting] internalized dual pressures to 'give in' to sex and to construct a flexible boundary between consent and nonconsent" (Fahs 2016, 72). Girls and women who experience this sort of sexual trauma often do not speak about it for fear of being blamed, even though those who go through "coercive sexual encounters experience a range of mental health consequences, including PTSD, depression, anxiety, mood disorders, sexual disorders, and borderline personality disorder" (Fahs 2016, 68). In fact, Breanne Fahs identifies sexual coercion as a "pervasive, pandemic, and almost universal experience in women's sexual lives," which makes Feyre's journey even more pressing and relevant to the lives of readers who would not otherwise have access to information about this topic (Fahs 2016, 74).

Though Feyre does not become truly conscious of this sexual coercion until later in book two, it is evident to readers in the way that she is stuck in a cycle of outbursts that lead to apologies, apologies that lead to making up (often intimately), and making up that leads her to forget—for a little while, anyway—the violence that started it all. Since, as scholars such as Kokesh and Sternadori argue, readers identify with characters in the novels they read, and sometimes use the experiences of their favorite characters to guide how they navigate their own lives, this representation of Feyre's relationship with Tamlin as coercive is an important one for them to see, since so often girls and women blame themselves for these kinds of encounters. It is valuable for them to see that she is experiencing the effects of trauma as a result of his controlling behavior, and to see the way that she comes to know her relationship as unhealthy—and heal from it—in subsequent chapters. Perhaps they will able to identify these symptoms and cues in their own lives, if they show up.

Tamlin quickly goes back on his word to give Feyre more freedom of movement throughout the manor and beyond. She begs him to let her join him on a patrol into town. He denies her, citing her inability to sleep through the night and the fact that she can barely stand being around other people. She reminds him that he promised he would give her more space. He tells her she is a liability. She feels herself cracking, and so asserts her will and tells him she is going whether he likes it or not. He responds with a powerful show of magic: "'No, you aren't.' He strode right through the door, his claws slashing the air at his sides, and was halfway down the steps before I reached the threshold. Where I slammed into an invisible wall. I staggered back, trying to reorder my mind around the impossibility of it . . . I slammed my hand into the invisible barrier. No movement—nothing but hardened air. And I had not learned about my own powers enough to try to punch through, to shatter it . . . I had let him convince me not to learn those things for *his* sake. . . . He'd locked me in here" (Maas 2017, 122–123). She is literally trapped in the home. Tamlin has shielded the house so that others can come and go, but she cannot leave until he lifts the barrier. She has flashbacks of being locked in a cell in Under the Mountain.

Tamlin literally trapping Feyre in the manor in this way, blocking her in so that she cannot leave the house, has even more nuance than the mere fact that he has imprisoned her. By imprisoning her in the house, he is locking her in the domestic sphere. He is signifying to Feyre that her place is in the home, not by his side, not in the field, not in battle. He is demonstrating to her that she is not his equal. From the moment that Feyre arrived at the Spring Court, she has never been Tamlin's equal. As a human under his protection in Prythian, he always held her life in his hands. Her well-being was always the product of his good will, and as such was always contingent and reliant on Feyre behaving. He has always told her how to behave: from how to dress or what to eat for dinner, to how to act grateful for the gifts he gives her, to rules about not leaving her room under various supposedly "dangerous" circumstances. He has always told her where she could go, in the house, on the manor grounds, and in town. Feyre has always pushed against these restrictions, telling Tamlin that she does not want to be his pet, or his trophy, or his prize. She believes that she wants to be his Lady, and they are engaged at this time in the series, but she has to constantly subdue her own desires in order to fulfill that role. By trapping Feyre in the house, Tamlin is trapping her in domesticity, in wifehood, and he is fully objectifying her into the silent prize that he wishes her to be. Containing her in his home is symbolic of the way that Tamlin sees Feyre, as subservient and fragile. It is very telling that at this moment, Feyre literally cannot breathe. Her reaction is to reach out with all the power she can muster—power that she has not been practicing, because Tamlin told her it was a bad idea to let other Lords know that she had it—to try to escape. She cannot break the wall

Tamlin has erected, but she is able to conjure darkness from her despair, and she grows hidden from view. She appears as a black hole, or a tornado of darkness.

That Feyre does not want to be subservient or unequal, and that she does not want to stay at home while Tamlin takes care of the Spring Court, is emblematic of who Feyre is as a girl, especially in terms of the ways that she is pushing against normative gender roles. She has always been a huntress, an agent of her own life, and the protector of others. It feels wrong for her to follow Tamlin's rules, and to capitulate to his desires about their life together. He dreams of her being his Lady, safe and protected in his home, there for him when he returns from running the affairs of the land. Feyre's relationship with Tamlin is always uncomfortable for its coercive undertone, but it is also unsettling for the way that he tries to mold her into a model of domesticity that she is not and does not want to become. Many of their arguments stem from this fact, and his trying to control her actions and movements. It is unsurprising that Feyre leaves Tamlin when she has the chance, to escape the confines of the domestic prison that he wishes to keep her caged in; and it suits that Feyre's chosen home becomes the Night Court, where there is open sky, fresh air, and few walls to contain her.

Rhysand, High Lord of the Night Court—with whom Feyre has a bond due to his bargain to help her Under the Mountain—sends his cousin Mor to rescue Feyre from being trapped in Tamlin's manor. Though Feyre does not realize it yet, the Night Court is the total opposite of the Spring Court in every way. This is where she will find true and unconditional belonging. In stark contrast to the Spring Court, Rhysand foregrounds choice and individual autonomy over all else. At this point in the text, Feyre knows him mostly as "Amarantha's Second," from the time that she spent imprisoned in Under the Mountain, but the reality is far darker. In actuality, Rhysand was coerced, manipulated, and magically forced to serve as Amarantha's lover for fifty years, the entire reign of Under the Mountain, as "punishment" for his role in killing Tamlin's father, who was one of Amarantha's closest allies. She was powerful enough, with the help of the cauldron's magic, to imprison and weaken the High Lords of all seven Courts. Rhysand gave in to Amarantha's demands in order to protect his people. Furthermore, Rhysand, as the heir of the daemati ("those who can walk into another person's mind as if we were going from one room to another," a mind reader and manipulator) line of High Lords of the Night Court, was able to keep his home city of Velaris secret and protected from Amarantha, and from the other Courts (Maas 2017, 150). As the most powerful High Lord in Prythian, Rhysand selflessly gave his strength to the protection of his people during Amarantha's reign and allowed himself to suffer as her sex slave to maintain the ruse.

I shared that story out of the chronological order in which it is shared in the book, because it is critically important to understanding the context of

Feyre's experience in the Night Court from the first moment she sets foot there. Rhysand sends Mor to rescue Feyre from Tamlin's manor specifically because he had imprisoned her. If he had entered the Spring Court himself, it would have been a declaration of war. But Mor entering and exiting—using passageways that belong to no Court—was technically allowed by the rules of engagement. However, Rhysand clearly and carefully tells Feyre that she is free to stay in the Night Court, or return to the Spring Court, that the choice is hers. She is not being kept in the Night Court against her will. The freedom to choose, to be her own person, is the most important cue that Rhysand gives her. Through that simple gesture, Feyre begins to realize all of the ways that she was trapped and blinded in the Spring Court. "I must have been a fool in love to allow myself to be shown so little of the Spring Court . . . there's a great deal of that territory that I was never allowed to see or hear about and maybe I would have lived in ignorance like some pet" (Maas 2017, 156). Recognizing for the first time the ways in which her life with Tamlin was not comprised of choices freely made of her own will, she realizes: "I'm thinking maybe he knew that—maybe not actively, but maybe he wanted to be that person for someone. And maybe that worked for who I was before. Maybe it doesn't work for who—what I am now" (Maas 2017, 156). Feyre sees the depth of her captivity, and Tamlin's drive to "protect her," and realizes she does not want it. It is her first step toward a life of agency and consent, of control over her body and her decisions.

Feyre's first experience with agency and consent begins in book two when, after the tantrum of fury during which Tamlin trapped Feyre in his house, she chooses to live with Rhysand—the High Lord of the Night Court, and Tamlin's sworn enemy. There, given physical and emotional space to move and breathe, and the time for the luxury of curiosity, for the first time ever she learns about what she likes, what she wants, who she wants to be, and who she wants to be with. The development of a healthy relationship with firm boundaries with Rhysand demonstrates to her that her past had always been conditional, and she had never known freedom. She realizes, in her own time, that Tamlin's obsession with her caused her harm. Freedom and equality, that toward which she has had to claw her own way, become conditions that she would fight for with her whole being.

The Night Court is a healing space for Feyre. Her quest to save Tamlin from the clutches of an evil queen had her imprisoned in darkness, beaten, tortured, drugged, humiliated, and forced to fight for her life as sport. And in the months after, she was imprisoned in Tamlin's manor. Traumatic experiences have a profound impact on many different areas of functioning, and include "adverse interpersonal trauma (e.g., abandonment, betrayal, physical assaults, sexual assaults, threats to bodily integrity, coercive practices, emotional abuse, witnessing violence and death)," and also "subjective experience (e.g., rage, betrayal, fear, resignation, defeat, shame)" (van der Kolk

2005). Furthermore, the relationship between trauma-inducing experiences and psychological distress, including post-traumatic stress disorder (PTSD) is well established, and "symptoms include re-experiencing the traumatic event, hyperarousal, rumination and emotional numbing" (Rahim 2014). Feyre is traumatized and plagued by nightmares. She loses sleep, and she loses weight. She has panic attacks, and she sometimes finds it difficult to breathe. Sometimes she does not get out of bed.

But in Rhysand's Night Court she finds a city of starlight, vast open space, shimmering stars, cool, comforting darkness—like a restful sleep. Furthermore, everyone in the Night Court has things to heal from. Rhysand, from repeated, decades-long entrapment and sexual assault by Amarantha; Mor, from betrothal to an evil man, and being left for dead by her own family; Cassian, from a low class status emboldened by his birth out of wedlock, abandoned and unloved, ostracized from his people; and Azriel, imprisoned in a windowless cell in his father's own dungeon until he turned twelve years old. Here, Feyre develops, hones, and embraces the vast powers that were bestowed upon her when she was turned into a High Fae. Since each High Lord contributed some of their own unique power, Feyre finds herself able to wield them all, making her the most powerful High Fae living. This ability, and responsibility, begins to shift her perspective on her life and her role, especially as a protector. As she begins to allow herself to be immersed in the Night Court, she begins to realize that she has the capacity to protect those she is beginning to love.

Rhysand wants Feyre to work for him but wants her to be empowered to make the choice herself. When she meets his "inner circle," she finds connection with them, all of them having experienced trauma in their lifetimes and having forged a found family with each other. Cassian offers to provide weapons training to Feyre, which she accepts because she does not want to be weak and defenseless ever again. Having been convinced by Tamlin not to develop her powers or train in battle, Feyre was left without any protection when Tamlin used his magic to lock her in his manor. She is determined never to let that happen again: "I would not be weak again. I would not be dependent on anyone else. I would never have to endure . . . because I was too helpless to know where and how to hit. Never again" (Maas 2017, 177). She knows that a war with Hybern is imminent—Amarantha was a General for Hybern, and now that she is gone they have received word that the King of Hybern is developing plans to take over Prythian and then move on the human world—and that she is potentially the best weapon they have against him. It is interesting for Feyre to have gone from a helpless human kidnapped by Tamlin in book one, to being someone that is stronger and more capable than everyone else: "I was not a pet, not a doll, not an animal. I was a survivor, and I was strong. I would not be weak, or helpless again. I would not, *could not be* broken. Tamed. . . . I want to know how to fight my way out. I don't want to have to wait on anyone to rescue me" (Maas 2017, 226–228). She trains hard in physical battle with Cassian, in magical training with Rhysand, and in flying on shapeshifted wings with Azriel. In the same way that she was a highly skilled huntress as a human, one whose skills saved her family from starvation, she develops into a formidable fighter as a Fae as well. She chooses to work with Rhysand to fight the imminent war.

In many ways, Feyre is returning to the person she was before she met Tamlin. She was always a huntress and a protector and amplified as High Fae those skills give her extraordinary capacity. She rejects the domestication of Tamlin, and a relationship in which she does not have an equal partner. She embraces her newfound magical powers, because they will enable her to be able to serve as a warrior and a protector of her friends, her sisters, her realm, and all humans. Feyre comes to understand herself as a strong, independent agent. She never has to feel like she cannot fight back ever again, and she does not have to settle into an identity as a girl or women that does not fit her own goals for her life and her future. Girls reading about Feyre's empowerment here might be drawn to her physical strength, her capacity to both fight and protect those she loves, and her resilience in overcoming a toxic relationship.

Feyre's relationship with Rhysand (in books two and three) is worth exploring in a few ways. He cares that she feels safe. His townhouse in Velaris is warded and shielded, so that only those she wishes to enter may do so: "You are safe here; and safe anywhere in this city, for that matter. Velaris's walls are well protected and have not been breached in five thousand years" (Maas 2017, 136). He notices that she is unwell. She is not sleeping, she is not eating, she never smiles, she lacks interest in hobbies; she is a shell of herself in the months following her departure from the Spring Court. He spends many nights holding her hair back when she wakes in the night, memories of her past suffocating her, and heaves in the toilet. He changes her sheets, he draws her baths. He offers her space, provides support, challenges her to build up her physical and emotional strength, and waits. He, too, is recovering from horrible trauma, and intense imposter syndrome. He recognizes that his feelings may never be reciprocated, and he focuses on finding ways to enable her happiness. He teaches her to read, he takes her on adventures, he encourages her love of art, and he introduces her to food—a particularly special thing for someone who had lived in poverty for so long.

She grows attracted to him during book two, and though it takes time to revive her sexual interest in the wake of her traumas, she grows curious about Rhysand and attempts to seduce him. At every step of every sexual intensification that they have, he asks for clear, unambigious, verbal consent. Having been the victim of rape by a woman who held both magical and manipulative power over him, Rhysand has no tolerance for anything less than that. And, relating to his abiding interest in her happiness, he also takes seriously

Feyre's sexual pleasure. In every sexual encounter that they ever have, he asks her what she wants and works enthusiastically and passionately on behalf of her sexual and emotional satisfaction and fulfillment. The importance of this detail to the consciousness of young adults and teenagers in our contemporary political moment is crucial. Janice M. Del Negro writes "the young adult is measuring the world every day, seeking the right disguise, the right armor, the right path, the right energy that will protect and propel them through life. If the stories we tell create our reality, the importance of providing a strong narrative voice to young adults cannot be underestimated" (Del Negro 2017, 95). In this series, Sarah J. Maas offers not only a strong heroine narrative, but a heroine who is granted curiosity, agency, and intense sexual pleasure—and, equally unusual, a male lover who loves to give her that.

In their article "Bodies and Agentic Practice in Young Women's Sexual and Intimate Relationships," Claire Maxwell and Peter Aggleton study subjects age sixteen to eighteen, and examine "how young women describe and understand their bodies, how the body is imbued with power, and the ways bodies appear to lead and be integral to practices which are agentic" (Maxwell and Aggleton 2012, 306). Specifically, they find that the more connected young women feel to their bodies, the more likely they are to practice agency in their sexual relationships, in particular in their quest for sexual pleasure. In the study, the authors found that it was "an inequality of power between themselves and their partner [that] provoked an emotional reaction which appeared to motivate them to 'take action,' 'take power back,' and in this way be agentic" (Maxwell and Aggleton 2012, 310). This is a critical correlation to Feyre's story, and the way that she claims agency over her body in the aftermath of her trauma. Feyre's concept of self comes from personal understanding of the dynamic of power in her relationship with Tamlin, and the negative bodily sensations she experiences once she recognizes the coercive nature of their relationship. Maxwell and Aggleton note that "young women's narratives of sex and their bodies within their sexual and intimate relationship experiences might further inform our developing understanding of agentic practice" (Maxwell and Aggleton 2012, 311). With Rhysand, Feyre seeks equality and sexual pleasure, offering her a way to claim, and then embody, the practice of agency in her relationship, which in fact shifts understanding of gender relations within the novel: Feyre as equal, as powerful, and as having agency over her body and her life.

As well, Rhysand encourages Feyre to be his equal in all things. When they become mated (which is the acceptance of a magical bond between two Fae), and then marry, she becomes High Lady of the Night Court alongside his High Lord title. Within the text, there had never been a High Lady in the history of the High Fae, and it is the subject of both awe and consternation. The Kingdom becomes theirs, she owns half the assets, and she is never coerced into taking actions. Maxwell and Aggleton write that "[t]he sexual body and an emerging understanding of one's sexuality from bodily experiences may therefore have the potential to shift understandings of gender relations, and of how power is understood within sexual and intimate relationships and this could be a . . . way in which bodies can become central to sustained agentic practices" (Maxwell and Aggleton 2012, 318). Feyre's equality as a sexual partner spills over into equality in her relationship, and gives her the capacity to seek out equality in all spheres of her life, constituting what Maxwell and Aggleton describe as "assertive, refusing, proactive, and interrogative strategies . . . the grammar of a more inclusive theory of agency that goes beyond the inadequacies of framing practice as affirmation and/or resistance" (Maxwell and Aggleton 2012, 319). When Feyre is able to reclaim connection to her body in the aftermath of trauma, she is able to experience sustained agentic practice that carries over into all parts of her life.

The joining of Feyre and Rhysand in this way symbolizes another layer of feminist revisioning of fairy tales in this series. That Feyre leaves the Beast (Tamlin) and is able to see the ways in which he manipulated her in their relationship is one step. Next, that Feyre is given time to feel that trauma, and then heal from it in the Night Court, without the intervention of men, is crucial to her journey. When she partners with Rhysand, it is after a great deal of deliberate thought; she does not want to be with anyone that she cannot be fully herself with, and she does not want to cede control of her autonomy to another in any way. And so last, when they choose to marry, they rewrite eons of tradition—in which there was never, in the history of Prythian, a High Lady—to marry and lead the Night Court as fully equal partners. This is crucial, in the context of other fairy tales retellings in the twenty-first century which rarely find ways to revise marriage plot. As Rosalind Sibielski writes of modern revisions to Cinderella, feminist critiques of fairy tales often focus on the "marriage plot," which hinges on "its ideological function in affirming patriarchal conceptions of marriage, in which women have an unequal and subordinate status." As such, she explains that is it significant when revisions rewrite that marriage plot, especially when it is "marriage on her own terms and to a man of her own choosing. In this way, the marriage plot within the fairy tale shifts from a signifier of women's oppression under patriarchy to a signifier of women's empowerment" (Sibielski 2019, 599–601). For Feyre, marriage to Rhysand centers her empowerment as an equal partner and offers her the pathway that she needs to exercise agency to forge a community of consent and healing for all people in Velaris.

The way that sexual pleasure gives way to healing, and then to empowerment, is evident in the way that Feyre chooses to become a protector. In order to have the power to defeat the King of Hybern, who has the cauldron and the enhanced magic that comes from that, Feyre must retrieve an object that has been hidden for millenia, called the Book of Breathings. It is connected to the cauldron, and, according to ancient legend, instructs the reader how to wield the cauldron's greatest magic. Feyre's unique powers and skills give her the ability to retrieve it, and it is the key to turning the tide of war at the end of book three. Tamlin convinces himself and others in his Court that Feyre has been mind-tricked into believing that she loves Rhysand; Rhysand's daemati talents are notorious, and people who do not know him tend to believe the worst about him. Tamlin believes that Rhysand has even tricked Feyre into believing she has a mating bond with him. He allies with the King of Hybern to draw Feyre to Hybern, to the cauldron, which she intends to steal from the King.

As an act of war and retaliation, the King captures Feyre's sisters and places them in the cauldron, an object of unimaginable power, without actually knowing what would happen to them, and they are forcibly turned Fae. Their forced conversion to Faehood is a violation of their bodies, a permanent, irreversible reminder of a choice they never made. It nearly breaks one sister, Elain, who is engaged to a fae-hating human, and who becomes a seer in the change. It enrages her other sister, Nesta, who vows to kill the enemy King for what he has done. For Feyre, her sisters become like her in more ways than just their Faehood; they, too, are now the victims of trauma, of the erasure of agency. Tamlin also asks the King to forcibly break the mating bond between Feyre and Rhysand, believing that Feyre will return to Tamlin if given the opportunity to make the choice "freely." Feyre, infuriated by Tamlin's betrayal of Prythian and of her sisters, concocts a plan to trick Tamlin into believing that she had, in fact, been manipulated by Rhysand, and tells him that she truly loves him and wants to return to the Spring Court. The ruse works and Tamlin takes her "home." At the end of book two, Feyre is living undercover as a spy in the Spring Court, where she can learn about Hybern's armies and plans.

One mechanism that feels restorative in this series of YA books is violence carried out against predators who disempower others by ripping away agency and choice of their victims, which is especially evident in book three, *A Court of Wings and Ruin*. This is, in fact, one of the Night Court's central motivations, to "right" these wrongs perpetrated against those who, for a wide variety of reasons, find themselves vulnerable and unprotected. Furthermore, they shelter victims of horrific assaults, giving them space and time to heal emotionally and physically, and then offering them a safe place to resume their lives. For example, Rhysand offers sanctuary in the Great Library of Velaris to priestesses who have experienced violence and trauma. One such faerie, Clotho, was attacked by a group of males, beaten and tortured repeatedly so that even a healer could not fully heal her. They cut out her tongue so that she could not tell people who had harmed her, and they smashed her hands so that she could not write their names. When Feyre asks

Rhysand why the males did not just kill her, he tells her "Because it was more entertaining for them that way. That is, until Mor found her. And brought her to me" (Maas 2018, 216). As a daemati, Rhysand was able to read Clotho's memories to see who attacked her. He let Mor hunt them, and then Mor stayed with Clotho for a month while she healed physically and emotionally. The males had healed her as they hurt her, which made many of her injuries permanent. Rhysand tells Feyre that "to heal her, the wounds would have needed to be ripped open again. I offered to take the pain away while it was done, but . . . she could not endure it—what having the wounds open again would trigger in her mind. Her heart. She has lived down here since then—with others like her. Her magic helps with her mobility" (Maas 2018, 217). Now the library serves as a sanctuary, as all of the priestesses there have endured traumas. The priestesses have full control over who visits and can stay for as long as they like. That way, they can heal from their trauma without interference from those who would cause them harm. Those who use the library must take binding oaths that they will do no harm while they visit. "Choice," Feyre notes. "It had always been about my choice for him. And for others as well. Long before he'd ever learned the hard way about it" (Maas 2018, 217).

The Great Library is a space of deep healing. Instead of trapping people inside, as Tamlin did with Feyre in the Spring Court, the Great Library is a place of protection. No one may enter without the express permission of the survivors inside. This is a space of comfort, support, and love, and is significant in the way that the existence of this place reflects on Rhysand. It was Rhysand who evicted the male "librarians" who had been entitled to the library as their space for generations and warded it for Clotho and other women like her, who needed a place separate from men. Rhysand enabled the priestesses to set their own rules, to control access and usage to the space and to the books. This is another way that Velaris is a community of consent and healing.

As Feyre launches her escape from the Spring Court in book three, she comes across Lucien (Tamlin's Second, and someone Feyre had once thought was a friend) in the woods as she is leaving. He has been immobilized by Ianthe, who is a priestess known to manipulate and trick men into bed with her; in fact, Rhysand had shared a memory with Feyre in book one where Ianthe had attempted to seduce Rhysand, in hopes that he would marry her, ignoring his clear verbal and physical cues that he was not interested in her. When he would not fall for it, she moved on to Azriel, and then Cassian, until Rhysand threw her out of the Night Court and banished her from ever returning. Now, she is angry that Lucien will not sleep with her (something Feyre suspects Ianthe has demanded of Lucien many times over the years). When Feyre finds them, Ianthe has trapped Lucien with wrist bands that nullify magic, and she is holding him against a tree "as Ianthe surveyed him like a snake before a meal" (Maas 2018, 85). In front of Feyre, Ianthe reaches toward Lucien's pants "not for his own pleasure, but simply to throw it in my face that she *could*" (Maas 2018, 86). Feyre uses the daemati powers that she developed from receiving Rhysand's life force when she was resurrected as Fae and enters Ianthe's consciousness: "A mask of decay. That's what it felt like to go inside that beautiful head and find such hideous thoughts inside it. A trail of males she'd used her power on or outright forced to bed, convinced of her entitlement to them. I pulled back against the tug of those memories, mastering myself. 'Take your hands off him'" (Maas 2018, 86). The daemati power means that those whose minds are attacked in such a way are incapable of resisting, and so she obeys. Feyre tells Ianthe to smash her own hand with a large rock, "the hand she's put on him, on so many others," which she does (Maas 2018, 87). Feyre tells Ianthe that she will never touch another person against their will again, that she will never convince herself that someone wants it when they do not, that she will never know another's touch unless it is fully consensual. She tells Ianthe that she will forget what happened, but that "every time you look at your hand, you are going to remember that touching people against their will has consequences, and if you do it again, everything you are will cease to exist. You will live with that terror every day, and never know where it originates. Only the fear of something chasing you, hunting you, waiting for you the instant you let your guard down" (Maas 2018, 87). During her time in the Spring Court, Feyre had learned that Ianthe had also been the one who suggested to Tamlin that he sell her sisters out to the King of Hybern, as added incentive for Feyre to leave with Tamlin. She wishes Ianthe to live a long life, and never know a moment's peace.

Amarantha and Ianthe are both women who use their power to rape men. They have both allied with the powerful King of Hybern, and in so doing were granted strong magical powers. As such, they are instruments of the patriarchy, which for a while allows them to thrive. In the case of Amarantha, she works for the King of Hybern to do his dirty work in Prythian. In return, her powers are augmented by the cauldron's magic, such that she can overpower all of the other High Lords in Prythian. Amarantha is protected by the King of Hybern, and by the cauldron's magic, because of her loyalty to the King's goal of controlling all of Prythian's courts through dampening the powers of their High Lords. Amarantha controls all the High Lords of Prythian through a magical spell that weakens their magic and allows her to overpower them. This works until Feyre outsmarts Amarantha, by solving a riddle that would break Amarantha's power over Prythian. By outsmarting Amarantha, Feyre is overturning patriarchal control. That leaves the door open for Tamlin to kill Amarantha, and this breaks the tie that the King of Hybern has over Prythian. Feyre solving the riddle, leaving Amarantha vulnerable, and Amarantha being killed by Tamlin chips away at the patriarchal domination within the series that is represented by Hybern's forces trying to conquer and dominate Prythian.

Ianthe has a similar role, in terms of her relationship to patriarchy. Ianthe has allied with the King of Hybern as well, and as such she has been given power and protection. She betrays Feyre, Tamlin's guards, and Tamlin himself in order to do Hybern's bidding, and as such she is given a high-level rank in his army and is granted free reign of the camp. After Feyre breaks Ianthe's hand and breaks into her mind to ensure that she never touches another man without his consent, the King of Hybern finds a way to untangle Feyre's spell and heal Ianthe's hand. She then becomes intensely loyal to him. When Ianthe dies by the Weaver's hand (the Weaver is represented as an old blind woman who lives in a cottage in the woods, and weaves fabric out of human flesh), it is another example of woman's cunning power overcoming patriarchy's brute force.

Even Tamlin, ultimately, is completely broken by Feyre for all the times that he coerced, manipulated, and trapped her. While she is embedded as a spy in the Spring Court she sets a trap, a web of seemingly innocent or spontaneous circumstances that lead Tamlin's Guard to mistrust him; that sow even deeper insecurity into Tamlin's confidence and leadership. When she escapes the Spring Court, she takes Lucien with her to the Night Court, meaning that Tamlin loses his best friend, his Second, and his most trusted ally. As word gets out about what happened, about all that Tamlin had done working with the King of Hybern to forcibly get Feyre back against Feyre's wishes, the Spring Court crumbles. Tamlin is left alone, broken, and angry. At first, Tamlin blames Feyre for the war that has begun: "'I bartered my lands to get back the woman I love from a sadist who plays with minds as if they are toys. I meant to fight Hybern—to find a way around the bargain I made with the king once she was back. Only Rhysand and his cabal had turned her into one of them. And she delighted in ripping open my territory for Hybern to invade. All for a petty grudge—either her own or her . . . master's'" (Maas 2018, 418). Feyre refuses his story, retorting: "'You don't get to rewrite the narrative.'" When he learns that she has become High Lady of the Night Court, he tries to convince himself and others that Feyre is power hungry—going wherever she can ascend the highest. He struggles to see anything beyond his own jealousy and rage. Though he is partially redeemed at the end of the book series, when he provides the seven courts with valuable intel about Hybern, fights for Prythian rather than Hybern, and helps resurrect Rhysand after he dies a hero in battle, Feyre's justice is total, justifiably vengeant, and unforgiving. Tamlin's demise is the just cost of Feyre's total freedom, independence, and right to choose her own path.

Kristina Deffenbacher explains that "[i]n response to threats and acts of rape, heroines . . . develop their supernatural powers and embrace their capacity for violence. The changes in these heroines and in their relationships offers a vision of gender identity that is not defined by rape and rapability, a denaturalizing inversion of readers cultural experience" (Deffenbacher 2014, 928). Feyre's development as a vigilante character is intricately connected to a contemporary feminist sensibility in which the performance of a violent fantasy of feminism—a vigilante feminism—serves as a corrective to the powerlessness felt by real girls and young women who feel like passive participants in their own disempowerment. This is characterized in this book as vigilantism performed by girls and women who have undertaken their own protection, and the protection of others, because they have been otherwise failed in that manner. They wield violence to make the world safer for others. For example, vigilante feminism aims to attack patriarchy by reappropriating its tools in agentic ways. It symbolizes social equality between men and women by claiming the tactics of what has traditionally been characterized as a violent masculinity. It is interwoven with the contemporary sensibility that the individual freedom and empowerment of girls constitutes a feminist rebellion.

In writing about twenty-first century adaptations of Cinderella, Sibielski affirms that "revisionist, popular media versions . . . reshape the fairy tale in light of, and in reaction to, American cultural responses to late 20th and early 21st century feminist activism." She explains that fairy tale revisions serve as a site of "ideological struggle over the forms that female empowerment can and does take . . . [as well as] the various ways in which these revisionist versions of 'Cinderella' deploy the fairy tale in order to interrogate the culturally contested role of feminism in women's empowerment" (Sibielski 2019, 585). Similarly, Feyre's disruption of gender roles and her use of violence and claiming of agency over her own life and body are ways that she embodies feminism and empowerment in this retelling. She notes that the "cultural function of providing platforms to work through upheavals in understandings of gender and sexuality is not new to fairy tales, nor is it unique to those revisionist fairy tales of the 21st Century" (Sibielski 2019, 591). Indeed, in both media and literature, fairy tales are popular fodder for retellings, and have found wide success with audiences who enjoy the reclamation of girls and women historically subservient to the patriarchy. When their characters flip the script, like Feyre does, it feels empowering for readers.

In *Comics, Trauma, and War*, Harriet E. H. Earle takes on the analysis of trauma in comic books, and uses it to draw "both clinical definitions and understandings of the impact of trauma on both the individual and the wider society" (Earle 2017, 25). She notes that comics, as a genre, have proven to be not only capable of representing difficult topics, but also well suited to it, as they "engage the difficulty of spectacle instead of turning away from it" (Earle 2017, 17). Specifically engaging the subject of the narrative of rape, she notes that "literature of trauma is written from the need to tell and retell the story of the traumatic experience, to make it real both to the victim and to the community. Such writing serves as both validation and cathartic vehicle for the traumatized writer" (Earle 2017, 41). Connecting this theory to comics, Earle argues that comics produce affect in readers, mimicking some part of the "feelings and experience of trauma," and those "affects within the reader . . . can assist in comprehension of the events and experiences discussed" (Earle 2017, 43). And though Earle is careful to separate the consumption of a traumatic narrative from the experience of a traumatic event (they are not the same), readers do play the role of trauma witness, which serves as healing for readers who have experienced trauma, or who are vicariously experiencing it through stories of people they know, or from the barrage of stories in the media. I find Earle's conceptualization of trauma in comics to be applicable to the reading of trauma in popular literature, as well, because it provides a carefully delineated frame through which to analyze the role of narrative in the lives of girls and young women who consume stories.

Earle's description of the psychological effects of trauma are useful in reading characters like Feyre, and later in this book, for Scarlett March (*Sisters Red*), Laura Kinney (*X-23*), and Jules (*Sweet/Vicious*), including her experiences with "flashbacks, nightmares, hypersensitivity, hyperarousal, unprovoked violent outbursts, evasion of certain situations or sensations, irrational anger, emotional and psychological numbing, and a disrupted sense of personal time" (Earle 2017, 31). When Feyre moves to the Night Court, she begins to unravel the conditions that had kept her imprisoned and coerced, as well as the extreme violence she faced at the hands of the Queen Under the Mountain. This is an important process for readers to have the opportunity to read about, because they may not otherwise have the opportunity to see the effects of violence on others, or, importantly, to see how others heal.

Readers are also playing the role of the witness. As Debra Jackson explains about "witnessing trauma," the process of "constructing a self-narrative, particularly after experiencing traumatic events, is an essential component of resubjectification, and it is an intersubjective process involving dialogue with an empathetic other, a witness to trauma" (Jackson 2016, 211). The stories of survivors are important, because they are an embodiment of agency, a way for survivors to control their narrative, which is a way of healing. In the telling of the story, details of sexual violence are often described in detail. Readers, therefore, become witnesses, and are able to empathize with the experiences of the characters while also recognizing that the emotional experiences of the heroines are not their own. This development of empathy is crucial for the young adult reader, as is the opportunity to deal vicariously with sexual violence and trauma, especially when, in a story like Feyre Archeron's, the protagonist heals.

The phenomenon of vicarious trauma is important to consider here. Vicarious trauma is something that social workers, activists, and teachers may experience as they work with people who experience trauma. They can take on the characteristics of burnout, fatigue, and in some cases PTSD. But vicarious trauma can also be a reality for girls and young women, who grow up bombarded with stories of sexual violence. Many girls and young women have experienced sexual violence firsthand, and so the effect of a story like Feyre's is one of identification. However, even girls and young women who have not personally experienced sexual violence have heard stories about it and have been conditioned to protect themselves from it, and it may be something that feels very present in their lives even without direct impact. Anastasia Higginbotham describes this phenomenon in "Sex Worth Fighting For," where she describes living in fear for her entire life, until she learned self-defense. She writes, "Though I have so far never been raped and never been physically attacked by a stranger, I have been lured, grabbed, tricked, stalked, harassed, coerced, and humiliated, and treated cruelly during sex" (Higginbotham 2019, 242). Because she had never been taught about healthy sexuality, for most of her life she did not realize that those behaviors fell on a spectrum of sexual violence, and she had been traumatized by not only what had happened, but what might happen. She describes: "I remained preoccupied by fears that something 'truly' bad would happen, and often imagined the gang rape and murder that would finish me off for good" (Higginbotham 2019, 243). So, she signed up for full-contact self-defense classes, and learned to fight back. She finds that after learning to protect herself, she feels safer in her own skin. She does not fear the streets as much, and she feels more confident. She sleeps better because she is not having anxious nightmares about her worst fears. For her, fighting is empowering, it is activism, it is her refusal to be vulnerable for having been born female. She concludes: "though there is no such thing as safety from an attempted rape in this world, I am all the weapon I need, and I sleep well" (Higginbotham 2019, 249). For girls who have experienced trauma, and for those who feel its effects vicariously, Feyre's story of healing and overcoming is a powerful identifier. The way in which she develops her own skill and strength so that she will never feel helpless again is empowering.

To empower, or to be empowered, is not the same as to feel empowered. I often come into contact with this critique when I am thinking about the relationship that readers and fans have to popular and literary content; are they being empowered to rise above oppression? Perhaps not. But they do feel better, like they can take on the world with a little more courage and confidence as a result of this material. We can gauge this impact by listening to fans, or by experiencing the emotional connection to fantasy material ourselves. That feeling connects us, connects fans, and offers a sense of belonging. Scholarship about young adult development tells us that stories have a substantial impact on the ways that they interpret and interact with real life stressors. For girls and young women who see strong heroines who value consent and agency above all else, that becomes possible. The feeling of empowerment, therefore, matters; it is what lingers and carries into their everyday lives.

NOTES

1. Copyright © Sarah J. Maas, 2017, *A Court of Mist and Fury*, Bloomsbury Publishing Inc. Copyright © Sarah J. Maas, 2016, *A Court of Thorns and Roses*, Bloomsbury Publishing Inc.

Chapter Two

"Choice is Your Weapon"

Violence, Empowerment, and X-23's Journey Toward Consent and Agency

As a clone of Wolverine, teenage superheroine X-23 was genetically engineered and raised in a lab to be a weapon.[1] With her strength, skill, mutant claws, and healing factor, she is nearly invincible. However, having been created as a weapon in a lab, she was raised from birth to be a soldier, trained to obey orders, and to live for directives. She was tortured all through childhood in order to make this conditioning stick, to obey without hesitation, to suppress empathy or identification with others, and to see herself, her body, and her mind as a weapon. When she begins to develop an instinctual resistance to orders to kill, particularly to killing children, the scientists controlling her develop a trigger scent to overpower her higher senses which sends her into a frenzied killing rage over which she has no control. Because of this manipulation of her senses, X-23 has no control over her life or her body as a child. In a cultural moment during which consent, via social movements like #GirlsToo and #MeToo, is prevalent in our consciousness, X-23 is a particularly interesting subject of analysis because her right to choice is denied to her, and even when she attempts to exercise it the trigger scent rips away her ability to consent. This chapter examines the story of X-23, and considers the way that violence serves as a corrective to her loss of agency and right to consent. I am interested in the ways that X-23 experiences violence as empowerment, as well as what is at stake when violence is embodied by her as a teenage girl. In this case study, X-23 reclaims agency through violence, and uses her past traumas to help her focus her strength on the protection of others, especially children and young women. X-23's story can be read through the frame of vigilante feminism, because choice becomes, in essence, her superpower, and through that she is empowered by violence. Though this experience does not radically reimagine patriarchal structures, it does radically interrupt a cycle of violence that leaves girls and women powerless in a violent world. X-23's pathway is dark, but when she escapes from the Facility that held her as a child she fights against her history of mindless violence to try to use her abilities for justice.

Carolyn Cocca, author of *Superwomen: Gender, Power, and Representation*, explains that "portrayals of female superheroes are embedded in particular moments in the history and the struggle over women's roles and women's power at particular times. Comics don't simply reflect 'real life,' though, nor do they simply affect 'real life.' Rather, they are part of real life, in that they are an institution in our world (like schools, or like mainstream news media) through which ideas about gender, sexuality, race, religion, disability, and power circulate" (Cocca 2016, 7). Thinking about comics as an institution that spreads ideas about gender and power is a useful frame for this analysis of X-23, because as a story about a child who is disempowered and abused, she takes control over her own life. Girls and young women are accustomed to realities in which their disempowerment does not offer a pathway to self-reclamation and agency, and so the long arc of X-23's story from 2003 to present can be both vicariously satisfying and personally cathartic. Cocca's analysis reminds readers that women and people of color are fiercely underrepresented in comics, and that underrepresentation is "happening in a world . . . in which sexual violence against women is something that occurs, statistically, every minute of every day, and women are still more often than not blamed for inviting it . . . in a world in which those whose voices have been silenced for years and years and years—the voices of those who have been never portrayed at all, or only portrayed in very small numbers, or only portrayed in objectified, stereotypical ways—are speaking up and being heard" (Cocca 2016, 15). X-23 is a troublesome subject of analysis because on the surface she is a child assassin, who only has the opportunity to become a vigilante for justice after many years of captivity. Surface readings are overly simplistic, however, and X-23's story is incredibly complex. She symbolizes the way that girls and young women feel growing up powerless in a violent patriarchy, as though their lives and choices are not their own, and the pathways to finding their true selves are blocked by many external factors. When she finds her true self and casts off the role she was assigned at birth, she becomes a vigilante feminist heroine.

Chronologically, in terms of publication year, X-23's story is told out of sequence. For the purposes of this chapter's analysis of X-23 based on her quest for choice, agency, and the right to consent, I have chosen to follow her comic representations in the order of her age, rather than in the order of their publication. For example, though X-23 first appears in the comic story *NYX* in 2003, and again in *Uncanny X-Men* (2004), it is the 2005 arc of *Innocence*

Lost, and the 2006 arc of *Target X*, that show us the painful story of her childhood. We also have the opportunity to see flashbacks to her early life in *New X-Men* (2006–2007), *X-23* (2010–2011), and *All-New Wolverine* (2016–2018) to help us understand the ways that the quest for choice was one that was deeply important to X-23 throughout her life. Methodologically, this chapter is the result of a close reading of more than 350 comics in which X-23 appears between 2003 and 2018. Since I recognized from her earliest appearances in 2003 that her characterization was as a child who is the victim of extreme abuse, I looked for moments throughout the comics in which her trajectory as a child under intense scrutiny and control with no agency begins to shift to one in which she is fully agentic and in control of her own life, identity, and values in 2016. This chapter does a close reading of key moments in her story that elucidate that pathway. Interspersed with that reading is an analysis of how X-23's story can be read as reflective of cultural norms about gender, and through a frame of trauma studies, childhood studies, and agency theory.

Innocence Lost begins with the death of scientist Dale Rice, who is killed by Wolverine as he runs from a lab where he has stolen Wolverine's DNA. The project that Dr. Rice had intended to begin then becomes the life's work of his son, Dr. Zander Rice. When Zander Rice is unsuccessful with the cloning process, the Director of the lab, which is named the "Facility," brings in Dr. Sarah Kinney, who is "the leading authority on mutant genetics" and whose "work in mapping the mutant genome may have great bearing on our project" (Kyle and Yost, *X-23* #1, 11). Her task is to create a viable clone embryo from the genetic sample retrieved from Wolverine. The Director entices her to work for them by telling her: "Unlimited resources and no political or legal restraints on your work. That's what we have to offer . . . however, there are sacrifices involved. We've all made them. Physically, you'd be totally cut off from the outside world, although you can still receive mail and phone calls . . . and you'd be committed for the life of the project. I also need to know if you can live with the moral implications of what you'd be doing here" (Kyle and Yost, *X-23* #1, 13). The total secrecy is exciting for Dr. Kinney as a scientist, but it also belies the off-the-grid nature of the work they are doing. As the Director notes, there are moral implications to unfettered scientific research and development. Sarah realizes that the Y chromosome is too corrupted to duplicate, but that by duplicating the X chromosome—and making a female genetic twin—she could have a viable embryo sooner. There is resistance to making a female weapon, but when she is given the go ahead to continue the work she also agrees to serve as the surrogate. As such, she carries X-23 in her womb, and becomes her mother.

Innocence Lost is told as a letter that Sarah Kinney has written to X-23, and includes both explanation of what happened to her, along with memories and flashbacks that show it. Sarah writes, "you deserve to know why we did

these things. . . . Your training was designed to strip you of your humanity . . . you were a weapon" (Kyle and Yost, *X-23* #2, 29). The explanations
that Sarah provides to X-23 indicate a child's life without agency. At seven
years old, X-23 sits in a bare cell wearing a pink dress, and Sarah explains:
"our orders were to keep you from gaining any sense of self . . . something
they said would compromise our ability to control you. We were never to
treat you as a child . . . only as a weapon" (Kyle and Yost, *X-23* #2, 30). Tests
show that X-23's intelligence and comprehension are off the charts, and that
she is in peak physical condition. As they watch X-23 grow and develop,
scientists simultaneously work to develop a "trigger scent," which is a mechanism that overrides X-23's brain function to send her into a compliant
killing rage (Kyle and Yost, *X-23* #2, 32). From the start, the trigger scent
research and development is intended as a way to "control" X-23.

Mutants usually develop their mutant characteristics around the time of
puberty, however, Zander Rice does not want to wait. Since X-23 is, to him,
a weapon not a child, he designs conditions that will force her x-factor to
kick in early; he poisons her with radiation until she almost dies, and her
healing factor activates to save her life (Kyle and Yost, *X-23* #2, 41). The
radiation poison is extreme torture, as is the process through which he
chooses to coat her claws with adamantium. To do this, he removes her claws
one by one, coats them, and then fuses them back in—all without anesthesia.
The nurses aiding him in the procedure question his ethics, and so he dis-
misses them. It becomes evident that X-23 is, for Zander, a stand-in for
Wolverine, who killed his father. Torturing X-23 feels like vengeance to
Zander, since she is made of Wolverines's DNA. He chides: "Are you
afraid? Do you feel, Weapon X? This is for my father" (Kyle and Yost, *X-23*
#2, 44–45). Her body heals more quickly than anyone anticipates. Now that
she has her healing factor, and her claws are coated with adamantium, Zander tests the trigger scent. Disliking how X-23's sensei has treated her with
kindness, he chooses to make an example of the teacher, and coats the weapons in his training room with the trigger scent. When X-23 picks them up,
she is sent into a killing rage and she kills her sensei. When she comes to, she
recognizes what she has done. This is another layer of Zander's cruelty,
taking away things she loves. Sarah notes that X-23 becomes less verbal,
emotionally distant, and worries that though her body always heals, her mind
may not (Kyle and Yost, *X-23* #2, 49–50).

When X-23 is ten years old, she is well-trained enough that she is ready
for a field test. She is sent undercover to infiltrate a speaking event that is to
be given by a presidential candidate, a target who is under the protection of
the military and the secret service—an impossible target. Disguised as a
disabled child she manages to get to the candidate, and she kills him, his
entire family (including children), all the guests, and the guards. The goal
was to advertise that no one was safe from this weapon: "Anyone. Any-

where, Anytime. The buying and selling of lives for profit. Not saving the world, or taking it over. No, this was about money. A lot of it" (Kyle and Yost, *X-23* #3, 60). Sarah realizes that her opinion, her influence, does not matter when it comes to the fate of X-23. For three years, X-23 is sent on missions to assassinate targets, and she succeeds without fail. No matter the target or the time limit, she always beats it.

After missions, Sarah often finds her non-communicative, and cutting herself with her own claws. As Kwasu David Tembo and Muireann B. Crowley explain, though "X-23 physically recovers within a day . . . this invasive procedure leaves lasting psycho-emotional trauma on X-23. That which afford her greatest strength is simultaneously the source of her greatest physical and psycho-emotional pain. The only effective outlet for X-23's pain is self-harm in the form of cutting" (Tembo and Crowley 2019, 95). As well, there is a link between "self-harm in youths and childhood trauma, physical abuse, and/or sexual abuse" (Tembo and Crowley 2019, 96). Self-harm is "a harmful way to cope with emotional pain, intense anger and frustration," and in this case it indicates that X-23 is suffering emotionally, though she appears to be in perfect physical condition (M. C. Staff 2011). Furthermore, cutting gives Laura a sense of emotional control, with X-23 expressing agency by "taking revenge against that which her oppressors most value, even though that object is her own body" (Tembo and Crowley 2019, 96).

Sarah is estranged from her family, and we see through a variety of flashbacks that it is because she was the victim of sexual abuse by her father as a child, and that her family did not believe her (Kyle and Yost, *X-23* #1, 13–14). Sexual violence is a thread that is pulled through X-23's story, from Sarah's abuse as a child, to X-23 after she escapes the Facility, and in a later story arc in which she saves girls from sex trafficking. When Sarah's niece Megan is kidnapped by a serial killer who is suspected to be harming girls before he kills them, Sarah realizes that X-23 has the capacity to save her. She takes X-23 from the Facility without permission, and they head to San Francisco where her sister lives. Using her sense of smell, X-23 can tell that the kidnapper entered through the window, and kidnapped Megan from bed. She can also track them through the city based on scent (Kyle and Yost, *X-23* #4, 85–86).

X-23's disguise as she embarks on her mission to rescue Megan is a cropped shirt, a short skirt, and pigtails, a young girl selling cookies door to door. She is sexualized in order to catch the attention of Megan's kidnapper. Even as a child, both X-23 and Sarah are aware of how sexuality can be used as a weapon. X-23 throws the kidnapper out the window (Kyle and Yost, *X-23* #4, 89–90). She then walks Megan out to Sarah, who tells Megan it was "all just a bad dream, and when you wake up you won't even remember it" (Kyle and Yost, *X-23* #4, 92). X-23 and Megan represent juxtaposed girlhoods. The girls are about the same age, but the innocence of Megan is starkly contrasted here with the lack of innocence of X-23. X-23 knows the evil in the world and knows what the kidnapper intends to do with Megan. Megan has been sheltered, however, and does not know about the world, so she can be told it is a dream to protect her from knowing about the real danger. When they return to the Facility, a television news program shown in the background notes that "a man who committed suicide yesterday by leaping from his apartment window has been linked to the kidnapping and murder of seven young girls in the bay area . . . in a related story, a missing girl was found alive and unharmed, ending concerns that she may have been the kidnapper's latest victim" (Kyle and Yost, *X-23* #4, 96). This confirms that Megan had been kidnapped by a serial killer, and that Sarah's intervention—by bringing X-23 to San Francisco—saved her life. On one hand Sarah used X-23 for a mission and asked her to kill a target, which continues to objectify her. However, in this case she saved her own niece from being his next victim.

A turning point moment happens for X-23 when Zander decides he wants to kill the Director and his family. He hands her the mission orders, and she kills the Director and his wife as ordered. However, her orders also tell her to kill their young son. When she finds the little boy in the closet, she stops. She decides to override her mission objectives, and she lets him escape (Kyle and Yost, *X-23* #5, 99–102). In this moment, X-23 realizes that she has some agency to resist; she was able to overcome the influence of her mission directive. This is also a critical moment for Sarah, as she realizes that there is hope that X-23 could live the life of a child instead of an assassin. Sarah writes to X-23: "somehow you managed to save Henry and to tell me the truth . . . which means there is hope . . . you showed me we failed . . . you are not a weapon . . . you are a child. Always remember you are not to blame. You did not pick this life. We . . . I forced it upon you" (Kyle and Yost, *X-23* #5, 114–116).

Sarah makes the decision to find a way to escape the Facility with X-23, and she asks X-23 to kill Zander, to complete a mission one more time for their freedom. She explains to X-23 "tonight what you do is right. Tonight what you serve is justice. Tonight, you take back the life we stole from you" (Kyle and Yost, *X-23* #5, 117–118). This notion of justice is important to X-23's development as a vigilante feminist heroine. So far in the comics, she has been a child assassin with no control over her life. She has not had the opportunity to exercise agency. The fact that she did not kill the Director's son is the first time she even tried to override her own orders. Sarah describing the killing of Zander as "right" and as "justice" sets X-23 up to be taught that there are particular times and contexts in which violence is the right thing to do: for the protection of herself, and the ones she loves. She is beginning to have the capacity to juxtapose assassination with justice, and it is going to provide her with the tools she needs to begin to make these kinds of choices on her own.

This moment is important to the development of X-23, because her choice not to kill the young boy demonstrates that she has the potential for agency. As Ingrid E. Castro and Jessica Clark explain in relation to the six-year-old girl character, Scout, in *To Kill a Mockingbird*, "agency is . . . formed in relationships" (Castro and Clark 2019, xiii). In that particular case study, they note that when "Scout punches a boy at school for insulting her father and kicks a man she perceives as a violent racist in the shins, she is not effecting rational change on the environment for her own ends as an autonomous individual but in recognition of relational and emotional ties that lead her to defend loved ones" (Castro and Clark 2019, xiii). X-23's claiming of the possibility of not following Zander's directive is a result of the relational and emotional ties that exist between her and the Director's young son. Furthermore, by killing Zander in the name of what Sarah deems "justice," X-23 connects violence to empowerment and choice. This is also an important moment for Sarah, as she realizes that "we can choose to be something other than what we have been forced to be. That we can be something better than what we believe we are" (Kyle and Yost, *X-23* #6, 121).

Sarah wants to start a new life, be a family. She expects to survive but Zander laced her necklace with trigger scent, and X-23 kills her after she blows up the Facility. As X-23 realizes what she has done, as her mother lay dying, Sarah tells X-23 that her name is Laura. By giving her a name, Sarah returns to her the identity that has been kept from her and gives Laura a chance to forge her own path. Sarah's letter to Laura is her last word: "You are a child, not a weapon. You are my child. You are my daughter, and I love you" (Kyle and Yost, *X-23* #6, 139). Laura is left alone in the world, without any sense of who she is or what she should do. She was not given a normal childhood, and so this moment is a break from the past and a step into the future, but it is entirely uncertain what she will do with it. On one hand, she has the whole world at her disposal. On the other hand, she is a child, completely alone in a world that will not understand her.

Innocence Lost is told from Sarah Kinney's perspective, in the form of a letter to Laura, her daughter, in case her plan is unsuccessful and she never gets a chance to tell her the truth about her life. *Target X*, however, is told through the flashback memories of X-23 herself. In this series, Avengers leader Captain America has arrested X-23, and has brought her in for questioning. With him is Matt Murdock, a.k.a. Daredevil, who Captain America has invited because he has the capacity—as an element of his superpower— to tell when people are lying. Captain America has questions for X-23 and wants to ensure that the answers she gives him are truthful. It turns out that Captain America had been on site as extra protection for Candidate Johnson, the Presidential candidate that X-23 assassinated when she was ten years old.

He discovered the massacre of twenty-seven "innocent people, twelve of them women and two boys, ages thirteen and fifteen" (Kyle and Yost, *X-23: Target X* #2, 29–31). As part of her mission plan, X-23 made it appear that she was buried among the bodies crying out for help, and Captain America carried her out of the room, where she escaped from right under his nose. She was the assassin, but he did not see through her disguise as a disabled child and he let her go. As such, Captain America feels like every murder she has committed since that day is his responsibility since he did not "see" her for what she was. His questioning of her now is his effort to understand who, or what, she is.

This story is also an opportunity for Laura to come to terms with who she is. As Castro and Clark explain, "characters, and the childhoods they inhabit, are brought to life through cultural spaces forged and accessed by children. In this case, it is the power of children to create spaces and places of their own in the adult world that demonstrates agency" (Castro and Clark 2019, xiii). When the story is told through the perspective of Sarah Kinney or other adult figures, it is challenging to locate the spaces that are Laura's own. However, *Target X* does that, and we are able to witness the world from the child's valuable perspective.

It is through Laura's flashbacks that we see the true degree of torture that X-23 endured through her childhood. She explains the nature of the trigger scent, about how it was developed for use on "targets that I could not be trusted to kill, or those that were considered exceptional" (Kyle and Yost, *X-23: Target X* #3, 58). They started the conditioning for it early; she flashes back to eight years old, her head submerged in liquid trigger scent while Zander Rice electrocutes the water. Again at nine years old, and at ten years old; with her healing factor, X-23 can be tortured with total abandon and impunity, because she heals from every wound. She is indestructible. However, she feels all the pain that is associated with that torture, and so when we see the past through her eyes, we can see the trauma of this on her soul, and on her psyche, even if we cannot see it on her body. At eleven years old the trigger scent sticks, and she reacts on instinct, without physical reinforcement. They test the scent first on a dog, and then on her favorite sensei.

Five days after Laura's claws were laced with adamantium (approximately nine years old), Rice introduces her to Kimura, her new handler. Kimura is a woman much larger than X-23, and she has she been specially engineered with super strength and impenetrable skin, even by adamantium. Rice tells her: "She will be your handler from now on. If you fail a mission or disobey orders again, you will answer to her. You can't kill her, animal . . . you can't even hurt her. We made her just for you" (Kyle and Yost, *X-23: Target X* #4, 90–91). Kimura punishes her regularly, when X-23 has any emotional reaction (like she had after she was forced to kill her sensei), when she reportedly did not make a rendezvous on time, and sometimes just because Rice lies in order to justify her punishment. And Kimura makes it a spectacle. In one image, we see X-23 getting beaten by Kimura, with a circle of guards standing around amused (Kyle and Yost, *X-23: Target X* #4, 92). Because she cannot die, she is dehumanized; this process is all part of making her a weapon.

Like Amarantha and Ianthe from *A Court of Thorns and Roses*, described in chapter 1, Kimura is a literal tool of the patriarchy. She is genetically modified, like Laura, but her modifications made her the perfect foil to Laura's particular powers—in particular, that she has skin that is impermeable, even to adamantium. Also, like Laura, Kimura is a product of the Facility, and the off-the-grid initiatives they are taking on in order to forge people into weapons. Kimura is an embodiment of the patriarchal control that the Facility has over Laura. The fact that she can torture Laura, but Laura cannot hurt her back mirrors the way that Laura was used in the Facility as an assassin without agency or choice, and also of how the trigger scent rips away her ability to resist orders. The power that Kimura has been granted as a tool of the patriarchy protects her from harm and grants her endless resources for her work. She is the only person that Laura actually fears.

At thirteen years old, Laura escapes from the Facility after she kills her mother. We know a bit about what happens to her when she is left alone in the world, from her brief appearance in the comic series *NYX*, where X-23 is a prostitute working for a pimp named Zebra Daddy, and her specialty is erotic cutting. We also see that she is cutting herself, on her arms. When Kiden, who will become a close friend throughout the brief series, first finds her, she is sitting in the midst of a bloody scene in which it appears that she has killed her client, but she says he committed suicide in front of her. That he said "I've done some very bad things in my life. Please tell my wife . . . tell my children . . . I'm sorry," and then stabbed himself (Quesada, *NYX: Wannabe* #4, 94). Tembo and Crowley note that X-23's "mutant body was exploited by the state and continues to be exploited by adults more broadly . . . as a child sex worker, the character is narratively and aesthetically positioned in such a way that exposes her to the irrevocable psycho-emotional trauma of statutory rape" (Tembo and Crowley 2019, 97). This experience is an added layer of trauma in Laura's life, and is one that will emerge from time to time as Laura works at various times to interrupt the sexual abuse and coercion of other girls and young women.

At fourteen years old, Laura makes her way to San Francisco to find her aunt, and her cousin Megan. Her aunt welcomes her with open arms, and Laura and Megan grow close. They are approximately the same age, and Laura has never had an opportunity to have a normal friendship, nor to visit family. Megan has been having nightmares about being kidnapped as a child; she can remember flashes of it, but her mother has told her that it was not real. Laura tells her that it was real, and that that she killed the man who was the monster (Kyle and Yost, *X-23: Target X* #2, 38–39). Megan is angry with her mother for being lied to, but it serves as a moment of bonding between Megan and Laura. Megan has had a hard time making and keeping friends as a result of her trauma, which is similar to how Laura has been unable to make friends based on her particular circumstances. Megan tells Laura, "You're my only friend" (Kyle and Yost, *X-23: Target X* #2, 44). Laura's relationship with Megan is crucial to her development of agency, and the capacity for agentic practice. Terri Suico articulates that the core principles of human agency (intentionality, forethought, self-reactiveness, and self-reflectiveness) "require a strong sense of self and a sound emotional base," which can happen during friendships between girls" (Suico 2018, 110). As well, "[f]or agency development to occur, individuals must be willing and able to resist," (Suico 2018, 111) something which teenagers are primed to do as they search for identity. Friendship, Suico argues, "offers personal and social frameworks for girls to develop agency" (Suico 2018, 110). Laura is rapidly developing a stronger sense of self vis-à-vis her relationship with Megan and is beginning to understand what is at stake in her ability to resist the Facility's control.

Laura confides to Megan that she is a weapon that was created in a lab, with adamantium claws and people looking for her. She also admits that the people who created her made her kill her mother, and when Megan asks for an explanation of how, Laura describes to her the trigger scent: "The ones who made me, they made a chemical . . . a scent . . . when I smell It everything goes black. And when I wake up everyone's dead" (Kyle and Yost, *X-23: Target X* #2, 51). These are important scenes for two reasons. First, Laura is coming into a sense of herself vis-à-vis her cousin, who is in pain from the trauma of the past, and in danger because of Laura's existence. Laura begins to understand that she will do anything to keep Megan and her Aunt Debbie from feeling pain and danger. Second, Laura explains clearly what the trigger scent does—she blacks out, she has no control. We hear from Laura herself what it feels like to be under the influence of the scent, a scenario in which clearly any capacity to consent or make choices is taken from her. Through her friendship with Megan, her growing love for her family, and her vocalization of the trigger scent's effect on her ability to consent, Laura is beginning to develop a more clear sense of self.

The Facility tracks Laura to her aunt's house, and Kimura deploys a team to retrieve her, and to kill Aunt Debbie and Megan. Laura is able to kill all of the agents that descend upon the house, but when Kimura shows up, Laura has difficulty protecting her family against her. Kimura snaps Laura's neck and taunts her: "How many people do we have to kill before you understand that you're a weapon, not a person? First Tanaka, then Sarah, and now I have to kill your new family here. Maybe if you watch Megan and Debbie die, you'll finally get the point" (Kyle and Yost, *X-23: Target X* #5, 103–104).

Kimura drags Laura to the basement and cuffs her to a beam with adamantium handcuffs, which she cannot break. Laura slices through Kimura's gun as she tries to shoot Megan, and Kimura gleefully announces that she will kill Megan with her bare hands instead. She taunts Laura with the fact that she does not have control over her life, or this situation: "Should I put my finger through her brain, or through her heart? You choose X" (Kyle and Yost, *X-23: Target X* #5, 110). Kimura uses the notion of "choice," which Laura has never been freely given, to torture her in this moment, explaining: "the only choice you have is brain or heart. But if you won't choose how Megan dies, I will." At this moment, Kimura begins to puncture Megan's heart with her finger. "Of course, you could stop her suffering. You could kill her X, it'd be merciful compared to this" (Kyle and Yost, *X-23: Target X* #5, 111). Megan is screaming in pain, and Kimura sets up this scene as though it is Laura's fault that it is happening this way, that Laura has choices about how to end it. But these are not real choices. Laura has never yet had the opportunity to make real choices. However, this is a key moment when Laura is out of options. She begged Kimura to stop, but she was not heard. She offered to trade her life for Megan's, but she has no value to Kimura in that way. The only thing she cares about in the world is being threatened, and so Laura cuts off her own hand to escape from the adamantium cuff that has her tied to the beam, and cuffs Kimura to the wall. She knows that will not hold her for long, but it gives them a few minutes to escape.

Kimura shrieks after Laura: "There's nowhere you can run I won't find you! You think you've saved her?! You're wrong! Megan is dead! Debbie is dead! Everyone you love will die! And I'll be the one that kills them" (Kyle and Yost, *X-23: Target X* #5, 114)! Laura knows that what Kimura says is true. She knows they will never stop hunting her, never stop threatening the people she loves. She makes a desperate attempt to kill Kimura by electrocuting the water that has been filling the basement, and in which Kimura is submerged. However, Captain America tells her that SHIELD was called in after the fire department found fragments of advanced weaponry and the remains of twenty-seven bodies in the wreckage, but that Kimura was not there. "Then she's still out there," Laura says, hopelessly (Kyle and Yost, *X-23: Target X* #5, 118).

In writing the first full-length study of conflict and trauma in comics, Harriet E. H. Earle explains that, as a genre, mainstream comics (which X-23's are, as part of the Marvel superhero universe) typically do not engage in nuanced representations of trauma. She writes that "it is not the desire of the genre to create psychological studies of the effects of violence and conflict on the self" (Earle 2017, 25). As such, Earle looks for ways to analyze trauma in comics by merging comics studies with trauma theory, "drawing both clinical definitions and cultural understandings of the impact of trauma on both the individual and the wider society" (25). Laura is a victim of repeated trauma throughout her childhood, and she is always aware that Kimura and the Facility are looking for her. She is always aware that there are forces that would like her freedom to be temporary. In discussing the differentiation between the concept of the "survivor" versus the "victim" of trauma, Earle writes that "survival becomes a part of the trauma because one is left with the knowledge of impending mortality and an intensified apprehension of the fragility of existence" (Earle 2017, 31–32). That is an apt way to characterize the ways that Laura perseveres despite her overwhelmingly terrifying reality of repeated child abuse—a reality that will continue for a few more years beyond this moment in her narrative.

One of the ways in which Laura copes with these repeated traumas is by locating and exercising choices about her own life when the opportunity is granted to her. For example, after Kimura's attempt to kill them, Laura helps Megan and Debbie escape to Canada, making them fake passports and directing them to a safehouse where they can get money and start fresh. Debbie tells Laura that before Sarah died her love for Laura had taken away the pain their abusive father had caused her. For so long Sarah did not love anyone, not their mother, not Debbie, and not herself, but Laura changed that. "You've saved us all, Laura. Thank you," letting her know that she loves her and that they will miss her every day (Kyle and Yost, *X-23: Target X* #5, 119). When Megan demands to know why Laura is not going with them, Laura explains: "Megan, don't you understand . . . they'll never stop coming after me. She'll never stop. Without me, you have a chance. I can't risk your life, not again" (Kyle and Yost, *X-23: Target X* #5, 122). This is a key moment of choice for Laura; she understands the circumstances of her own life and understands that there is a permanent target on her back. In order to ensure the safety of others, to keep those she loves safe, she lets them go.

Furthermore, after she leaves Megan and Debbie, Laura makes the choice to track down Wolverine. Her initial inclination is to kill him because she believes that they are both weapons that must be destroyed for the safety of humanity. Wolverine is willing to die, but he refuses to allow Laura to kill herself. He explains: "You didn't choose this life and there was nothing you could have done to stop what happened. . . . Your mother sent me a copy of a letter written to you. So, I know what happened . . . what they did to you and that it wasn't your fault. None of it" (Kyle and Yost, *X-23: Target X* #6, 140). He tells her: "No one should have to go through what you did, especially not a child. But now you've got a choice to make. Sarah's letter is in the pocket of that jacket. You know what the Facility wanted for you. Now find out what your mother wanted" (Kyle and Yost, *X-23: Target X* #6, 142). Choice is held out to Laura here as the future, as a possibility. It is an unfamiliar concept for her, having been told her whole life what to do, and she struggles with it. As Laura is thinking it over, however, SHIELD shows up and Captain America arrests her for the killing of Candidate Donaldson (her first mission, when she was ten years old) and the innocent people at his rally.

In answering Captain America's questions about all the people she has killed, Laura begins to consciously recognize what she has been through. Matt Murdock characterizes Sarah's letter as "a confession, written by one of the murderers you're after. Sarah claims responsibility for every death committed by this child. Every single one, including the execution of the other guilty parties at the Facility." He sees Laura to be as much of a victim as any person she was ever forced to kill. He also knows that SHIELD will use her as their own weapon if Captain American turns her in (Kyle and Yost, *X-23: Target X* #6, 147–148). Captain America ultimately chooses to take Laura to a bus station instead of to SHIELD, in effect setting her free to forge her own path. He sees her as a person, not a weapon, and he views himself as partly complicit in the way her life turned out: "The first time we met, I made a mistake and you ended up back in the hands of the people that made you a weapon. If I take you in now, new people will use you the same way the Facility did and I can't let that happen . . . not again." (Kyle and Yost, *X-23: Target X* #6, 151). Laura boards the bus, planning to head to the Xavier Institute where she can find Wolverine, and she finally has the opportunity to read her mother's letter. Here, for the first time ever, Laura can decide for herself who she is, and who she is going to become.

A few scenarios in subsequent comics can illustrate the ways in which Laura's journey henceforth is one toward a life she consents to, in ways that are authentic for her. After M-Day,[2] only twenty-seven of the mutant students at the Xavier Institute were left with their powers. As the depowered students were returning home, a bus was bombed by anti-mutant zealots killing forty-two of them. The students remaining at the Xavier Institute are in mourning, and they also live in fear of another attack. As such, Wolverine asks Laura to join the Xavier Institute for her protection, as she figures things out, but also to help protect the students there. Laura understandably has difficulty with human relationships, and social cues are foreign to her, but she is extremely logical and her senses are extraordinary. The students of the Xavier Institute are traumatized on so many levels. They are mutants, which makes them pariahs to much of society. Many of them have been rejected by their families. And after M-Day, they become hunted. Dozens of them are killed, and many of the remaining students witness the deaths of their friends. They feel like the X-Men are incapable of saving them, and so they are all working on figuring out how to save themselves. Many of the students have PTSD or depression. Since they all have their own baggage, most of them are able to see past Laura's origin as X-23, as a weapon, and give her space as she searches for her own identity. They are all learning how to make their own choices when only bad options are ahead of them. Because of all of this,

Laura develops ways to fit in, and to become a truly valuable member of the team.

Having been raised to believe her only purpose is to kill, Laura struggles with the nature of right and wrong when she is on her own. Her friends at the Xavier Institute help her develop her understanding of nuance, cause and effect, and self-control. A moment that is especially crucial to Laura's growing respect for herself and her capacity to be human comes after a mission in which the New X-Men save teammate Mercury from the Facility. A rare biometal found within Mercury's skin is valuable to the Facility in building a super-predator, and so they kidnap her and find ways to extract it from her. As we know from the way that the Facility treated Laura during her captivity, their methods are brutal. Mercury is physically and mentally tormented, which leaves her traumatized in the wake of the incident. However, the rescue operation gave Emma Frost (co-headmistress of the Xavier Institute, whose power is telepathy and telekinesis) the opportunity to see what kinds of circumstances Laura has survived, and to encounter Kimura. Emma is able to read Kimura's thoughts, and learns what a monumental feat it is that Laura is still alive and in control of her own life (Kyle and Yost, *New X-Men: Childhood's End Vol. 4* #36, 95–97). Her recognition of this reality helps Laura begin to see how much agency she is learning to exert over herself, and it empowers her to continue her journey toward self-discovery.

While Laura is at the Xavier Institute, Cyclops receives intelligence that the bus bombing that killed the depowered students was orchestrated by Matthew Risman, leader of a group called The Purifiers. Cyclops wants to secretly reassemble the X-Force to go after Risman; the X-Force is a secret mutant strike team that takes a proactive stance against threats to mutantkind, and—unlike the X-Men—they kill when necessary. Naturally, Cyclops wants Laura to join the team because of her healing factor, and her skills at tracking and assassinating. Wolverine tells Cyclops to leave Laura out of it: "Laura does not know how to choose . . . I brought her to Xavier's so she could start a new life. Learn how to be a real person, even after everything that went down with the kids. I'm not going to ask her to kill again. Forget it" (Kyle and Yost, *X-Force Vol. 1: Angels and Demons* #1, 11). Wolverine makes sure that Laura understands that the X-Force is not the X-Men: "you keep heading down this path, and any shot you had at being human slips further away. You do this, and you're X-23 again" (Kyle and Yost, *X-Force Vol. 1: Angels and Demons* #1, 19). However, since Risman is directly responsible for the deaths of forty-two of her peers, she is very willing to join this fight. At sixteen years old, this is one way of channeling her anger and her skill with violence, and it is, importantly, one that she chooses.

Unfortunately, it is a choice that leaves her left vulnerable and open to recapture by the Facility, led by her former handler Kimura. This time, they want to retrieve a blood sample from her so that they can re-start the Weapon

X program, the program that created her, and which was ended when Laura destroyed the Facility at age thirteen. The torture that Laura endures is extreme; to prove her point that Laura can never escape from her or the Facility, Kimura strings Laura up by her arms and legs, and cuts off her arm with an electric bone saw. In this story, the Facility has been secretly infiltrated by an undercover SHIELD agent, Agent Morales, who has been tracking X-23 for years, trying to piece together and comprehend the body count she has left in her wake (not unlike what Captain America did during *Target X*). When she first meets X-23, she exclaims how young she is, that she is really just a kid. "No she's not." Kimura retorts, "She's a weapon" (Kyle and Yost, *X-Force Vol. 3: Not Forgotten* #18, 82). The Facility never saw Laura as a person, and their cruelty toward her is limitless.

When Laura and Morales attempt to stage an escape, Morales demands accountability from Laura: "Did you just do it because you like it? I really want to know because you seem pretty capable of making your own decisions. . . . You commit those kinds of crimes there has to be something in it for you." Unlike Kimura, when Morales looks at Laura she *does* see a person, and therefore she projects responsibility and guilt onto her as a result. But Laura has had time to grow, and to begin to come to terms with her lifetime of abuse and her utter lack of control. "You don't know what you are talking about," Laura says. "The Facility created me to be a weapon, killing was all I knew. I didn't know how to say 'No.'. . . But if I ever did say no, they had a way to make me kill. A chemical trigger" (Kyle and Yost, *X-Force Vol. 3: Not Forgotten* #18, 118–119). This is an incredibly important scene, as Laura comes to terms with, and verbalizes, what consent has meant to her. It has been literally meaningless in her past because every time she exercised any hint of resistance, of saying no, her will was overpowered by the chemical trigger. This is a violent assault on Laura, and when she would awaken from that drugged state and see the carnage, she actually did feel remorse. This psychic trauma was noted by her mother when she resisted verbalization after her missions, and when she began cutting herself. Tembo and Crowley write that "despite the quasi-invulnerability her mutant powers afford her, X-23's healing factors cannot undo the immeasurable psycho-emotional trauma she sustains. We describe this condition as one of tragic irony because the agency of near invincibility in X-23 . . . ostensibly ensured by radical physical resilience, gives no psychological or emotional guarantee" (Tembo and Crowley 2019, 98). But until she escaped from the Facility when she was thirteen years old, there was no point to that remorse, because there was no escape from that control.

Laura's handler, Kimura, was engineered just for her, with skin that is impenetrable, even by adamantium. For Laura, Kimura is indestructible, and because of her healing factor, their relationship has generally consisted of Kimura torturing her. Laura feels all pain, but heals. She has had all of her skin melted off, limbs decapitated, neck snapped—all torturous, tormenting injuries that always healed. One of the reasons that I was drawn to analyze X-23/Laura Kinney through the lens of trauma and agency was to reclaim her narrative from this violence. She is the victim of such extreme child abuse, that I felt the responsibility to witness it, and to locate her voice in the story. Harriet E. H. Earle explains this interaction between reader and comics by explaining that:

> comics uses its arsenal of formal representation techniques to produce affect in the reader and, in doing so, mimics (some part of) the feelings and experience of trauma. I do not claim that these texts fully represent the experience of trauma; it would be nearly impossible for them to do that. Nor do I claim that these texts aim to traumatize readers. Trauma is a firsthand experience that reconfigures the self and (usually) arises from a situation in which the individual's life was in serious danger; such experiences do not occur when reading a book. Rather, I wish to show how, through careful formal and representational techniques, the comics herein discussed create affects within the reader that can assist in comprehension of the events and experience discussed. (Earle 2017, 43)

In this scene, as Laura and Agent Morales manage to escape from the Facility, Kimura uses a dying walkie talkie to torment Laura: "I want you to know . . . I'm never going to stop. Never! . . . I'll find your little X-Men classmates . . . your telekinetic boyfriend . . . I'm going to kill them all" (Kyle and Yost, *X-Force Vol. 3: Not Forgotten* #18, 141). In one of the most heart wrenching sequences in her comics representation, Laura's face falls as she hears this, because the viciousness is unearned. She did not ask for her life. She tried to leave it and incurred the wrath of Kimura for so doing. "There's nothing I can do," she gasps, as she begins to cry and collapses to the ground (Kyle and Yost, *X-Force Vol. 3: Not Forgotten* #18, 142). Laura's story, and the trauma that she endures throughout her childhood, does produce affect that leads to deeper understanding of and empathy with Laura's trauma for readers. This particular scene is another turning point moment, and at the end of this issue of *X-Force* Laura leaves the group, returning to the Xavier Institute where she hopes to find some peace.

In a later series, in *All-New Wolverine*, Laura describes Kimura as the only person who scares her. Kimura was created by a clandestine private lab well outside the purview of government regulation, and the Facility openly courted Dr. Sarah Kinney with the fact that they did not adhere to a code of ethics in their research and development. Laura is abused and exploited during her time at the Facility. However, the people there are the only comparison she has to a system of justice. Zander Rice hates her, but he is in charge. Kimura exists to torture her, and she doles out punishment for supposed transgressions. Tembo and Crowley note that "Despite all the traumas

X-23 endures in the Facility, it is also a space of learning for her. Within its walls, she acquires skills, expertise, and knowledge that no youth (let alone average adult) would acquire in a lifetime . . . the fact that learning occurs under carceral construction means that X-23's initial expressions of agency are structured and guided by the interests of white adult males who oversee her 'education.'" They also note that she is "subordinate to the operations and operators of power" (Tembo and Crowley 2019, 86). As a child, these are the only figures of authority in Laura's life. Because of this, it makes sense to read these stories about her experiences within the context of real-world justice systems that fail to protect those in their care.

For example, in a 2019 article in *The New York Times*, titled "'You Have to Pay With Your Body': The Hidden Nightmare of Sexual Violence on the Border," journalist Manny Fernandez reports "a sheriff's deputy in San Antonio was charged with sexually assaulting the 4-year-old daughter of an undocumented Guatemalan woman and threatening to have her deported if she reported the abuse," and "In West Texas [in 2016], two teenage girls reported that they had been sexually assaulted by a Customs and Border Protection officer, who they said forced them to strip, fondled them, then tried to get them to stop crying by offering chocolates, potato chips and a blanket" (Fernandez 2019). In July 2019, an Ohio parole officer was arrested for sexually assaulting three women whose cases he oversaw, and faced "charges of rape, gross sexual imposition and two counts of sexual battery after three women said he victimized them while they were on parole between June 2016 and July 2017" (Miller 2019). In August 2019, two New York Police Detectives were found guilty of misconduct for having sexual intercourse with a woman in their custody, before releasing her without arrest (Bote 2019). And, in 2016, Oklahoma City police officer Daniel Holtzclaw was sentenced to 263 years in prison for sexually assaulting thirteen African American women who were in his custody (McLaughlin and Sidner 2016). In her book *Fight Like a Girl*, Megan Seely describes the culture we live in as one in which rape and gender-based violence are condoned, actively and also by inaction. The impunity with which the various law enforcement officers acted is evidence that "we currently live in a culture where many women are afraid to fight back, where most women are taught that we can't fight back, and where some are even disempowered and believe that we are not worth fighting for. We live in a culture where, on a conscious, semiconscious, or unconscious level, men are encouraged to see women as property and believe that we exist for their amusement and convenience" (Seely 2007, 187). And these are but four of the countless cases citing behaviors that are gross abuses of power, and which target girls and young women.

Such violence against women is unfortunately not uncommon, though it is underreported and underprosecuted. In *Down Girl: The Logic of Misogyny*, Kate Manne reads Holtzclaw's crimes within the broader context of misogyny, noting: "He was betting on the fact that his victims wouldn't report him and that, even if they did, they wouldn't be able to bring him to justice—his being a police officer" (Manne 2018, 23). As explained in the introduction, Manne describes misogyny as a political phenomenon that "operates within a patriarchal social order to police and enforce women's subordination and to uphold male dominance" (2018, 33). Laura can also be read within the context of misogyny and the patriarchal order. The fact that she was going to be born a girl was deeply contested from the start (the Facility wanted a clone of Wolverine, not a female genetic twin), and it is possible to read her treatment by the doctors and scientists at the Facility, and by Kimura, as gendered. It is possible that she could have experienced a heightened objectification as a result of her gender, given that it was a point of contention from her inception. What Laura and the girls and women described in the previous paragraph experienced is torment and torture at the hands of men who were supposed to protect them, and who failed to do so. Laura's story echoes these injustices, but unlike real girls and women, Laura has superpowers that allow her to fight back and to protect others from a similar fate.

The comic series *X-23*, which debuted in 2010 and was written by Marjorie Liu, is a story about the aftermath of Laura's choice to be part of X-Force, and her journey toward healing from past traumas. This particular story arc offers Laura opportunities to reflect on herself and her past in order to move forward as her own independent person. Laura is plagued by anxiety, depression, and horrible nightmares. In *The Killing Dream* (2010), Laura dreams that Wolverine has been possessed by a demon, and he is tormenting her. In her dream, he tells her what she fears most: "You're lost. You hardly know how to function. You keep to yourself. You sleep in the woods. You cut yourself because it's the only way you feel anything. You're the clone of a killer. You've always suspected what that means. You're practically soulless. I know these things Laura. Souls have a taste. Souls are full of light. But inside you there's nothing but darkness" (Liu, *X-23: The Killing Dream* #2, 46). She resists his characterization and tells the dream-demon-Wolverine that he is wrong. This is Laura's unconscious way of working through her own fears that she is soulless, that she is broken, and that she is only a killer.

Her psychological attempt to come to terms with her past so that she can heal from it has Wolverine-as-demon taking her "home" in her unconscious. In her dream, she finds her way back to the Facility where Laura meets her "true self" who appears in the form of her own silhouette of starlight, buried so deep inside that even the doctors could not touch it (Liu, *X-23: The Killing Dream* #3, 56). Her true self shows Laura the truth of her past, that she was tortured, brainwashed, and conditioned. The memory shows Laura with her arms, legs, and head cuffed to a chair, eyes forced open, and a doctor exclaiming that her empathy scores are still too high. "She's been resistant from the beginning," someone says, "It'll take something extreme if you want to break her" (Liu, *X-23: The Killing Dream* #3, 58). The doctors ask Laura's mother—Dr. Sarah Kinney—for her recommendation on how to break her, and Sarah chooses a puppy experiment (Liu, *X-23: The Killing Dream* #3, 60). Laura realizes that while it may be true that her mother loved her, it is also true that her mother hurt her. Sarah obeyed "the men in white" by participating in the Laura's sadistic conditioning. Here, Laura is given a puppy to love. Then she is told that she must kill it instantly. When she hesitates, she is told that it will be tortured and killed slowly while she watches. Horrified, but resolved not to let the puppy suffer, Laura complies. Laura realizes that she was a construct of men in white coats, but that she was born as a human too. Her true self tells her:

> remember who you are. Know yourself. Know who you could be. Do not be afraid. . . . You were not born empty, Laura. It took effort to make you that way. It took many hands and minds. It took years. You fought them, every step. But they outnumbered you. And you were so young. You had no choice. But you have a choice now . . . believe in yourself. Choice is your weapon. Belief is your weapon. No one can hurt you, if you remember that. You have been through the worst. And you were not broken. You will never be broken (Liu, *X-23: The Killing Dream* #3, 62–63).

This idea that choice has become Laura's weapon is crucially important to her journey to healing. After agency and choice have been taken away from her for her entire life, she begins to recognize the difference between what choices have been hers and what have not. In this scene, she needed to experience this psychological journey in order to see that she fought for herself even when everyone, including her mother, was trying to control her.

This scene is about healing from trauma. Laura asks her unconscious why she must see this again, and her true self tells her that she needed to see this past again so that she could believe in herself, so that she can choose herself. So that she understands that she can never be broken. In describing the effects of trauma, Debra Jackson explains that disaster, violence, and trauma "overwhelms the person's ability to understand and cope with events" (Jackson 2016, 206). Laura's traumatic past is known to her, but it is emotionally inaccessible to her because she has not yet had the time to narrativize and process what happened to her during her childhood. Jackson explains that when "a traumatic event occurs, the full realization of its impact is not immediately accessible." There is a period of "latency" between the time of the trauma and the "full emotional impact of the event" (Jackson 2016, 206). This can be hours, days, or decades, and it "traps the survivor in a cycle of repetitions and reenactments that makes the traumatic event contemporaneous with the present" (Jackson 2016, 207). She describes the variety of cognitive, affective, and physical symptoms of post-traumatic stress disorder that "interrupt their daily lives: feelings of helplessness, loss of control, anger, dissociation, numbing, denial, insomnia, nausea, heightened startle response, and hypervigilance, as well as revisiting the experience through nightmares, flashbacks, and/or hallucinations" (Jackson 2016, 206–207). Laura's depression, anger, nightmares, flashbacks, and hallucinations clearly demonstrate that she is experiencing PTSD. Jackson explains that this "involuntary repetition" of traumatic events helps to generate a "voice that is released from the wound, which bears witness to the trauma" (Jackson 2016, 208). *The Killing Dream* is a literal manifestation of this voice released from the wound bearing witness to the trauma, the voice being her "true self" and Laura's journey into her unconscious mind as her bearing witness. This is another turning point moment for Laura, as her psyche works through her past traumas to help her understand who she is. She fears that she is innately evil, soulless, but her memories of her past traumas show her that she has always fought against that conditioning.

Jackson also describes the way that survivors of trauma sometimes describe "the trauma as splitting them into two distinct selves. . . . Many other survivors describe their experience as a kind of death, not only in terms of facing a life-threatening event, but also in the annihilation of their sense of personhood" (Jackson 2016, 208). In *The Killing Dream*, Laura's "true self" is literally represented as another self, a silhouette of starlight who tells her "I am you." As Laura fights the demon in her nightmare, her true self tells her "You can defeat him. You can push him away forever. All you need to remember is who you are. Know yourself" (Liu, *X-23: The Killing Dream* #3, 56). Her torture and conditioning was supposed to erase her personhood; the Facility's need to erase the humanity in X-23 is the main impetus for her torture there. The "splitting of the self," however, "is not simply an effect of destruction, it is an enigma of survival" (Jackson 2016, 208). For Laura, the "true self" made of light was buried deep inside, "in a place deeper than your heart. Deeper than your silence. I am the part of you the scientist's never touched" (Liu, *X-23: The Killing Dream* #3, 56). Throughout the various comics arcs, Laura's past is fragmented, with different parts available to her at different times. It seems incoherent at times. But Jackson notes that this is how trauma is experienced, "in fragmentary ways" (Jackson 2016, 210). This reliving of past events, and this conversation with her "true self," is Laura's way of surviving, and of learning how to connect with herself. Importantly, Jackson explains that to recover one's subjectivity, one must reestablish "one's embodied agency, including the ability to authoritatively tell one's own story" (Jackson 2016, 211). *The Killing Dream* is a way of witnessing Laura's trauma, of putting together the pieces of the narrative of her childhood, so that she can begin to heal. The fact that choice is now her weapon and her superpower is agentic for Laura; she can begin to embody agency, possibly for the first time in her life, and move forward in ways that are authentic for her.

This descent into her nightmares where she encounters Wolverine-as-demon is also a symbolic marker of her heroine's journey. The heroine's journey in comics is a way for the superheroine to "realize her personal power and claim it, whatever society says" (Frankel 2017, 4). As Valerie Estelle Frankel explains in *Superheroines and the Epic Journey*, external forces including "the patriarchy (often as the government or the heroine's calculating creator) and a world of misogyny" will try to stop her from completing her quest. In the case of Laura's nightmare, she is literally confronted with her creator, in the guise of her genetic twin from whom she was cloned, and the government-like entity where she was born and raised, the Facility (Frankel 2017, 4). The simple definition of a heroine's journey "involves a descent into death or a representation thereof, then emerging strong in a metaphor for growing up or overcoming life's trials" (Frankel 2017, 6). Frankel notes that this journey appears in nearly all superheroine comics, and it is evident that it is central to Laura's story as well. Her emergence from her nightmare (a hell-like representation of death), where she refuses to accept the demon's assertion that she is soulless, is symbolic of both growing up and overcoming life's trials. It is also a turning point moment after which Laura's journey toward healing, empowerment, and ultimately agency over her own life follow.

Laura's process of healing re-connects her to herself, and a few more catalyst moments in her story will lead her to claim agency over her own life. After the interlude with the demon in her nightmare, Laura leaves the Xavier Institute. She tells Storm: "I want to make my own life. Before someone else makes it for me. Again" (Liu, *X-23: The Killing Dream* #3, 70). On her travels, somewhere in the Southwest, she encounters a teenage girl in a diner, named Alice, who has a black eye. Laura believes that Alice is trying to lure Laura out of the diner, to get in a car with a man in the parking lot. This reminds Laura of her own experiences when she was thirteen years old and had just escaped from the Facility, when she worked for a pimp to survive on the streets. Laura tells Alice: "I had a pimp once. But he never asked me to lure girls to him. If he had I would have said no. I was lost . . . but not that lost" (Liu, *X-23: The Killing Dream* #4, 78). Alice runs out of the diner and gets into the car. Laura follows the car down the road, and witnesses the man killing Alice, as he mutters: "You don't say no. You don't say no to anyone. You do your job. You should have done your job. You should have kept your stupid mouth shut" (Liu, *X-23: The Killing Dream* #4, 81).

This scene is essential to Laura's own coming to terms with her identity as a vigilante feminist superheroine. Alice was vulnerable and reminds Laura of herself. When the man kills her for not doing what she was told, Laura takes it very personally—she identifies with Alice, and the murder is unjust. Laura has a growing sense of what "just" killings are, and they are to protect herself or those she loves. She chose to exercise this justice when she was protecting Megan and her Aunt Debbie, and again when she joined the X-Force to avenge forty-two of her classmates. When Laura approaches this scene, the man tells her that he did not mean to kill Alice. Laura replies, "Yes you did," and he shoots her, so she kills him. Since Laura will heal from the gunshot wound, she is not really protecting herself in this scene. Rather, there is no other way to get justice for a murder like Alice's; she is an orphan, and she is without protection. There is no one to witness her life or her death, or to make sure that the man is appropriately punished for what he has done. When Laura kills him, this is the first time that she has killed someone on her own, fully of her own volition. As a child assassin, she was under orders; at her Aunt Debbie's house, her family was under direct and immediate threat; on the X-Force, she was on a mission. But in this moment, Laura has left the Xavier Institute specifically so that she can make her own life, so that no one else makes decisions for her. Killing this man who has murdered Alice is Laura making the choice to wield violence on behalf of other girls who are the past and future victims of this man, and to end his life. A few moments later, Gambit arrives on the scene, claiming that he tracked her to make sure she is okay. Laura explains that she killed the man because he deserved to die. When Gambit asks Laura if she was fit to judge him she replies that there was no one else there who could. He asks her if she can live with that, and she says yes (Liu, *X-23: The Killing Dream* #4, 88). The vigilante feminist superheroine must be the judge, jury, and executioner for men like this one, who wield violence against girls and women with impunity. In this scene Laura begins to come to terms with that role and chooses to take it on.

In the penultimate issue of Marjorie Liu's run of *X-23*, Jubilee takes Laura dancing at a club. Immediately, Laura senses a man tightly grasping the shoulder of a terrified looking woman. Laura recognizes him as someone who used to run with her pimp, Zebra Daddy—whose death she orchestrated two years ago. He thanks her for having Zebra Daddy killed, telling her that he has taken over Zebra Daddy's territory. Laura responds that she will kill him. The pimp chides her: "Tough girl. . . . You really think you can handle all my boys? Or maybe you have some tricks . . . you can show them for old time's sake. I remember Zebra Daddy used to give us discounts, but I never had you—" Laura growls, "Not me, or anyone else ever again" (Liu, *X-23 Vol. 3: Don't Look Back* #20, 77). The pimp escapes, and the woman who was working with him is terrified. Laura asks her where he keeps the other girls. She tells the woman that if she does not get the other girls out now, they will never get out (Liu, *X-23 Vol. 3: Don't Look Back* #20, 79). When Laura and Jubilee arrive at the house where the girls are being kept, they find a full-scale human trafficking situation—dozens of girls and young women—and they realize that they are in over their heads. Laura knows innately that she has to get them to safety but knows she does not have the means to do so. This story is a full circle arc: in 2003, we see X-23 as a prostitute in New

York, and in 2012, she has the opportunity to rescue others like her. As they exit the house, they find themselves swarmed by SHIELD, led by Natasha Romanoff, who takes the trafficked girls to safety. Natasha tells Laura that she is valuable, and skilled, and offers her a place in the Avengers (Liu, *X-23 Vol. 3: Don't Look Back* #20, 83). SHIELD and the Avengers are doing a different kind of work, directly intervening to help people, and she thinks that Laura would fit in. Here again, Laura has choices about the direction of her life and what she wants to do with it, and this particular choice leads her to a major change. She arrives at Avengers Academy shortly thereafter, where she finds friendship, support, and purpose.

For Laura, violence—when chosen, and when used on behalf of the protection of others—serves as a psychological corrective to her lack of agency and inability to consent throughout her life. For her, violence is experienced as empowerment, particularly when utilized to exact justice. That will be her role in the Avengers. In claiming agency over and through violence, Laura resists victimhood, and refuses to be passive and broken—though that is often what people expect her to be, especially because of her age and gender. Laura's particular skill set takes her from a place where violence is seen as dishonorable, to a place where she is empowered by it, and valued for it.

After Wolverine dies, Laura takes on the mantle of *All-New Wolverine*, in his honor. Now that Laura has control over her life and her choices she has a no-kill policy, though her work often still lends itself to violence. Before his death, Laura and Wolverine had grown close, and Laura refers to him as her father. He left his things to her, including his apartment, a secluded cottage, his mantle, and she misses him. Laura learns that a company called Alchemax has been making clones of her and engineering them not to feel pain. Most of them are mysteriously dying, but Laura rescues the ones who are alive. She takes one of them in to live with her, named Gabby, giving Laura the opportunity to be a caregiver and mentor to someone the way that Wolverine was for her. Gabby joining her is unexpected, but it turns out that this protective relationship, like the one she had with Wolverine, is something Laura very much wants to pass along. Laura's desire to protect Gabby in this way is a key way to read her as a vigilante feminist superheroine, who is by definition someone whose actions are done on behalf of others, to make the world a safer place for girls and women. That Laura has expanded her life to fit a child and give that child the safety and security that she herself did not have until she met Wolverine when she was sixteen years old demonstrates her prioritizing others over herself.

The *All-New Wolverine* arc is the final, critical piece of the puzzle toward tracking how Laura develops the capacity for choice and agency over her own life. Laura learns that someone has recreated the trigger scent, and she and Gabby go into hiding (Taylor, *All-New Wolverine Vol. 3: Enemy of the State* #13, 7). She is the victim of a set-up, as water bomber planes blanket the whole town where she is hiding with trigger scent (Taylor, *All-New Wolverine Vol. 3: Enemy of the State* #13, 24). She blacks out, and when she comes to, everyone is dead and she thinks she killed them. The water bombers had returned to a warplane that was flying the Madripoor flag, so Laura heads to Madripoor to find out who set her up and why (Taylor, *All-New Wolverine Vol. 3: Enemy of the State* #14, 41). When she arrives in Madripoor, she learns that the trigger scent has been developed by Kimura, who is there with a plan to capture X-23 and use her as her ultimate weapon so that she can take over the world.

Kimura's first mission for Laura is to kill Tyger Tiger, who is vying for control of Madripoor. Laura refuses, threatening to kill herself first. Kimura shows her photo evidence that she has tracked down Megan and Aunt Debbie. It took Kimura years to find them, but she did find them, and if Laura does not do what Kimura demands, Kimura will murder them; or worse, she will force Laura to murder them, and video tape it so that she will have to watch how they begged her to stop (Taylor, *All-New Wolverine Vol. 3: Enemy of the State* #15, 81). Laura agrees to work with Kimura, in exchange for the protection of her family. Kimura begins re-training Laura with trigger scent, submerging her in it while she is subjected to torture and strain. She has developed a torturous prison that is designed just for Laura, a cross between a sensory deprivation tank and an iron maiden. In it, Laura is submerged in trigger scent, floating, with spikes jutting out of her body. It is designed to ensure that Laura does not know where she is, or when it is, or who she is, but just that she is constantly in pain (Taylor, *All-New Wolverine Vol. 3: Enemy of the State* #15, 83). This condition of torment is then supposed to lend itself to success when she is dumped into a space where there are people around; Laura theoretically will be so enraged and in pain that she will lash out and kill everyone.

Kimura tests it on Tyger Tiger's stronghold, and what she finds is that Laura has developed the capacity to resist the trigger scent's instinct to kill. Instead of killing the people in the room, she electrocutes and immobilizes them (Taylor, *All-New Wolverine Vol. 3: Enemy of the State* #15, 89). This is a huge realization, and an incredible feat, because Laura is so much more in control of herself that she is able to resist forces that used to totally dampen her ability to resist. Laura finds out that she had been set up back in the town that had been blanketed in trigger scent. Rather than kill innocent people Laura had stabbed herself through her own brain. Kimura had to make it look like Laura had done it in order to make her feel enough guilt that she would seek out Kimura in Madripoor. This development is crucial to the growth and development of Laura's sense of agency, because, as Suico argues, "for agency development to occur, individuals must be willing and able to resist" (Suico 2018, 111). Laura's resistance to the trigger scent is a form of agency.

Laura is rescued from Kimura by all the people she loves: Gabby, Gambit, and her boyfriend Warren. She has the allyship of Tyger, who is grateful that Laura did not kill her. And lastly, her friends have brought Jean Gray with them. Jean has an idea to telepathically reprogram Laura's mind so that she can fully overcome the trigger scent and be truly free. They place Gabby and Laura in a protected room with a vial of trigger scent and a cute bunny—both hopefully deterrents to Laura's killing rage (Taylor, *All-New Wolverine Vol. 3: Enemy of the State* #16, 103). Jean Gray waits outside the door, and when Gabby douses herself with the scent, Jean Gray goes into Laura's mind. She finds that when Laura blacks out for the trigger scent she goes back to a memory of herself as a young child sitting with her mother, Sarah Kinney, as her mother reads her *Pinnochio*, the book that her mother had hidden inside a copy of *The Art of War* so that Laura could have access to something that was meant for a child. Laura tells Jean that the door is locked, that she cannot get out. Jean tells her to try again, that the door is actually unlocked. Laura is a bit resistant to giving up this moment, this memory of feeling safe with her mother, but she overcomes it, opens the door, and literally finds her way out of the trigger scent's influence (Taylor, *All-New Wolverine Vol. 3: Enemy of the State* #15, 113–115). From that moment onward, the trigger scent is useless on her. This is a kind of freedom she had never allowed herself to even imagine.

For Laura's entire life, Kimura has been the only thing she has feared. Kimura is the only person that she cannot kill, and she lives to torment Laura. Even without the trigger scent's control over her, Kimura still has infinite ways to cause her pain—Laura has an entire lifetime of examples of the sadistic, cruel torture that Kimura has exacted on her. Furthermore, Kimura knows where Laura's family is hiding. Knowing that Kimura will never stop being a threat to her and her loved ones, Laura figures out how to kill Kimura. Kimura is engineered to have super strength, and she has impermeable skin. She has even reprogrammed her own mind so that she is not susceptible to magic or mind manipulation. But she has to breathe; and so Laura drowns her. This is her last act of killing to free herself, her family, and everyone she might ever love from the monster who has brutalized her since she was nine years old (Taylor, *All-New Wolverine Vol. 3: Enemy of the State* #16, 136–138). She moves forward now without any barriers to agency over her own body and life. Her total psychic freedom is the ultimate safety, and it will allow her to be whoever she wants to be. As Castro and Clark write in the introduction to *Representing Agency in Popular Culture*, "it is the power of children to create spaces and places of their own in the adult world that demonstrates agency" (Castro and Clark 2019, xiii). The first thing she does when Kimura is no longer a threat and she knows that she, herself, is no longer a threat either, is go to Megan and Aunt Debbie to let them know that they do not have to hide anymore (Taylor, *All-New*

Wolverine Vol. 3: Enemy of the State #16, 140). Once Jean Gray helps Laura psychically break the influence of the trigger scent, and Laura kills Kimura, there are no more barriers between herself and full ownership over her own body. And that capacity for agency leads her to become a powerful advocate on behalf of others, making the world safer on her own terms.

For readers, watching Laura arrive in this place can also be meaningful. As Maud Lavin writes in *Push Comes to Shove: New Images of Aggressive Women*, which examines audience and viewer interaction with aggressive women, "the representation of violence acts on the subject in very different ways than action violence. It is representations of violence, particularly of women and girls committing violence" that has a productive impact on audiences (Lavin 2012, 108). It is "a welcome antidote to seeing too many female characters as victims in past movies" (Lavin 2012, 122). This is in line with Megan Seely's argument in *Fight Like a Girl*, that telling stories and showing images of girls and women using violence will positively impact their confidence, and their sense that they are worth fighting for. When all we see is violence enacted against women, without them ever fighting back, it sends a cultural message that violence against women is normal, as is women's passivity in the face of violence. As Lavin notes, "the myth of feminine passivity is dead. Or should be" (Lavin 2012, 238).

Jeffrey A. Brown notes that "the increased visibility of . . . modern action heroines is a progressive change and models for viewers and readers an image of strong femininity, as well as a belief that women can in fact be their own heroes. But, as with any wide-ranging trend in popular culture, the figure of the action heroine also needs to be considered as more than just a harbinger of evolving gender politics. . . . The action heroine exists at the center of a precarious set of beliefs about gender, sex, ethnicity, age, violence, and power" (J. A. Brown 2015, 6). Indeed, it would be both reductive and troublesome to read X-23 as a mere signal that woman can be their own heroes. That is a significant aspect of her story, but it requires a lot of unpacking to get there. Typically, assassins do not get a pass to be heroes; but under the circumstances of Laura Kinney, when we pull back the layers and read her character as a child who is not given choice until she is a teenager, it becomes clear that we need a more nuanced way to read her. One part that Brown identifies is "how the current wave of action heroines is redefining femininity through a struggle with stereotypical and historical ideas about womanhood," which Laura certainly does (J. A. Brown 2015, 7). The scientists at the lab were resistant to creating Laura in the first place because they wanted a male clone of Wolverine. X-23's existence as a genetic twin was troublesome to them because they could not imagine that a girl would be as capable of a weapon as Wolverine; it turned out she was even more capable, as she outperformed Wolverine in test runs in the lab. But for X-23, it is not the fact that she is a female genetic twin of Wolverine that makes her story so important; rather it is the quest for choice and agency once she could no longer be forced to kill on command.

As a scholar, I am also a reader, and the way that I have chosen to trace Laura's story along a trajectory of trauma, healing, empowerment through violence, and ultimately finding agency over her own body and life is somewhat resistive. It is an act of witnessing to share X-23's story in the way that I have chosen to do throughout this chapter, reclaiming her narrative and her agency and locating the places where she exercises choice in ways that allow her to grow and be empowered to be better and to help others. It is painful to witness child abuse, which is at the core of the story of Laura Kinney. It is difficult to psychologically come to grips with drugging young girls to take away their ability to say no, which is what happens to X-23 when she is used as a weapon against her will. But that is central and essential to her story. Choosing her future, as well as how to reconcile her past, is her *raison d'etre*. Laura Kinney is a survivor, and deserves recognition for that.

NOTES

1. The quote in the title comes from Marjorie Liu's *The Killing Dream* #3, page 63, and refers to the moment in which Laura realizes that choice has always been denied to her, but that in reclaiming her right to it she is gaining power over her own demons.

2. M-Day refers to a day on which hundreds of thousands of mutants were depowered or killed. The Scarlet Witch attempted to rid the world of the mutant gene by casting a spell, "No More Mutants," which ended up de-powering a massive majority of mutants. Called "the Decimation," this action reduced the mutant population down to a few hundred, as most mutants were depowered and some others were killed as a result of losing their powers. In total, 986,618 mutants were either depowered or killed by the Decimation. (https://marvel.fandom.com/wiki/Decimation)

Chapter Three

Hunting Wolves

Violence, Agency, and Empowerment in Jackson Pearce's Retold Fairytales Young Adult Fantasy Series

Both the *Sisters Red* and *Sweetly* books in the Retold Fairytales series of young adult novels by Jackson Pearce have at their core the existence of werewolves, called Fenris.[1] They can transform anytime, day or night, full moon or no moon, and they hunt girls and women. In their human form they are imperceptible as wolves, except to the eyes of a trained hunter, and wear the bodies of very good-looking, sweet-talking, suave men.[2] The Fenris prey on girls in a sexualized way. In all four novels in the Retold Fairytales series, the Fenris charm young women, woo them, attract them, and then they eat them.[3] They are strengthened and titillated by fear, and so they are well practiced in luring girls into spaces where they are cut off from safety, and terrifying them at the moment of their transformation. They transform into werewolves for the sole purpose of eating their prey, and on the rare occasion that they are interrupted in that process, usually by a hunter, they are weakened and ravenous until they are able to feast. The longer they go without feeding, the wilder they become, and the more victims they devour. The girl heroines in this series emerge as hunters fighting against creatures cloaked as men that wish them harm. They train themselves as weapons focused entirely on the eradication of this threat. Cultural fear about sexual predation permeates this series, but instead of adapting to it the girls fight it. And not only that, they protect other girls in doing so. The girls, always sisters in these stories, take on the burden of knowledge about the Fenris, and commit themselves to destroying them. This chapter considers the ways in which the traumatic circumstances of the heroines' youth serves as a catalyst for them to develop into teenage vigilante feminist super/heroines. They carry the knowledge that monsters really exist, and they take on the burden of eradicating that threat so that no other girls and women ever have to go through what they went through. Furthermore, they do this by honing their bodies and their senses, by learning how to hunt the hunters. Their capacity to fight instills in them an agency that is defined by their resistance to fear, and by the critical importance of their purpose in the world. They are empowered by their use of violence, and by making the world safer for others.

Sisters Red, a retelling of Little Red Riding Hood, is told from the perspective of teenaged sisters Scarlett and Rosie March, who survived the wolf's attack in their grandmother's cottage when they were children. Scarlett, having fought the wolf to protect her sister, is badly scarred. She won the battle and killed the wolf, but she lost an eye, and carries the memory of her encounter all over her body. Their survival, and the knowledge that they now carry that monsters really do lurk in the darkness, has hardened them into fierce wolf hunters. *Sweetly*, a retelling of Hansel and Gretel, is told from the perspective of Gretchen, an eighteen-year-old girl who finds herself a guest at the home of a candy shop owner. Twelve years ago, she and her brother Ansel survived an attack by a witch in the woods, but her twin sister was lost, and was never heard from again. When she meets a handsome woodsman in her new town, she begins to unravel the reality of the community she is visiting, which has a terrifying history of the annual disappearance of eighteen-year-old girls. As fairy tale retellings, these stories function in an important way to disrupt the cycle of violence against girls and women. As Maria Nikolajeva explains, "social structures are represented in literature, as well as how texts reflect the time and society within which they were produced. Sociohistorical studies of fairy tales provide good examples. By comparing versions of the same tale, we can draw conclusions about the views on childhood and other social values during the time the tales were told or written" (Nikolajeva 2005, 73–74). In the case of this chapter, these twenty-first century fairy tale retellings demonstrate the ways that girls and young women are coded as agentic in the face of their violent circumstances. And Janice Del Negro speaks directly to their importance for teens, who "are drawn to these tales and to reinterpretations of these tales, deeply engaged by their exposure to them in contemporary media. Their willingness to step into the fantastical as limned by these supernatural, romantic, and tragic tales allows them to interact with powerful emotional moments in the safety of a narrative frame" (J. M. Del Negro 2017, 99). Specifically, Del Negro articulates the success of discussions about sexual consent that are triggered by reading early versions of Sleeping Beauty, in which it is literally a sleeping girl who is kissed by a prince without any care for what she may have wanted (J. M. Del Negro 2017, 99).

In chapter 1, I explored the ways in which fantasy violence can "bolster confidence" and present "an empowering challenge to overcome" (Gackenbach, et al. 2016, 92–93). This is especially important for young adults, since, as Johnson and Campbell note, they are "looking for ways to grow into adulthood," and see the worlds of fantasy as a space to resolve their anxieties (Johnson and Campbell 2016, 34). Janice M. Del Negro and Melanie A. Kimball explain that "stories shape personality, develop empathy, create community, change minds, and alter consciousness" (J. M. Del Negro 2017, ix), and Del Negro also argues that "[s]tories that depict . . . heroines overcoming extraordinary odds are critical to the emotional health of all listeners, but to no one more so than adolescents who are tentative and uncertain of their own emotional survival" (J. M. Del Negro 2017, 97). Kristina Deffenbacher talks about the role of texts in combatting rape culture, noting: "stories of women warriors suggest the possibility of women not just facing and surviving rape but also facing down and successfully fighting rapists, and rape culture itself" (Deffenbacher 2014, 932). Finally, as explored in chapter 1, Sarah Hentges explains that because of their "power to unsettle dominant discourses" and "afford the potential for subversion," "the texts that girls consume, as well as the texts that we consume about girls, are important for an understanding of the roles that girls play in life and in our imaginations" (Hentges 2018, 54). She acknowledges the power of characters and books, especially as fans, noting "what we find in the characters of books not only helps us to see ourselves more clearly, these stories also help us escape into another world where we can see other women fight similar battles" (Hentges 2018, 76).

This chapter provides analysis of another book series in which teenage vigilante feminist super/heroines experience trauma, find agency, and are empowered—through violence—to help other girls and young women. This analysis conducts a close reading of two of the four novels in the Retold Fairytales series, tracing moments in the texts in which the heroine subject is first faced with the imminent threat of the Fenris, and then chooses to become a fighter to hunt the monsters, to protect other girls and women. Through this choice, she is empowered by her physical capacity for violence, especially in her skill at killing Fenris. As well, through this choice she directly impacts the safety of others by reducing the threat of Fenris in their communities. Taking on the role of hunter and protector, these heroines claim agency over both their bodies and their lives. In the Retold Fairytales Series, the Fenris stand in for sexual predators; the way that they select, hunt, and eat girls is sexualized. This will be recognizable to readers as another mirror on rape culture, and the empowerment that the heroines in these stories experience by learning how to fight can be vicariously satisfying for readers.

SISTERS RED

The front cover of the novel, *Sisters Red,* by Jackson Pearce, asks "Who's Afraid of the Big, Bad Werewolf." A retelling of Little Red Riding Hood, it takes its inspiration from the fairy tale about wolves disguised as men who trick and lure girls and women in order to devour them. The novel's opening chapter, "Prologue: A Fairy Tale, Seven Years Ago," describes the first time Scarlett and Rosie March encounter a Fenris, a predatory wolf who eats girls and women. On this day, a Fenris finds its way to Scarlett and Rosie's grandmother's cottage in rural Georgia. Fenris like their girls young and pretty, and so this one is consumed by desire for eleven-year-old Scarlett, as she twirls in her red party dress. When he learns that the girls are home alone with their grandmother, he transforms into a wolf and kills her before turning his attention to them. After her grandmother is killed, Scarlett realizes she is the only thing standing between the wolf and her sister, and she is reborn as a hunter that day. Instinct takes over, as she cracks a hand mirror and pulls out a shard of glass to use as a weapon. Scarlett gets her first glimpse of the wolf, and it is terrifying. He has enormous, hollow eyes, and a mouth filled with long, pointed fangs. His back arches so sharply that it appears broken, his shoulders are hunched, and his feet—with claws as long as fishing hooks—turn in. His nose elongates until it appears canine, and his lips spread wide across his face. He lurches toward the girls on his paws. As she stares into the eyes of the monster, she repeats to herself: "I am the only one left to fight, so now I must kill you" (Pearce 2010, 8).

At that moment, Scarlett becomes the hunter. Having grown up listening to her grandmother's bedtime stories about Plato's cave—of how the shadows on the wall are actually real, and that leaving the cave for the light means one must be brave—in this moment she has seen the sunlight, and in the light there are monsters. It is something that forever changes her, it is something she can never unsee, and it is something which she can never ignore. Scarlett's trauma is not only marked by the loss of this innocence, and by the death of her grandmother at the hands of a Fenris, but she is also badly injured during the attack. The Fenris scraped her deep across the right side of her face, leaving her scarred and without an eye. He left deep gouging marks on Scarlett's body, forever marking her by his encounter, and making her a physical outcast—as well as an emotional outcast, marked by her new knowledge. From this moment forward, she feels responsible, now that she knows, to protect other girls from the fate of the Fenris, girls who do not know and who cannot fight. It becomes a duty to her, it becomes her identity. She commits her life, full-time, to being a hunter, honing her body into a strong, deadly, hatchet-wielding weapon until she is the best at it.

In the first present-day scene in the book, we meet Scarlett, now seventeen-years-old, luring a Fenris who is hunting his prey in town. She carries a hatchet and wears a red cloak: "the cloak serves multiple purposes—the color of passion, sex, and lust is irresistible to wolves, and the fabric hides the instrument of their death. And perhaps most important, wearing it feels right, as if I've put on a uniform that turns me into more than a scarred-up orphan girl" (Pearce 2010, 10). She plays Red Riding Hood to the Fenris' wolf, but in this story, there is no ambiguity about why red is the color the wolves are attracted to. It turns them on, and when they get aroused, they cannot help but begin to transform. And Scarlett never kills a Fenris who is not fully trans-formed, just in case her instinct fails her and it is actually just a human man with evil intentions stalking her. She has never been wrong, but as a hunter, this is her ritual. Here, we learn how much wolves look like charming men, as Scarlett describes a Fenris that she is hunting. She describes him as "nor-mal," "nice," like a high school football player. She notes that this is by design, a key part of the illusion: "it's hard to lure young girls to their doom if you look like a psychopath. You have to look kind, put together, clean-cut. Show them pretty hair and stylish clothes and most girls won't look close enough to see that your teeth point in a very canine way or recognize that it's hunger your eyes are lit with" (Pearce 2010, 11). He smiles at her. Scarlett notes that "a normal girl would think about touching him, would think about kissing him, about wanting him. A normal, stupid, ignorant girl" (Pearce 2010, 22). Scarlett feels both envy and annoyance for the "normal" girls. Envy for their innocence, their ability to live their lives without the knowl-edge that monsters lurk in their midst, and their unmarred skin. She hunts Fenris not only because she knows they exist and she has the capacity to do something about it, but because she knows that no one else is looking out for girls in the world. She hunts Fenris to protect other girls, to keep other families from having to feel the pain of loss that she has had to endure. She fights to protect their ignorance.

The way that Scarlett's identity is wrapped up with her role as a fighter, and the way that she copes with trauma and her fear of physical helplessness by becoming a Fenris hunter, is in line with the many arguments presented in this book's introduction, that the capacity for wielding violence in protection of others makes women and girls feel more safe. Alison Graham-Bertolini, for example, argues that passive resistance is not an effective way to ward off predators, and that the gendered nature of nonviolence is a product of the patriarchy that wants to keep women in a subordinate place (Graham-Bertoli-ni 2011, 165). Megan Seely argues that women need to reclaim their histori-cal role as warriors (Seely 2007, 186). Amana Fontanella-Khan posits that aggressive vigilante tactics have measurable effects on community change in India (Fontanella-Khan 2013, 264). And, Jocelyn Hollander demonstrates that self-defense training "helps to change the root conditions that allow violence against women to flourish" (Hollander 2016). The way that Scarlett identifies with her physical role as a hunter and with her duty to protect others mimics all of these ways, historical and contemporary, that violence serves as a mechanism to empower girls.

Fenris are instinctually drawn to the "prettiest" girls. They are drawn to perfumes, to sparkly make-up, to the delicacy that allows them to overpower the girls and terrify them. Scarlett's frustration is deeply intertwined with the reality that she has witnessed over the years, that Fenris are especially drawn to feminine girls who are dressed in red, or who are wearing skimpy club clothes. With these sorts of details, it is clear that the Fenris of the Retold Fairytales series are an allegory for predatory men, for the cunning, calculated rapists who live in our world, unseen until it is too late. As well, Pearce takes on the challenging terrain of the "sexy clothes" myth that enables rampant victim-blaming in American culture and society. In 2014, in response to a tweet suggesting "women should dress modestly to avoid rape," *XOJane* journalist Christine Fox posed a question on Twitter: "If there are any women on my TL who are victims of sexual assault & don't mind sharing something . . . what were you wearing when you were assaulted?" Her question yielded answers from thousands of women and men, and a #WhatWereYouWearing campaign was born. Her goal was to start a conversation on the pervasive habit of victim blaming. Fox wrote, "Something incredibly therapeutic and cathartic happened that I'm sure none of us could've expected . . . in real time we debunked the 'well, what was she wearing? theory'" (quoted in Smith 2014). It is both common for people to assume rape victims were dressed provocatively to "ask for" rape, and for survivors to feel guilty for their role in their own rape. For example, writing for *The Oregonian*, Emily Smith tells the story of a nineteen-year-old girl who was raped by a co-worker she trusted:

> [She] experienced some of the same concerns that keep many victims from reporting. She felt stupid for hanging out with [the rapist] alone. She worried he would try to hurt her after she turned him in. Her fear of people blaming her for the rape persists. [The rapist] was always nice and friendly to her at work. But she still feels responsible for becoming his target. . . . "It was my fault. Just because—I should have known better." She struggles with how rape is treated in public, where comedians joke about it, where high school students record and share videos of it, where it is a mere word that does not adequately describe her experience." (Smith, 2014)

Sisters Red enters into this territory, where myth and reality meet. Survivors of sexual assault often blame themselves for what happened to them, as the above story in *The Oregonian* demonstrates. The "what was she wearing" defense has been used countless times to try to paint accusers in a bad light, to make juries question their character. Scarlett has witnessed the way that Fenris slobber over girls in skimpy clothes and wears a red cape to play to that weakness. But the reality is that Fenris—like rapists—are the ones responsible for the attacks, not the victims, no matter their behavior, and though that may be what lures them, Fenris kill girls no matter what they are wearing.

In 2017, Jen Brockman launched an exhibit, titled "What Were You Wearing?", at the University of Kansas, which showcased the stories of eighteen rape survivors displayed next to the clothing they were wearing when it happened. Brockman had spearheaded similar installations at the University of Arkansas and the University of Iowa, before opening this one. The art installation "aims to shatter the myth that sexual violence is caused by a person's wardrobe," and includes t-shirts, exercise clothes, dresses, and cargo shorts. For survivors, the exhibit is validating, as they "see their own outfits reflected on the wall, [and] see it wasn't their fault" (Stevens 2017). This is the same motivation for the creation of the SlutWalk in 2011, in which, as Jessica Valenti wrote for *The Washington Post*, "Thousands of women—and men—are demonstrating to fight the idea that what women wear, what they drink or how they behave can make them a target for rape" (Valenti 2011). Valenti reported that the SlutWalks started with a local march organized by five women in Toronto, and went "viral, with events planned in more than 75 cities in countries from the United States and Canada, to Sweden and South Africa. In just a few months, SlutWalks have become the most successful feminist action of the past 20 years." The event was initially organized after a police officer told students at York University that if they wanted to avoid rape, they shouldn't dress like "sluts." Describing themselves as "fed up and pissed off," a march that was anticipated to be one hundred ended up becoming a rally of three thousand. This issue strikes a deep chord of shared frustration for girls and women, demonstrated by the instant popularity of this sort of community action. Valenti wrote, "The idea that women's clothing has some bearing on whether they will be raped is a dangerous myth feminists have tried to debunk for decades. Despite all the activism and research, however, the cultural misconception prevails . . . [though] the sad fact is, a miniskirt is not more likely to provoke a rapist than a potato sack is to deter one" (Valenti, 2011) .

In the Retold Fairytales series, clothing will not stop a Fenris attack, but it does intensify their pleasure in committing the assault. Scarlett and her sister Rosie wear particular clothing to catch their eye, and they use this tactic to get the Fenris to turn more quickly. The Fenris *are* extremely attracted to all of the qualities of beauty that "normal" girls try to exude, and as the person trying to keep Fenris from hurting girls, Scarlett feels like they make her job more difficult when they capitulate to things like beauty norms and standards. She has nicknamed these normal girls, the ones who wear perfume and makeup and go to bars and clubs and dances, "Dragonflies:"

> They're adorned in glittery green rhinestones, shimmery turquoise and aqua-
> marine powders streaked across their eyelids. Dragonfly girls. Their hair is all
> the same, long and streaked, spiraling down their backs to where the tiny
> strings holding their tops on are knotted tightly. Their skin glows under the
> neon lights—amber, ebony, cream—like shined metal, flawless and smooth.
> (Pearce 2010, 208–209)

She is exasperated by them, and knows that they are unintentionally inviting danger. But she is also committed to protecting their right to be ignorant: "Ignorance is no reason to die. They can't help what they are, still happily unaware inside a cave of fake shadows. They exist in a world that's beautiful, normal, where people have jobs and dreams that don't involve a hatchet" (Pearce 2010, 208–209). The answer is not in changing what the girls wear— the Fenris will (and do) feed on any girl, regardless of clothing. The only way to end Fenris attacks is to eradicate Fenris, a seemingly endless and impossible task, not unlike eradicating rape by eliminating rapists. It would be so much easier if clothing were the problem; but it is not, these are real monsters, and the reality is that they will attack anyway because it is who they are and it is what they do. Scarlett knows that she is not going to be able to kill the wolves fast enough to save every girl. Though she is fully committed to hunting Fenris, she feels guilty for not doing enough, knowing that girls will die (Pearce 2010, 90).

The Dragonfly girls represent the embodiment of normative beauty, and the pressure women and girls feel to make themselves attractive to men. Because of her deformity, Scarlett is unable to be part of their world, and though she is annoyed by what she sees as their pettiness and narcissism, she also knows that if the trajectory of her life had been different, she and Rosie would have been like them. As Jessica Valenti explains in *Full Frontal Feminism*, women and girls suffer for beauty: "When you're taught that the majority of your worth is in how aesthetically pleasing you are to boys—and then boys tell you you're ugly—there's something soul-crushing about that . . . the ways in which our society keeps women obsessed with their looks serve a gross sexist purpose . . . we're taught to be forever worried about our appearance" (Valenti 2007, 198–199). Valenti argues that women and girls know the harmful consequences that adherence to beauty norms have on their bodies, psyches, and lives, but that they don't care (Valenti 2007, 197). Valenti echoes what Scarlett is thinking when she warily watches the Dragonfly girls: "We're expected to be hot—but if we are, we're vain and stupid. And if we're not hot, we're useless" (Valenti 2007, 211). Scarlett buys into this logic a bit, as she toes the line between admiration and condemnation of the Dragonfly girls for their choices.

We can also think of the Dragonfly girls as the personification of beauty norms. Valenti explains: "None of us want to be ugly; in fact, we all would really like to be beautiful—and it's killing us. Literally" (Valenti 2007, 197). She is talking about all the ways that we mutilate, starve, and modify our bodies to be (or feel) more beautiful. In *Sisters Red*, however, the Dragonfly girls' quest to be beautiful, to glitter and smell good, is also literally killing them. Scarlett notes the ways that these girls will attract the Fenris, because the Fenris hunt attractive, sweet smelling girls; these factors enhance their arousal, which heightens their pleasure in the kill. The Fenris, here, are the embodiment of patriarchal standards of control over the bodies of women and girls, and of the culture industry that profits off of them. Valenti writes: "It's important to remember why some folks need us to feel ugly. It serves a specific purpose: to make us spend, to distract us, and ultimately make us disappear" (Valenti 2007, 209); in *Sisters Red*, the girls literally disappear.

Scarlett's identity is intertwined with her role as a hunter. Her experience at eleven years old, when her grandmother was killed and she was left alone to protect herself and her sister, has traumatized her. The way that Scarlett has experienced trauma deeply impacts the way she develops as a character. As explored in chapter 2, Debra Jackson explains that the "full realization of its impact is not immediately accessible" (Jackson 2016, 206–207). There is a period of time between the traumatizing event and the full emotional impact of the event, which "traps the survivor in a cycle of repetitions and reenactments that makes the traumatic event contemporaneous with the present" (Jackson 2016, 206–207). The loss of her grandmother to a violent death, and the wolf's subsequent attack on Scarlett and Rosie, feel at various times quite present, and at other moments, quite past. Scarlett's symptoms are obviously post-traumatic stress disorder (PTSD), which is clinically characterized by "feelings of helplessness, loss of control, anger, dissociation, numbing, denial, insomnia, nausea, heightened startle response, and hypervigilance, as well as revisiting the experience through nightmares, flashbacks, and/or hallucinations" (Jackson 2016, 207). Scarlett hunts to gain the control that she lost, and she feels angry most of the time. She is numb to feeling any kind of emotion (love, sexual desire) for anyone but her sister, and on only a platonic level, their friend Silas. She suffers from insomnia and flashbacks: "the Fenris breaking down our door. My grandmother screaming in German. The feeling of his teeth on my arms, my legs, my face" (Pearce 2010, 34). Arguably, her obsessive physical training is a manifestation of hypervigilance. Jackson notes that many trauma survivors feel like they experience a sort of death, in the sense that their sense of personhood of selfhood is destroyed (Jackson 2016, 208). When Scarlett encounters the Dragonflies she poignantly feels the memory of the girl she could have been, and mourns it: "My world is a parallel universe to theirs—the same sights, same people, same city, yet the Fenris lurk, the evil creeps, the knowledge undeniably exists. If I hadn't been thrown into this world, I could just as easily have been a Dragonfly" (Pearce 2010, 109).

It is described as a kind of lust that makes the wolves react to pretty girls. They are attracted to the color red, which is sexual and sensual, and they are not able to control themselves. In the face of their prey, they sometimes cannot help but transform, with canines and claws growing, and fur appearing in patches on their bodies. This notion of being so attracted to something that they cannot control themselves marks the Fenris as not just predators in the sense of the fantasy genre, but correlates also with the predators in the misogynist rape culture in which the author is writing, and even that in which the story takes place. Kate Manne writes about the monstrosity that rapists take on in our cultural imagination, noting that we expect that "real rapists will appear on our radars either as devils, decked out with horns and pitchforks, or else as monsters—that is, as creepy and ghoulish creatures. . . . What is frightening about rapists is partly that they are by far the most likely to be men. Rapists are human, all too human, and they are very much among us. The idea of rapists as monsters exonerates by caricature" (Manne 2018, 199). The Fenris are monsters disguised as handsome, charming, attractive men, between the ages of approximately fourteen and forty-nine. They approach girls and young women with entitlement, confidence, and when they have trapped them, they attempt to instill fear in them. The Fenris love fear. It heightens the satisfaction of their hunt, and ultimately of their kill. This is an allegory of the way that the "boys will be boys" attitude pervades American culture and society.

In a July 2019 article in the *New York Times*, "Teenager Accused of Rape Deserves Leniency Because He's From a 'Good Family,' Judge Says," Luis Ferre-Sadurni documents a case of sexual assault that occurred between two sixteen year olds at an "alcohol fueled pajama party" in New Jersey in 2017. Of the details of the case, Ferre-Sadurni wrote that "the boy filmed himself penetrating her from behind, her torso exposed, her head hanging down. . . . He later shared the cellphone video among friends . . . and sent a text that said, 'When your first time having sex was rape.'" And yet, "a family court judge said it wasn't rape," and "also said the young man came from a good family, attended an excellent school, had terrific grades, and was an Eagle Scout." This was a teenage boy who had shared video of the assault with friends and had lied about that fact when confronted by the victim. Denying that this case was one of rape, the judge questioned the validity of the victim's level of intoxication, denied that the rapists actions were predatory, and dismissed his text as "just a 16-year-old kid saying stupid crap to his friends" (Ferre-Sadurny 2019). This case is emblematic of the way that misogyny operates to punish girls and women who come forward about sexual assault. As Kate Manne explains, people tend to defend men's innocence and honor, and "grant them a pardon prematurely," even going so far as to extend in many cases "the benefit of the doubt to the alleged perpetrator over his accuser-cum-victim, no matter how thin the basis for doubting her word may be" (Manne 2018, 178). The case came to light in 2019 because an appellate panel reviewed the case, finding that the judge "overstepped in deconstructing the circumstances of the case, making his own assessment of the boy's culpability and considering the defendant's prior good character." This is just one of many cases in which the virtues of boys and young men are held to a higher degree of value than the crime against girls and young women.

In the 2015 case *People v. Turner*, freshman at Stanford University Brock Turner was convicted of assault with intent to commit rape of an intoxicated/unconscious person, penetration of an intoxicated person, and penetration of an unconscious person, and yet was only sentenced to six months in county jail. Despite having witnesses to the crime, a full medical exam and rape kit, a statement within a few hours of the attack, and pressing charges within twenty-four hours of the assault, the survivor—Chanel Miller—still found her character and motivation questioned remorselessly during the trial. Though Turner was convicted, Miller describes in her memoir, *Know My Name*, what happened at the sentencing hearing. His father told the judge "Brock would do anything to turn back the hands of time and have that night to do over again," and he blamed the high-pressure drinking culture, and the poor influence of the upperclassmen in his fraternity at Stanford for his son's behavior. He shared that the "verdicts have broken and shattered him and our family," and that the sentence requested by the prosecution would be a "steep price to pay for twenty minutes of action out of his twenty-plus years of life" (C. Miller 2019, 231–232). Despite Miller's own ten page statement at the sentencing hearing that shared the irrevocable harm done to her body by the assault, and to her psyche, well-being, and family by the long, intense trial during which Turner maintained his stance that the interaction was consensual, (despite the fact that she was unconscious and unresponsive), he ended up serving just three months for "good behavior."

Throughout the duration of the case, supporters of Turner described him as coming from a respectable family, and was a kind, loving, and respectful person. They blamed the culture of alcohol consumption at parties (and spent a majority of the time arguing about how intoxicated the victim was), rather than on the rapists actions. The judge believed Turner, saying during the sentencing hearing: "I take him at his word that, subjectively, that's his version of events . . . I do find that his remorse is genuine . . . Mr. Turner came before us today and said he was genuinely sorry for all the pain that he has caused to Chanel and her family. And I think that is a genuine feeling of remorse . . . I think that he will not be a danger to others. . . . The character letters suggest that up until this point he complied with social and legal norms sort of above and beyond what normal law-abiding people do" (C. Miller 2019, 234–235). Kate Manne terms this phenomenon as "himpathy," which is described as "excessive sympathy sometimes shown toward male perpetrators of sexual violence. It is frequently extended in contemporary

America to men who are white, nondisabled, and otherwise privileged 'golden boys' such as Turner, the recipient of a Stanford swimming scholarship. There is a subsequent reluctance to believe the women who testify against these men, or even to punish the golden boys whose guilt has been firmly established—as, again, Turner's was" (Manne 2018, 197). The U.S. has a vast array of cases to choose from to demonstrate that judges, and others with power, worry overmuch about the potential consequences of ruining the lives of men who are accused of rape, rather than the effects of their actions on the girls and women they have raped. It is noteworthy that the judges in both of these cases were removed from the bench following public outcry of their decisions, potentially showing a shift in public sentiment that is hungry for stronger repercussions and more severe punishments.

The reason that the vigilante feminist super/heroine is of such high value today stems directly from this reality that the systems that are set up to protect victims of crimes like sexual assault are failing girls and women. That the cultural reflection of a fantasy story like *Sisters Red* is so evident is a signal of its ubiquity; everyone recognizes these entitled rapists in the suave approach of the Fenris to his next victim. Furthermore, this is a commentary on the valuation of girls in a misogynist culture. No one notices when lots of girls just disappear. As Rosie realizes while scanning the news for a string of murders that might lead them to Fenris, the Fenris attacks usually do not even make the news, unless the girl is beautiful or rich. When girls disappear, it is just written off as another statistic of a missing girl (Pearce 2010, 30).

Though Pearce does not note it, we would also need to add "white" to the description of the "wealthy" and "beautiful" girl that might make the news when she disappears. Girls of color going missing often does not only not make the news, it is also taken less seriously by police precincts when reported. That is the reality of a rape culture, where people have grown so sensitized to violence against girls and women that they do not even notice it. Harmeet Kaur writes that "data shows that missing white children receive far more media coverage than missing black and brown children, despite higher rates of missing children among communities of color" (Kaur 2019). In 2018, the FBI National Crime Information Center database included 424,066 missing children under the age of eighteen, of which 37 percent were Black, "even though black children only make up about 14 percent of all children in the United States" (Kaur 2019). Women's Media Center reported on a 2017 hashtag, #BringBackOurGirls, in order to draw attention to the epidemic of missing Black girls in Washington, D.C. It uncovered a "poorly rolled-out police notification system in D.C. about missing people and a history of neglect and invisibility of missing Black girls formed a perfect storm for a brief, widespread panic about what was happening to Black girls in Washington" (Lindsey 2020). This article reported that between 64,000 and 75,000 Black girls are missing in the United States, explaining that they are "uniquely vulnerable and too easily erased from public discussions about the alarming trend of missing people" (Lindsey 2020).

One night, on a hunt, Scarlett loses sight of a Fenris and a group of three young women, and she is too late to save one of them. She recalls their fear, their inability to breathe. Scarlett empathizes with them, remembering the feeling off wondering whether or not this is all just some horrible nightmare. She sees herself in them, wondering if she looked the same way—filled with terror and disbelief—when she saved her sister from the Fenris attack when she was younger. She feels terrible for not being able to protect the girls from the knowledge: "Nothing can help you, Dragonflies. Say good-bye to the world you knew, welcome to the mouth of the cave. I'm sorry I failed you. I'm so, so sorry" (Pearce 2010, 160). Scarlett's mind replays the night, seeing the dead girl's elbow on the ground, unattached from the rest of her body—the rest of her body devoured. The thought "mixes with memories of emerging from [her grandmother's] bedroom, covered in dead Fenris blood, hoping to run into [my grandmother's] arms only to see there was nothing left of her but a bloodied, shredded apron. It's as if the Fenris know to leave a small piece of the victim, a piece that always lurks in front of all the happy memories of the dead" (Pearce 2010, 160–161). This melding of the past and present when Scarlett is triggered by the Fenris attack is a typical trauma response. As described in chapter 2, Jackson explains that when "a traumatic event occurs, the full realization of its impact is not immediately accessible" (Jackson 2016, 206–207). There is a period of "latency" between the time of the trauma and the "full emotional impact of the event" (Jackson 2016, 206–207) This can be hours, days, or decades, and it "traps the survivor in a cycle of repetitions and reenactments that makes the traumatic event contemporaneous with the present"(Jackson 2016, 206–207). Even six years later, the violence of the Fenris attack at her grandmother's house is right with her in her consciousness, alongside the violence she witnesses in the present. Scarlett's identity as a hunter who hunts and kills Fenris is a way to cope with the impact of the feeling of helplessness she recalls from the day her grandmother died.

Scarlett's physical power, her capability to fight back against Fenris, is transformative for her, it makes her a survivor and an agent of her own destiny. As Claire Maxwell and Peter Aggleton write, "Young women who discursively position themselves as 'powerful' integrate their bodies within such an understanding, using this integration to shore up the possibilities of agentic practice" (Maxwell and Aggleton 2012, 306–307). As she grows more confident in her body's capacity, she moves from being a young girl who can never be stronger than the monster, to training herself in tactics and weapons that empower her to take that power back. She then chooses a life where she fights, because she feels like she belongs there. Maxwell and Aggleton articulate that, once one sees the body as powerful, "the physical body and acts of speech work together to open up opportunities for agentic responses and behaviours which could become more sustained," integrating into both the girl's narrative and her actions (Maxwell and Aggleton 2012, 313). Scarlett's identity is wrapped up with her role as a Fenris-hunter, and the way she carries that out in everyday life grants her agency over her life and choices.

Scarlett feels duty-bound to be a hunter. She tells her friend, Silas that she cannot sit back and assume someone else will kill the Fenris. She believes that it is their responsibility to "do good when we have the power to" (Pearce 2010, 111). Violence is empowering for her, as she is able to feel more confident and secure in her own body once she is physically able to defend herself against Fenris and protect others from their attacks. When she comes across three Fenris one night, Scarlett explains: "My heart swells. This is what I am meant for" (Pearce 2010, 113). The way that Scarlett claims agency over her body and her life and uses her skills at hunting to protect other girls and women, marks her as a vigilante feminist super/heroine. There is no mechanism of formal justice through which Fenris can be caught and punished, and so Scarlett must act on her own to track and destroy them. When she fails, girls die. Through this identity, she embodies agency and experiences empowerment when she uses her skill with violence to make the world safer for others. She explains: "How could I possibly try to pretend the sunlight doesn't exist, now that it's taken so much of me? And I'm not stupid—I realize what I'm giving up" (Pearce 2010, 39). Though she does not see an end in sight, she hunts in order to kill Fenris, who are monsters that kill girls and ruin the lives of families. She knows that there is not a finish line, exactly, to the work that she has taken on, unless she can some-how manage to kill every Fenris. She does not realistically think that she can accomplish that, but she dreams of a world in which all the fear and darkness are gone (Pearce 2010, 35).

What girls read is important to their identity development, since "emerging research in the areas of psychology and neuroscience points to the importance of stories in everyday life, how stories shape personality, develop empathy, create community, change minds, and alter consciousness" (J. M. Del Negro 2017, ix). It is important that young adult readers have opportunities to see characters who can heal from trauma, and who are agentic. As Del Negro explains, "Stories that depict heroes and heroines overcoming extraordinary odds are critical to the emotional health of all listeners, but to no one more so than adolescents who are tentative and uncertain of their own emotional survival, despite any surface glamour to the contrary" (J. M. Del Negro 2017, 97). Additionally, Sarah Hentges argues that "the texts that girls consume, as well as the texts that we consume about girls, are important for an understanding of the roles that girls play in life and in our imaginations" (Hentges 2018, 54). She elaborates that "What we find in the characters of books not only helps us to see ourselves more clearly, these stories also help us escape into another world where we can see other women fight similar battles" (Hentges 2018, 76). For Scarlett, honing her body into a weapon and hunting Fenris is a way of healing, controlling her environment, and feeling like she has agency over her own life. It is empowering to her. Rosie says of Scarlett: "It's not a sickness, it's a passion. I now realize, a passion to hunt the same way a painter must paint or a singer must sing. It's her blood and her heart" (Pearce 2010, 320). The hunt, which is inherently violent, is a calling for Scarlett. She feels whole when doing it. She is empowered through violence, which allows her to exercise agency over her body and her life.

SWEETLY

In the second novel in the Retold Fairytales series, *Sweetly*, a loose retelling of Hansel and Gretel, Jackson Pearce introduces another community preyed upon by Fenris. At the start of this novel, young twin sisters and their older brother are walking in the forest. One of the twin girls carries a fairy tale book with her like a guidebook, because they are looking for the witch's house, rumored to be in these very woods. As they walk, the older brother drops jellybeans along the trail. When they hear cracking branches and the sound of an approaching figure, they turn to see an enormous monster—the witch—with yellow eyes. They clasp their hands together, so they do not lose each other in the dark forest, and they run. The witch gives chase. The older brother realizes that they are being slowed down by clasping hands, and they will all die if they do not let go. He breaks free just as he sees the edge of the woods. He enters the house, to find that only one of his sisters made it out of the woods with him.

That witches are real, but no one believes them, is a curse with which Ansel and his surviving sister Gretchen must live. They are terrified of the woods, of being alone. Gretchen, having lost the other half of herself when her twin disappeared, feels lost throughout her life. Their mother dies of grief, and their father remarries. Their stepmother does not like them. Soon, their father dies, as well, and when Gretchen is eighteen years old, they are kicked out of the house. They head East from Washington, where they have lived all their lives. Gretchen wants to move to the East Coast, to the ocean where there are no forests for witches to hide in. They only have a couple hundred dollars, and Ansel's old truck. They break down in South Carolina, just a few hours west of the ocean, out of money and unable to pay to have the truck towed or fixed.

They find themselves in the small town of Live Oak, a vestige of the Confederacy where the pride of the town is a small museum containing the boots of Robert E. Lee, and where no one wants to talk to outsiders, especial-ly young ones. It is not long before they learn that young folks, young women in particular, seem to disappear from Live Oak. Some say the miss-ing young women have moved to the city, never to turn back or call home again. Others believe they have been taken or killed. When Gretchen and Ansel arrive in town looking for work, they are directed to the home of Sophia Kelly, a house in the middle of the woods far from town which she also runs as a candy shop (Kellys' Chocolatier) out of the front part of her house. When she invites them to stay a few days to fix things up around the property, so that they can pay to fix the truck, they are quite literally staying in a house of candy deep in the woods, a clear allusion to the fairy tale from which the novel draws its inspiration.

As Gretchen and Ansel spend time with Sophia, they grow more comfort-able and feel more secure than they ever have. Part of it might be the candy, which seems to have the power to calm nerves and soften anxiety. But mostly, it is that they were blamed as children for losing their sister in the woods. That pain, coupled with the trauma of the loss, and compounded by the grief in a home where first their mother, and then their father died, has left Gretchen and Ansel lost. With Sophia they are welcomed and loved and folded into the comings and goings of Live Oak. For the first time in a very long time they feel wanted.

There is talk about Sophia in the town. Some people blame her for the disappearance of the girls, because they started leaving right after she came home from college. She came home because her father had been murdered in their house, supposedly mauled by a pack of angry dogs. Folks did not know for sure how he died, but that was what it appeared to be. Shortly after, Gretchen's sister went off to college, and never returned again, even to visit. And since the disappearance without a trace of eight teenage girls over a span of two years cannot be explained, they blame Sophia. As Jed Wilkes, a local man from Live Oak, says of Sophia: "People think she's either the patron saint of candy, or the first sign of Live Oak's end days" (Pearce 2011, 18). Sophia's story seems to be as tragic as theirs; her mother died of cancer when Sophia was young, and now her father and sister are gone as well.

Each year since she moved back to Live Oak, Sophia has hosted a Choco-late Festival. It is an invite-only, formal party to which teenage girls are invited. To liven it up, Sophia invites guys from "out of town," to show the girls a good time, and to introduce them to people outside their small com-munity. It is the party of the year, and when Gretchen and Ansel arrive in Live Oak, it is only eight weeks away. Between that and the Fourth of July celebration, Sophia has more than she can handle to do in the candy shop, and she invites Gretchen and Ansel to stay with her until after the Chocolate Festival. The candy shop is so calming, and the candy seems to calm their anxieties when they eat it, so they agree to postpone their departure to the beach to stay and help Sophia. When Gretchen takes party invitations to the Post Office to mail them, she spots a row of photos on the back wall, depicting smiling girls. Above each of their faces is marked "Missing Person Alert," and she realizes that she is looking at the girls who were lost after the Chocolate Festival. She counts them—eight girls—and she scans the names: Layla, Emily, Whitney, Jillian, Danielle, Allie, Rachel, and Taylor. These are the girls whose lives the people of Live Oaks believe Sophia has ruined (Pearce 2011, 63–64). Gretchen fantasizes about helping them, finding them, about being the person who solves the mystery of the missing girls. She memorizes their names so that they will not be forgotten, unlike her twin sister about whom none of her family was allowed to speak after she went missing in the woods.

One evening, while Gretchen is sitting on the porch, staring into the woods, she becomes emboldened to reclaim her life. All her life she has avoided forests, scanned the tree-line for monsters that might emerge from its edges, knowing that forests were not safe. Now that she is eighteen and living in a new place all the way across the country, she wants to take back her agency. After eating a candied lemon peel, a concoction that Sophia told her is supposed to help with courage, Gretchen walks to the edge of the woods, willing herself to enter. She tells herself there are no witches. When nothing immediately jumps out at her, she enters the woods. She reaches a creek, and the sound of the water rushing over the rocks is so soothing that she sits down. She notes the moonlight pouring down through the treetops, reflecting in the creek, and she sits, noting how serene and beautiful the scene is.

She realizes suddenly that the creek is actually deafening, and as she strains to listen to the forest, she senses something in the woods with her, describing the sense of becoming overcome with a sense of dread. "Something rustles, something large enough that I hear it over the creek's rapids . . . I stiffly turn to see whatever it is that's moving. Whatever it is that's waiting for me on the other side of the creek. It's a man. And he has yellow eyes" (Pearce 2011, 81). He has perfect white teeth and sweeping blond hair. Gretchen tries to make herself believe that it is just a man standing in front of her, but the yellow eyes are the witch's eyes from so many years ago, the day that her twin sister was taken away from her in the woods near her home in Washington. She runs, he chases her, and as he does he transforms. The description is similar to the one Scarlett gives during her first encounter with a Fenris; the shoulders hunch forward, the mouth grows too long for the face, and it has claws and long teeth. But she specifically notes his eyes, which are yellow and precisely the same as she remembers from childhood, when she and her sister and brother were attacked in the woods in Washington, when her sister never made it out of the forest alive. When she looks back again, "there is no man behind me. Just a monster. Head slung low to the ground, teeth jutting up through hanging black lips. His ears are plastered back on his head. Each time he takes a small, careful step toward me, his claws click and scratch at the pavement. The yellow eyes are locked on me" (Pearce 2011, 84). Gretchen is being hunted, the helpless prey of a hungry monster. She makes it to the main road but knows she cannot outrun her attacker.

In this terrifying moment, Gretchen is miraculously saved. A man emerges from the woods with a gun and shoots the monster. The monster slumps over, a heap of blood and fur, and then explodes into darkness. Gretchen feels "too many emotions, and my body has shut down. Where was the man with the gun twelve years ago? Why did he save me and not my sister? Why do I get to survive" (Pearce 2011, 85)? Instead of feeling relief at the vindication that the witches are actually real, she first feels survivor guilt. The first time she saw the witch as a child, she was the twin who made it out of the woods, and now, the second time she sees it, she has been rescued from what she had always believed would be her fate. The man with the gun is Samuel Reynolds, brother of Silas Reynolds, who is a main character in *Sisters Red*, and one of a long line of woodsmen. Some of his brothers are good with a knife, an axe, but he is good with a gun. He is there, in Live Oak, hunting the werewolves, the Fenris, as he explains to Gretchen. "I thought they were witches," Gretchen replies, as he explains that these werewolves have nothing to do with full moons, silver bullets, or red capes. Samuel tells her: "Sophia Kelly is the only witch in Live Oak. I've been trying to convince everyone in Live Oak the Fenris exist for the past two years. All it's gotten me is a reputation for being a lunatic" (Pearce 2011, 89).

Gretchen has spent her entire life waiting for the witch to come claim her, scared that it would come back to finish the business of taking her sister so many years ago. When she encounters the Fenris in the Live Oak woods, she realizes that she was right that it was her destiny to see the monster again. She thinks, "I didn't die. Not in the forest, not after, even though I was afraid. Terrified that the witch would come for me, terrified of vanishing. Terrified the exact thing that happened last night would happen. And it did. But I didn't die" (Pearce 2011, 95). She was astounded to meet Samuel Reynolds, a person who "didn't run from the monster—*he walked up to it*. And shot it. That's all it took to destroy everything I've been afraid of for twelve years, everything that could make me disappear" (Pearce 2011, 95). Knowing that the monsters can be destroyed gives her the idea that if she could learn how to shoot a gun, she "wouldn't have to be afraid anymore. I wouldn't have to be afraid of anything ever again" (Pearce 2011, 95). Her survivor guilt makes her feel like she is cheating death, saving herself and potentially other girls, when she could not save her own sister. She says to herself: "Staying like this, being the victim—that won't bring her back" (Pearce 2011, 95). She believes she can feel stronger, empowered, if she learns to shoot. She decides to ask Samuel Reynolds to teach her how to use a gun.

Samuel tries to talk her out of it. He does not teach people how to use guns, firstly, and secondly, he fears that actively hunting Fenris will be more dangerous than trying to avoid them. Gretchen pushes: "I don't want to be afraid anymore . . . I'm sick of thinking I'll end up like my sister or the girls who disappeared here" (Pearce 2011, 104). No one in Live Oak believes him when he tries to tell them about the Fenris, and he has become a pariah in town because he tries to convince people that the missing girls are dead, and that Sophia Kelly is to blame. He decides to help Gretchen because having a person in his life who believes him is worth something to him, and he understands her core rationale for wanting to be safer in a world that she knows is filled with monsters.

There is evidence to back up that the way Gretchen feels, that learning how to physically defend herself could make her not only physically more capable of self-defense but also give her a sense of agency and control over her life that was taken from her in the forest as a child. Jocelyn A. Hollander writes about the importance of self-defense training for sexual violence prevention, and the basic premise can connect here, as well. As she writes: "women's self-defense training aims to arm women with the skills to avoid, interrupt, and resist assault . . . most teach awareness, physical fighting skills, and escape tactics . . . [and some] also teach verbal assertiveness and empowerment skills" (Hollander 2016, 207–208). In going through this training, women not only learn defense and fighting techniques that match their body type, but they also gain a sense of agency over their own bodies that they feel has been lost by the looming threat of violence. Evidence shows that the training "produces deep and sustained changes in the women who complete it . . . [and it helps] them feel more confident in all areas of their lives" (Hollander 2016, 217). The training transforms "women's sense of themselves," "empowers women, expanding rather than limiting their freedom," and "fosters changes in women that may have ripple effects that go far beyond the individual to all they interact with and the culture as a whole" (Hollander 2016, 220). That Gretchen refuses to live in fear any longer, that she chooses to learn a way to defend and fight, is in line with the role that self-defense training has for girls and women who live under threat in a rape culture. And, as explored earlier in the chapter when talking about *Sisters Red*, the Fenris represent sexual predators.

Samuel is in Live Oak because three years ago he fell in love with a girl there, and when you live in Live Oak, you stay there. Two years ago, she disappeared: Layla, one of the eight missing girls on the Post Office wall. Gretchen pieces together that the missing girls were taken by Fenris, and Samuel shares that they were all taken within a few days after the Chocolate Festival, which is why he thinks Sophia Kelly is involved. However, Gretchen has doubts of Sophia's involvement because, as she has been living with her, she has come to believe that Sophia's younger sister, Naida, who supposedly left for college right after their father died, might actually be the first of the disappeared girls—the one who originated the pattern. As Gretchen and Samuel practice shooting, she asks why he stayed after she was gone, with no friends, and no one in town trusting him. "Someone has to protect everyone else," he says. Gretchen begins to try to solve the puzzle of the missing girls. She wonders what it is about these girls that made them special, because knowing that "maybe means no one else has to vanish" (Pearce 2011, 146). She becomes focused on this as a solution. Her sister, and these Live Oak girls, were killed by Fenris. Now that she knows, she wants to save others from that fate, become a skilled hunter so she can protect herself and others, and keep any more families from having to go through the pain of losing their daughter. Gretchen's intent is to be the vigilante feminist super/heroine protector these girls need, to make their world safer for them to live, and to eradicate the threat to their safety.

As the days pass, and Gretchen and Ansel are still staying with Sophia, Sophia grows more and more insistent that Gretchen stay for the Chocolate Festival. It is a fancy affair, one that Sophia has started preparing for a month in advance. She hangs strings for paper lanterns up in the trees in the back yard, she begins making delectable and unusual chocolate treats, and she mails out fancy invitations with RSVP cards. She is obsessed with the RSVPs, staring at them, sometimes seeming sad as she looks at them. She tells Gretchen that "not enough" girls are coming and worries that her reputation in town will ruin the party. The tradition is that girls who are graduating from high school that year wear red dresses. We know from the Fenris lore shared in *Sisters Red* that the Fenris are aroused by the color red, it heightens their excitement and makes their hunt more satisfying. The girls in town who are planning to attend the party shop for those dresses with great care, and talk about them with pride; though Gretchen does not yet know why or how, these girls are being set up to be as irresistible as possible to Fenris. Younger girls in town anticipate their invitation to the party when they are a bit older. Since Gretchen is eighteen, Sophia insists that she wear a red dress along with the Live Oak high school graduates, and she finds one of younger sister Naida's that fits her well.

When Gretchen is skilled enough with a gun that she can hit a moving target, Samuel agrees to take her hunting. They walk through the woods for hours, and eventually they do find a Fenris target. When Gretchen shoots it, and kills it, she feels happy: "I grin, I laugh, I shout all at once and a feeling of warm freedom sweeps through me. I don't need to be afraid anymore" (Pearce 2011, 234). Gretchen has lived her whole life in fear of the "witch" returning to kill her; she has feared forests, and being alone, and she has lived with unbearable survivor guilt. The feeling of release—of freedom—that she feels when she is capable of shooting and killing a Fenris is healing for her, and it empowers her. Her embodiment shifts from being a passive participant in her own life, to being an agent of her own destiny. The violent act of shooting and killing a Fenris provides her with the purpose that she needs, which is to protect other girls and young women from being taken and killed.

Gretchen and Samuel try to unravel the puzzle of the missing girls and their connection to Sophia. They learn a few things. First, Naida was a twin, whose sibling died in the womb. That meant that Naida and Gretchen had something huge in common—a twin who died—and Gretchen begins to worry if she, too, might somehow be in danger. Second, someone has been delivering shells to Sophia, and every time she receives one, she gets upset. Gretchen also finds shells in the back shed, in a box, eight of them. On a hunt, after Samuel kills a Fenris who is drawn to Gretchen, they find that he was carrying a shell, and they realize that it is the Fenris who have been delivering these shells to Sophia. There are eleven in all. Eight shells in the shed, match the eight girls who disappeared after Sophia Kelly's Chocolate Festival. Together, they piece together that the eleven new shells must mean that eleven more girls are going to be taken or killed this year. After weeks of stress and anxiety over the RSVP count, Sophia tells Gretchen that twenty-three girls are planning to attend the party. Not knowing what relationship this all has to Sophia, but realizing the wolves must be planning to attack at—or shortly after—the Chocolate Festival, Gretchen begs Sophia to cancel the party: "the four of us can go anywhere you want. We don't let any more girls disappear. But you have to stop the festival. You have to cancel it" (Pearce 2011, 265). Not only does Sophia refuse to cancel it, but she still insists that Gretchen stay for it: "There is so much desperation in her voice. . . . Her eyes are wide, and she chokes on each breath" (Pearce 2011, 265).

Gretchen and Samuel concoct a plan to arrive to the party late and armed, in hopes of saving the girls who are in danger. When they arrive they find Sophia in the kitchen talking to an angry Fenris. They overhear him telling her that he is disappointed that there are "not eleven." Sophia responds: "But there just aren't eleven this year—one of the girls didn't show up. Look out there—there are plenty of seventeen-year-olds! I can make up for it next year" (Pearce 2011, 279)! Gretchen suddenly realizes that Sophia already knows about the wolves, the shells, and what is really happening to the Live Oak girls. Not only does she know about it, but she is involved with it. Eleven shells are the Fenris' instructions; Sophia sends them home with a shell, and with that they are marked to die. When Gretchen and Samuel confront her, Sophia breaks down and explains to Gretchen that the Fenris killed her father, and then came back and took her sister, but they did not kill her. The Fenris told Sophia that they would give her sister back someday, if Sophia cooperates with their demands. Specifically, the wolves want Sophia to provide them with a harvest of girls who are eighteen years old each year: "They want girls at eighteen. The closer to eighteen, the better. It's their favorite age—they say it's when a girl's blood is sweetest. They leave the younger ones—wait till the next festival. They take the ones in the red dresses" (Pearce 2011, 285). Then she tells Gretchen that she is number eleven, which is why Sophia was so desperate for Gretchen to remain and to attend the festival.

When a hungry Fenris enters the room and begins to turn into a wolf, Samuel shoots him. He does not die, though, he rears back and runs outside. Suddenly the party erupts into chaos. The handsome "guys from out of town" begin to transform into wolves, and the girls begin to scream. Samuel and Gretchen begin to fight. Sophia tells Gretchen the gruesome details about why her sister Naida was taken instead of killed. When a twin dies, they absorb the soul of the other twin so that they have two souls inside them. That rare circumstance allows the Fenris to kill one soul by biting the living girl in the heart, and then the other soul slowly dies while the girl is kept in the ocean, until she becomes dark—a kindred evil like the Fenris, but different. Subordinate. The turned creatures become the Fenris' playthings—sex with a mortal kills them, so they imprison the turned twin girls as their sex slaves. Gretchen realizes that she is a twin who has absorbed the soul of her sister, too, and the Fenris pack leader can also smell that on her. He wants her to live so he can take her to be with Naida, so that Gretchen can become one of their sex slaves. As Gretchen and Samuel slaughter the Fenris pack, and girls begin escaping, the leader grabs Sophia and tries to bargain with Gretchen. He tells her they will leave, and let everyone live—Sophia, Samuel, Ansel, and the remaining girls—if Gretchen will go with them. In order to kill the pack leader, she must shoot him between the eyes, but he is using Sophia as a human shield. To kill the Fenris, Gretchen would have to shoot through Sophia. Sophia begs her to do it and choosing justice (for what Sophia has done in cooperating with the Fenris) and the lives of the girls (who can still be saved), Gretchen does it, and Sophia dies.

Sophia, like Amarantha and Ianthe in chapter 1 and Kimura in chapter 2, is a tool of the patriarchy. She has made a deal with the Fenris to protect her sister, and as long as she does what the Fenris ask of her—which is to trick and trap teenage girls for the Fenris to prey upon each year—she is granted their protection. But what they ask of her is too much to bear; the guilt that she feels for being a weapon of the patriarchy has left her despairing, and she would rather die than see another group of girls killed. The lead Fenris turns on Sophia when it realizes how valuable Gretchen is to him; as a twin who has absorbed the soul of the other, she can become a Fenris toy. Sophia seems grateful when Gretchen figures out her secret, and she begs to die. When Gretchen kills Sophia to kill the lead Fenris, she is saving countless other girls' lives as well as her own life. She is also, at least temporarily, destroying the embodiment of patriarchy in this town.

At this moment, Gretchen's role as a vigilante feminist super/heroine is apparent. As Laura does in chapter 2, when she kills the man who murders Alice, the quest for justice in these worlds is elusive. There was no one but Laura to decide the fate of Alice's killer, just like there is no one but Gretchen who can take this shot and decide the fate of Sophia, who is responsible for the deaths of at least eight girls. Laura is able to live with herself making this decision to protect others. Gretchen is, as well. Killing the leader of this Fenris pack will mean that the girls at the party now will be safe; it means that Gretchen will not be captured and turned into a sex slave; and it means that other girls will be protected from Sophia's future parties, which are just fronts for this sadistic hunt. All of Gretchen's physical training and practice with the shotgun have gotten her to this place, where she is no longer paralyzed by her past. She is capable of using her own body to wield a weapon to protect other girls from the fate of her twin sister, and this is empowering for her. In this moment, she has claimed agency over her own body and life and accepted the role of protector of others.

The parallels between the Fenris and rapists is clear, and the metaphor of "hunter and prey" reflects the way that rape culture is represented in contemporary U.S. society. In the documentary film *The Hunting Ground* (2015), director Kirby Dick and producer Amy Ziering track down stories of college students who have been raped, and whose schools failed to adequately protect them after they reported their assaults. There is no pretense about what the documentary title means—the college campus *is* the hunting ground, where the rapists are the wolves, hunting their prey, sometimes with unapologetic, proud impunity. The film notes that 8 percent of men in college are responsible for 90 percent of all assaults; they are serial rapists. One such man, "his face blurred out, describes how easy it is to be a serial rapist given the prevalence of alcohol and new students. 'The number of victims is endless,' he says" (Burr 2015). And it is not only male rapists who are represented as wolves in American culture; fraternities are represented in the media as wolf dens, with their young men howling at passing women as a symbol of masculine virility. The documentary is a representation of a reality, but it tells us what the Retold Fairytales series tells us—that there are wolves among us, often dressed as handsome, good looking suave men who prey on college women. As with the Fenris, they are well practiced in luring women into spaces where they are cut off from safety. In fact, the Fenris desire young women most at eighteen years old, because it is when they are the "sweetest tasting." Similarly, as *The Hunting Ground* elucidates, college freshmen, eighteen-year-olds, are most vulnerable to sexual assault during the first months of college, at this age they are imagined as fresh meat, as easy prey, and are disproportionately victims of sexual assault during the first ninety days.[4]

In *Sweetly*, Gretchen finds her destiny in saving other girls from her sister's fate. This is a manifestation of the impact of the trauma she has experienced, as sometimes the effect of trauma on a person is to create a "splitting of self . . . that trauma is not simply an effect of destruction, but an enigma of survival. One's identity becomes bound up with, or founded in, the death one survives" (Jackson 2016, 208). If we think about Gretchen as the "one who survives," in the forest when her twin sister was taken, or again in the Live Oak woods when the Fenris hunts her, it makes sense that her identity becomes wrapped up with that survival. When she learns that Fenris are involved in a complicated and grotesque plot to lure and kill eighteen-year-old girls, she wants to protect them. She learns how to shoot a gun, practicing until she has good aim, shaping herself into a hunter, so that she can protect others, particularly because there are no other systems set up to do so. When she learns that the Fenris want her because, as a twin whose sister has died, she has the unique capacity to become a dark creature and a sex slave, the battle takes on a personal twist; Gretchen is saving herself from becoming a victim of repeated sexual assault. The severity of this reality sharpens Gretchen into the hunter she wants to become, and she saves dozens of girls through her use of violence. As with Scarlett in *Sisters Red*, and Feyre in *A Court of Thorns and Roses*, the way that Gretchen chooses to see her body as powerful, and to use it to fight back against monsters, is a reclamation of agency over her own body, life, and choices. When her power becomes central to her new narrative about herself, she becomes the agent of her own destiny as well, a vigilante super/heroine fighting to make the world safer for others.

The way that girls and women fight these battles matters, as "these stories position self-determination as the key to women's individual empowerment, and they feature protagonists who model such empowerment through their portrayal as either assertive, outspoken women that defy cultural stereotypes of female passivity, or else as characters who develop into such women as the narrative progresses" (Sibielski 2019, 593). Scarlett and Gretchen both grow into models of self-determination who defy conventions of female passivity, but importantly, they also use that growth to protect others. Rosalind Sibielski affirms that when protagonists speak out against the "injustices perpetrated against others" they link "their empowerment to their willingness to stand up for the rights of others, and not just in the face of infringements to their own individual personhood" (Sibielski 2019, 594). This is crucial to an analysis of Scarlett and Gretchen as vigilante feminist super/heroines; their actions are not solely their own, or for their own benefit. They do not seek power for the sake of power, or violence for the sake of violence. Their violence is done for the protection of other girls and women, to keep them from having to face the Fenris predators.

Studies show that young adult readers tend to relate deeply to the characters they read about in novels. Readers spend more time with a novel than they do with a film or television show, and so the potential for readers to identify with literary protagonists is amplified. Beth Ann Goodenberger explains the notion of "experience-taking" in *Then and Now: A Look at the Messages Young Adult Fiction Sends Teenage Girls in the 1970s and the 2000s*, which occurs when "The character's world, actions, dialogue, and beliefs, are all experienced by the readers" (Goodenberger 2015, 2). Though the phenomenon does not occur every time a person reads, when it does happen "young women can become heavily influenced by the female protagonists in young adult novels" (Goodenberger 2015, 3). In this way, "young adult novels can make a tremendous impact on the reader, influencing and even altering their behavior and thinking" (Goodenberger 2015, 3). As Goodenberger argues, and as other scholars such as Melanie Kimball and Janice M. Del Negro corroborate in their study, "Teenagers are already at a vulnerable point in their lives as they transition to adulthood, and they are easily influenced during this period. For teenage girls, the female protagonists they read about can provide them with a guide to not only an adult, but also a woman" (Goodenberger 2015, 3). Readers "derive their own interpretation of a text based on their personal life" (Goodenberger 2015, 3). Between experience-taking and the reader-response process of personal meaning making, "it is easy to see how a novel can drastically affect the lives of vulnerable teenage girls" (Goodenberger 2015, 4).

One of the ways that girls are vulnerable is in the way that their lives are steeped in a misogynist landscape in which violence against women and girls is normalized. As Kelly Oliver notes in *Hunting Girls*, "we live in a rape culture that valorizes lack of consent and sexual assault, especially of young high school and college age girls, but we also have images of ever-younger strong girls wielding weapons who can take care of themselves" (Oliver 2013). The Fenris stand in for sexual predators in the Retold Fairytales series, and so the ways that Scarlett and Gretchen overcome trauma in order to reclaim agency over their lives and bodies is meaningful for readers. It offers them a mechanism through which they can imagine themselves through the protagonists, as teenage girls who are fighting back. Maria Nikolajeva explains that "social structures are represented in literature, as well as how texts reflect time and society within which they were produced. Sociohistorical studies of fairy tales provide good examples" (Nikolajeva 2005, 73). This is particularly important with the stories examined in this chapter, as the Fenris stand in for sexual predators, amidst a contemporary cultural context in which one in four women will experience sexual assault in her lifetime. Scarlett and Gretchen fighting against Fenris reflect a time and society in which violence against women and girls is normalized, or even, as Oliver argues, valorized. However, by honing their bodies into weapons and taking on the roles of hunters, Scarlett and Gretchen offer vicarious ways to experience the empowerment of defeating their attackers.

NOTES

1. The other three texts are: *Sweetly* written in 2011 (a retelling of Hansel and Gretel); *Fathomless* written in 2012 (a retelling of The Little Mermaid); and *Cold Spell* written in 2013 (a retelling of The Ice Queen).

2. In *Sisters Red*, there is reference to a boy as young as fourteen, and men closer to fifty with gray hair. The age of the Fenris depends upon the age in which they are located and turned. They are described as "frat boys," "rock stars," "chiseled," "charming," "attractive," and "disarming."

3. Similarly, in the section titled "Moral" in Charles Perrault's *Little Red Riding Hood* (1697), he wrote of wolves that: "Some are perfectly charming, not loud, brutal, or angry, but tame, pleasant, and gentle."

4. Partially excerpted from *Marvels and Tales* article with permission from Wayne State University Press.

Chapter Four

"I Know How to Do Things Most People Don't"

Rape and Vigilante Justice on a College Campus in MTV's Sweet/Vicious

Sweet/Vicious aired on MTV in 2016–2017 and follows the fictional story of Jules, a young woman at Darlington University who has trained herself as a "real life" vigilante in order to take down men on campus who have sexually assaulted young women and gotten away with it.[1] Having attempted to use the justice system on campus and seeing it fail her, Jules has forged her body into a tool of vigilante justice, using violence to take down attackers in the hope that she can make them feel a fraction of the fear and helplessness that their victims have felt. Though not technically super-powered or magical, Jules possesses extraordinary strength and capacity well beyond that of a "normal" girl; she is small in stature, but she spends a summer training in self-defense so she is able to attack and subdue men much larger than her. It is clear that her characterization is being drawn from comics, particularly from vigilantes like Batman. Jules embodies a deeply satisfying vicarious catharsis for any woman who has ever felt like their strength could not match that of men, and because she is ostensibly able to achieve this through rigorous, but totally human, means, she represents the fantasy that girls and young women can be their own vigilante heroines.

This chapter examines the story of Jules and her partner/sidekick Ophelia to consider the ways that vigilantism shows up on a college campus as a way to balance the scales of justice, by conducting a close reading of the first season of *Sweet/Vicious*. Treating it as a visual text, my analysis traces key moments in the development of Jules and Ophelia as vigilantes, and as a team, working together on behalf of the protection of other girls and women to eradicate rape culture on their campus. It tracks the way that they experience trauma, and then use violence as a mechanism for empowerment and healing, and for reclaiming agency over their lives and bodies. As well, this chapter situates *Sweet/Vicious* within the real-world context of sexual assault on college campuses, in order to theorize about the effect that a show like *Sweet/Vicious* might have on the identity development of viewers. Finally, it situates Jules and Ophelia as feminist vigilante super/heroines, which is particularly impactful for viewers who have experienced their own trauma, because the stage upon which their violence is enacted is a realistic college campus, recognizable as relevant for its real-world correlaries.

In the introduction, I shared the argument that Kristina Deffenbacher makes about the importance of texts that "engage issues of sexual violence and female agency in a space that is at once like and safely beyond their world" (Deffenbacher 2014, 924). As well "stories of women warriors suggest the possibility of women not just facing and surviving rape but also facing down and successfully fighting rapists, and rape culture itself" (Deffenbacher 2014, 932). Furthermore, Jessica Kokesh and Miglena Sternadori specifically describe the role that viewer identification with characters on screen had on identity development (especially in young adults), including a "one-sided relationship that consumers of any media . . . may establish with characters. In a parasocial relationship, audience members use media to gain an 'intimate, friend-like' relationship with a desired media character" (Kokesh and Sternadori 2015, 143). Furthermore, audiences can experience narrative transportation, which is "positively related to their previous knowledge of an issue . . . and the degree of perceived realism" (Kokesh and Sternadori 2015, 143), suggesting that a show like *Sweet/Vicious* could be especially impactful to girls and women who have experienced sexual violence, or who feel its effects vicariously. Finally, these factors—identification, parasocial interaction, and perceived realism—suggest that texts have a significant influence on readers and viewers (Kokesh and Sternadori 2015, 152–153).

Jules is a rape survivor. Throughout the first season of the series we learn that Jules was raped by her best friend's boyfriend, a young man that she was friends with and whom she trusted. After they have both been drinking at a party at his fraternity, Jules wanted to rest for a bit and asked him if she could take a nap in his bed. It never occurred to her that she was in danger, because she felt safe with her best friend's boyfriend. When he assaults her, she unambiguously says no. He covers her mouth, holds her throat, and he is much larger than her. When Jules realizes that she cannot move, and that she is being sexually assaulted, she goes still, disbelieving her own reality. For Jules, not only is her body violated, but her sense of identity is totally compromised by the betrayal of her trust in a friend, in a space where she had felt safe. She feels completely powerless, because neither her words nor her body could remove her from that situation. The strength and skill that Jules develops when she trains in self-defense not only allows her to feel some modicum of safety in what she now knows to be a violent world, but it gives her the capacity to "right" some of the wrongs that have been done to other victims of sexual assault at Darlington University. She chooses to become a vigilante for the justice that she does not see on her campus, or in her community.

In thinking about the place of vigilante justice as a tool that gives power back to women in cultures that enable violence against women, Aaronette White and Shagun Rastogi articulate that "some forms of women's vigilantism are legitimate acts of violence in specific political contexts where local judiciaries fail to protect women against gross human rights abuses" (White and Rastogi 2009, 316). Darlington University is a stand-in for all of that; the University, the campus police, and the District Attorney's office all know that sexual violence at Darlington University is an epidemic, and they all play an active role in suppressing reports, failing to fairly adjudicate, or neglecting to press charges against offenders. It is represented as a lawless land, a space between myth and reality where campus judiciaries have the power to brush felonies under the carpet. And so, reading Jules and her partner Ophelia (dubbed the Darlington Vigilantes) as perpetrating legitimate acts of violence—within this fictional setting—is deeply powerful. It suggests that college campuses are not so unlike (symbolically, at least) the paternalistic, patriarchal, misogynist cultures in which the real life women that White and Rastogi are writing about live.

The relevance of the central story of *Sweet/Vicious* relies on two realities. First, sexual violence is rampant on college and university campuses. Second, that colleges and universities are notorious for not taking sexual violence seriously when reported. Both of these realities are rooted in evidence. The American Association of University Women (AAUW) notes that "university and college women are disproportionately affected [by sexual harassment and sexual violence] impeding their safety, comfort, access to education, and ability to participate in campus life" (American Association of University Women 2020). A 2019 report by the American Association of Universities, titled "Campus Climate Survey on Sexual Assault and Misconduct," was designed to assess the incidence, prevalence, and characteristics of incidents of sexual assault and misconduct, as well as the overall campus climate regarding perceptions of risk, knowledge of resources available to victims, and perceived reactions to an incident of sexual assault or misconduct. The survey is the largest of its kind, having received data from 181,752 students. According to this survey, 25.9 percent of undergraduate women experienced nonconsensual sexual contact by physical force or inability to consent since entering their institution of higher education, as well as 22.8 percent of transgender, genderqueer, or non-conforming (TGQN) people (Cantor, et al. 2020, ix). The statistics varied widely across institutions in the study which makes the data a little difficult to generalize. For example, the distribution of the percent of undergraduate females reporting nonconsensual sexual contact involving force, incapacitation, coercion, or absence of affirmative consent since entering the school was 14–20 percent at five of the schools included in the study; 21–25 percent at sixteen of the schools included in the study; and 26–32 percent at twelve of the schools included in the study. The higher numbers (21–25 percent and 26–32 percent) at 85 percent of the schools suggests that on most campuses, the problem is even larger than generalized data suggests, because some schools with lower rates skew the numbers low. When coercion and lack of ongoing voluntary agreement is added to the list, the percentages skyrocket, with 39.4 percent of women and 40.2 percent of transgender, genderqueer, or gender non-conforming fourth year students reporting experiencing that since first enrolling at school (Cantor, et al. 2020, 42). Furthermore, 59.2 percent of female, and 65.1 percent of transgender, genderqueer, and non-conforming undergraduates reported being sexually harassed. The most common form of sexual harassment includes inappropriate comments about their body, appearance, or sexual behavior, followed by making sexual remarks, or insulting or offensive jokes or stories.

In the first episode of *Sweet/Vicious,* viewers watch as Jules scales the outside wall of a fraternity house to access the second-floor bedroom of a male student at night. She wears all black gear, and uses a voice altering device to make herself unidentifiable. She punches him in the back of the head, knocking him out of his desk chair. When he tries to grab his phone, she tears it out of his hand. When he stands to defend himself with a stick, she disarms him, snaps the stick, and kicks him in the gut so hard he flies backward and breaks the door of his closet. He offers her money, thinking he is being robbed, and she kicks his wallet out of his hand. "Truth or dare?" She asks him. When he looks confused, she says, "Truth it is," and flicks open a knife before kneeling before him to show him a photograph on her phone. "Do you know this girl?" She asks him. The man looks horrified, "I don't know who that is." She slaps him across the face, "Say her name!" He tells her that the girl's name is Beth. She moves the knife up his leg, toward his crotch. "Did you have consent? Think about that. Think about the music that you played to drown out her screams. Think about the tears in her eyes as you held her down, and forced yourself into her." He is crying, and he begs her "No, please no, I'll do anything," which leads her to punch him in the face again. "I'm sorry. I thought no meant yes?" she tells him, "You didn't stop when she said no, though, did you?" When he does not answer, she punches him in the face again until he cries out "No, no I didn't stop. I didn't. I'm so sorry. I didn't mean to hurt anyone. Please." She tells him, "If you ever do that to anyone else, I'll be back." Then she gives him his phone back and instructs him to call 911 and tell them that he has been assaulted and he needs a paramedic for his leg wound. Then she sticks her knife in his thigh, and leaves through the window, warning him "Don't pull that out until they get here. It's gonna get messy." As she walks away from the house, she takes off her black gear, loosens her long blond hair, and uncovers the frilly pink and white rose sweater that she is wearing beneath. Playing into gender stereotypes about who a violent vigilante could be, Jules is the last person anyone would suspect of committing such a violent crime (*Sweet/Vicious*, season 1, episode 1, "The Blueprint").

One month later, we are introduced to Ophelia, who is a contrast to Jules in many ways. Where Jules is a blond sorority sister on a scholarship who cares about her grades and does not drink alcohol, Ophelia is a green-haired computer hacker who cheats her way through college, never goes to class, openly smokes pot and sells it at work, drinks hard, and enjoys sex without strings. One evening, as Ophelia is walking through campus openly smoking a joint, she is spotted by a campus police officer—Officer Barton—who begins to chase her. While escaping, Ophelia accidentally turns down an alleyway where Jules is fighting another rapist. In this case, we see Jules openly fist-fighting a man who is significantly larger than her, but she manages to flip him, twist his arm, and break his fingers. Ophelia recognizes him as Tommy Cope and calls out his name in surprise. Jules sees her and pushes her up against the wall, twisting her arm behind her back. Ophelia exclaims, "You are so strong!" before assuring Jules "I'm not trying to stop this! He date raped someone in my dorm freshman year, he's a garbage person." Jules lets her go and turns around to kick the man on the ground one more time. "Who *are* you?" Ophelia asks, intrigued. As she hears the campus police approaching on foot, Ophelia urges Jules to run. Jules scales the fence at the end of the alley and gets away just in time, and Ophelia kicks Tommy while he is down. She notices that Jules has dropped a locket on the ground. When Officer Barton finds her with the male student on the ground, she says, "Clearly, this wasn't me" (*Sweet/Vicious*, season 1, episode 1, "The Blueprint").

As a character that is the opposite of Jules, Ophelia seems to emulate the composite girl in Mary Pipher's 1998 study, *Reviving Ophelia: Saving the Selves of Adolescent Girls*, which was updated and reprinted in 2019. In that study, Pipher found that many teenage girls were turning to dangerous behaviors like heavy-drinking, drug use, sexual activity, and party-going in order to quietly rebel against the strictures of their parents, and against gender norms that felt stifling. She writes: "Drug and alcohol use are appealing to teenage girls, who are often confused, depressed, and anxious. Alcohol and marijuana are popular because they offer teenage girls a quick, foolproof way to feel good. Amphetamines help girls avoid hunger and eat less. Plus, imbibing often enhances status with friends" (Pipher and Gilliam 2019, 287). Ophelia uses all of these—a heavy-drinker (including during the daytime), a frequent drug user, a proponent of casual sex where she prefers not to know her partner's name, and a hard partier (again, even during the daytime). Her green hair specifically enrages her mother, who seems to otherwise care very little about who Ophelia is or what she does. Pipher also explains that "heavy use is a red flag that points to other issues, such as despair, social anxiety, problems with friends or family, pressure to achieve, or negative sexual experiences" (Pipher and Gilliam 2019, 288). Though brilliant, Ophelia avoids class, which is likely another way to push back against her parents' expectations.

The first scenes of *Sweet/Vicious* are jarring, because the audience is placed in a position of cheering Jules on as she beats up these men. Not only is she skilled at it, but she is significantly smaller than the men that she is overpowering. There is a sense of vicarious satisfaction in watching Jules take them on, because it is wish-fulfillment for girls and women who do not feel capable of defending themselves physically. As Maud Lavin notes in *Push Comes to Shove: New Images of Aggressive Women*:

> Historically, in U.S. culture, women's aggression has been repressed, frowned upon as inappropriate behavior, or branded as low class. In the mass media, women's exercise of aggression has at times been represented as a punishable offence. In contemporary U.S. culture, though, a large shift visible in the representation of women's aggression appears . . . there's been a cultural turn since the 1990s: feminine aggression is now often celebrated. In cultural manifestations ranging from indie grrl rock to consumerist Spice Girl culture, from video game action heroines to mainstream sports movies, from street activism to national political figures, there exists for the first time in the nation's history, albeit unevenly, a growing, heavily viewed array of positive representations of aggressive women. (Lavin 2012, 3)

Jules' use of violence in these scenes taps into that notion of a positive representation, because we know that she is beating up rapists who have evaded justice. Lavin notes that "cultural representations of feminine aggression can be complex and messy signs of hope, and can contribute to friction so key to collective and individual action," (Lavin 2012, 4) which is what Jules' actions within the television show are going to accomplish—she brings hope to survivors, she disrupts the status quo that enables rape, and she builds a collective who are ready to intercede to eradicate sexual violence.

Officer Barton takes Ophelia back to his office for questioning, since she was a witness to the assault on Tommy. He asks her to describe the assailant, "his height, his build, any defining features." Because of the violent nature of the attack, and the large size of the person who was attacked, the officer's assumption is that the assailant is male. Since Ophelia found the locket on the scene, she suspects that the assailant is female, but does not tell him that. She tells him that he was tall with a large build—neither of which is true; Jules is short, and small in stature. Ophelia's best friend, Harris, is a law student. Ophelia tells Harris about the attack she just witnessed, which she describes as "brutal," unlike anything she had ever seen. And she notes that both of the recent attacks on campus have been on frat guys and wonders aloud whether they were not random. Harris says: "Whatever comic book scenario you're playing out in your head right now, quit it. This is dangerous. And stupid. And crazy." Ophelia promises not to do anything dangerous or stupid. However, with the locket in hand, she really wants to get to the bottom of who the person is that she saw beating up Tommy (*Sweet/Vicious*, season 1, episode 1, "The Blueprint").

Ophelia returns to the campus police station, with a ruse that she lost her earring in Officer Barton's bathroom the night before. As he goes to help her look, she finds the campus police file on Thomas Cope (Tommy) and finds out that he had been investigated for sexual assault. The victim of the rape reported to campus police that she believed she had been drugged and assaulted in her dorm room. Though there were no bruises, she woke up naked in her bed, and could not remember getting there. "No foul play" was found after the investigation concluded, and the case was closed. Ophelia assumes that the attacker she encountered in the alley must have been the girl that Tommy raped, Sasha Mitchell, and Ophelia goes to Sasha's dorm room to return the locket and talk to her. However, when she gets there, she learns that Sasha dropped out the previous semester, and was no longer even in the state. Ophelia catches a break in her investigation when a couple of sorority sisters approach Ophelia to buy marijuana, and she notices that the necklaces they have on are identical to the one that she found at the scene of Tommy's attack. She offers to deliver the marijuana to their party, and when she arrives, she asks if any sisters have lost their necklaces. Jules recognizes Ophelia from the night of Tommy's attack, and she shoves her down into the basement to ask why she is stalking her. She pulls out a knife, holds it against Ophelia's throat, and tells her that if she interferes in her life again, she will have to hurt her. Ophelia takes the opportunity to swipe Jules' phone and install tracking software on it. By searching her phone, she can see that Jules has been monitoring the news about Carter Fisher, a Darlington baseball alum who has been accused of sexual assault by three separate girls. Ophelia makes a guess that Carter is next on Jules' list, and she tracks down his address and goes there (*Sweet/Vicious*, season 1, episode 1, "The Blueprint").

When she arrives, Jules is in the process of fighting with Carter in his garage, but unlike the previous times, she is losing this fight. Carter holds her to the ground by her throat, pulls her mask off her face, then knocks her out, exclaiming "Stupid bitch. I'm going to kill you." Ophelia sneaks up on him from behind and hits him in the head with a hammer—a blow that instantly kills him. When Jules awakens, she finds Ophelia, and learns that she killed

Carter. Jules is scared and angry, because killing people is not what she does. Ophelia reminds her that Carter was about to kill Jules. Ophelia wants to go to the police, but Jules tells her the police will not help her. They clean the scene, wrap Carter up in a canvas cloth, and put him in the trunk of her car. Jules asks Ophelia how she knew where to find her, and Ophelia tells her that she put tracking software in her phone. Jules is impressed with Ophelia's skills. Ophelia asks Jules how she knows how to do what she does. Jules replies: "I know how to do things most people don't. There is stuff happening out there and no one is doing anything about it. People are just getting away with awful things. I'm trying to make some of that right." "That's the plot of Batman," Ophelia replies, "Okay, so what do we do next?" to which Jules answers, "There's no 'we.' I work alone." Ophelia reminds Jules that her plan would not have worked tonight, she would have been dead. "So what, you want me to teach you everything I know" (*Sweet/Vicious*, season 1, episode 1, "The Blueprint")? The reality is that Jules cannot continue to work alone. The work that she wants to accomplish—making right some of the awful things people get away with—is a huge undertaking. Having a partner, and being part of a team, will allow her to be more effective at that job. Also, this is where her actions move from the actions of an individual to the actions of a collective.

The killing of Carter Fisher is not the main subject of the television show *Sweet/Vicious*. It is a sub-plot that serves as a mechanism to create the circumstances for a vigilante team-up, and also to create a counter subtext that compares and contrasts various ethical justifications for breaking the law when the law fails to provide adequate protection. Neither Jules nor Ophelia are interested in killing people. Carter was supposed to get beaten up for raping three young women, just like Jules' other missions. When he gains the upper hand, however, he intends to kill Jules. Ophelia showing up at the right time means that Jules does not become another murder statistic. But since Jules intentionally sought out Carter to hurt him (violent vigilantism is, after all, against the law) they decide that it does not matter that his death was ultimately self-defense. They justify his death by making him a very "bad" guy, a repeated rapist who intended to kill Jules. They never intended to kill him, and they have no intention of killing any of the other rapists they go after. The sub-plot of Carter Fisher's death (including where to bury the body, whether the detectives will find evidence of them at the garage where he died, and the fact that Jules begins dating Carter's step-brother) means that *Sweet/Vicious* is not a perfect story of vigilante justice done retributive-ly. They do not make all the right choices. But nevertheless, overall, it has many layers to peel back about campus rape culture, systems that fail to protect survivors, trauma, survival, and empowerment.

Ophelia identifies their next case when she meets Hailey at the police station. Hailey tells her that she is there because she was sexually assaulted and is thinking about making a report. She is upset because she has been there all morning, and no one is making it easy for her. She is alone. She ends up leaving, so Ophelia hacks into the Darlington University Title IX records and locates her report. Hailey reported that she was hanging out with a basketball player, Damon Avery, at one of their teammate's houses, and they did some shots. After making out a little bit, Damon followed her to the bathroom, and forcibly raped her. She reported that she told him no, but that he didn't listen. Ophelia begins to make a plan to make Damon Avery the next target (*Sweet/Vicious*, season 1, episode 2, "The Writing's On the Wall"). Ophelia sneaks into the men's locker room, locates Avery's locker, and installs tracking software on his phone. She assembles a file on him and presents it to Jules. Jules says "There is no next guy. We're done here Ophelia, a person is dead." Ophelia resists Jules characterization, "A rapist is dead. A rapist who would have killed you. So, forgive me for not wanting to pour one out for that scumbag. What happened to making things right, to helping people?" Jules says the whole thing was a huge mistake, and that she just wants to go back to her old life. Ophelia asks Jules if her friends know what really happened to her, and when she does not answer, Ophelia tells her: "I see you. For who you really are." Jules is scared, though, and asks Ophelia not to contact her again.

Ophelia tracks Hailey and follows her to a campus bathroom. Inside the bathroom, Ophelia finds a wall covered in graffiti. It says, "STAY AWAY from Kappa Alpha Omega," "Don't drink the jungle juice," "No means no," "I believe you!!", "You are not alone," and the names of nineteen men. Ophelia returns to Jules and tells her she has found something that she needs to see. Ophelia tells her that if after seeing the wall she can just walk away, then she will never bother her again. "We are doing this for different reasons, but that doesn't mean there aren't people out there who need our help. The school needs its Batman." Jules adds Nate Griffin's name to the wall. Ophelia hands her Avery's file again, and this time Jules nods in agreement. This is the beginning of their vigilante partnership (*Sweet/Vicious*, season 1, episode 2, "The Writing's On the Wall").

Dressed in black gear, with voice alteration boxes, Jules and Ophelia find Damon Avery practicing shooting baskets in the gym alone. They hit him in the head with a basketball, and then trip him so he falls to the floor. "You picked the wrong guy!" he exclaims, before Jules kicks him in the face. They kick him a couple of times when he is down, and then when he stands, they knee him in the groin. Jules holds him down by kneeling on his chest, and she draws a knife and holds it to his throat. "You know the police may not have taken Hailey's claim seriously, but we do. It wouldn't be easy to get drafted with a looming rape charge against you. Touch a woman without consent again, and we will be back. They are about to leave, having done no serious or permanent damage, but Avery calls out to them, "Psycho!" So, they turn around, hold him down, and Jules breaks his right arm. "Have a good season!" she responds (*Sweet/Vicious*, season 1, episode 2, "The Writing's On the Wall").

Vigilante feminist super/heroines, by my definition, are heroines who work on behalf of girls and women who are otherwise failed by systems and left unprotected. They take over in violent worlds, in worlds where violence against them is real, but in which girls feel like they have no power. Their actions directly challenge the status quo of violence. The vigilante feminist character is one who takes on the role of avenger and protector of girls and young women, who are threatened by violence because those who are supposed to protect them (families, law enforcement, campus judiciaries) fail to do so. In the stories that I am analyzing, the vigilante feminist is a teenage super/heroine who has herself experienced violence, trauma, and a loss of agency in the aftermath. The reclamation of her body, and her agency, through the quest to protect others, is empowering and healing for her. In the case of *Sweet/Vicious*, it is Jules—not Ophelia—who has experienced direct trauma. But Ophelia has experienced vicarious trauma. She knows many girls who have been sexually assaulted, she knows several of the girls that Jules avenges, and so she comes forward out of a sense of shared rage and injustice that comes from that secondary trauma, of being emotionally close to so many people who have experienced sexual assault that it makes her feel as though it is in the air she breathes. When she comes to her work as a vigilante, it feels just as real for her as it is for Jules—she tells her they have different reasons for being here, but their goals are the same.

Having lived in fear for her entire life, Anastasia Higginbotham describes the phenomenon of victims of vicarious trauma being empowered through full-contact self-defense in "Sex Worth Fighting For." She writes, "Though I have so far never been raped and never been physically attacked by a stranger, I have been lured, grabbed, tricked, stalked, harassed, coerced, and humiliated, and treated cruelly during sex" (Higginbotham 2019, 242). Because she had never been taught about healthy sexuality, for most of her life she did not realize that those behaviors fell on a spectrum of sexual violence, and she had been traumatized by not only what had happened, but what might have happened. She describes: "I remained preoccupied by fears that something 'truly' bad would happen, and often imagined the gang rape and murder that would finish me off for good" (Higginbotham 2019, 243). So, she signed up for full-contact self-defense classes, and learned to fight back. She finds that after learning to protect herself, she feels safer in her own skin. She does not fear the streets as much, and she feels more confident. She sleeps better because she is not having anxious nightmares about her worst fears. For her, fighting is empowering, it is activism, it is her refusal to be vulnerable for having been born female. She concludes: "though there is no such thing as safety from an attempted rape in this world, I am all the weapon I need, and I sleep well" (Higginbotham 2019, 249).

The field of critical trauma studies "has been forged through shared intellectual considerations of 'modern' catastrophes such as war, genocide, forced migration, and 9/11, alongside everyday experiences of violence, loss, and injury." Its varied modes of inquiry rely on "centripetal tensions: between the everyday and the extreme, between individual identity and collective experience, between history and the present, between experience and representation, between facts and memory, and between the 'clinical' and the 'cultural"(Casper and Wertheimer 2016, 4). Furthermore, the field relies on "*critical trauma theory*. Here, the category of trauma is not taken for granted, but rather unraveled and interrogated to assess the political and cultural work that 'trauma' does—both in the world, as well as for those (like us) doing the interrogating" (Casper and Wertheimer 2016, 5). Jules embodies individual trauma, and Ophelia embodies collective trauma. Jules has experienced rape, and Ophelia has grown up in a society that represents the devaluation of girls and women, where young women that she knows are being sexually assaulted at an alarming rate. For Jules, trauma is the history that collides with the present in ways that become politicized; her personal experiences have shown her that girls and women are not being protected in the way she thought they would be, and she has mobilized to fill that gap. For Ophelia, sexual violence permeates the campus culture around her, and when she confronts that reality, she wants to fight against the forces that converge to cause harm. Though her trauma is vicarious, it feels no less real to her than Jules' does. In fact, the sort of "witnesses" like Ophelia, who know survivors and listen to the stories of those who have experienced trauma firsthand "may experience nightmares, bouts of depression, and feelings of despair, numbness, and suicidal thoughts. Psychologists refer to these effects as a form of trauma called compassion fatigue, secondary trauma, or vicarious trauma" (Jackson 2016, 224). As such, Jules and Ophelia work together to use that trauma to spur them into formulating solutions that allow them, and others, to feel a bit more safe.

Jules agrees to train Ophelia in defensive and offensive tactics (*Sweet/Vicious*, season 1, episode 3, "Sucker"). Ophelia has innate skill with knife throwing, and she is a very fast learner. With their official team up, each time a new name is added to the wall, Jules and Ophelia do research and reconnaissance to make sure they have the right person, and then they go after them. This work is empowering for them. It allows them to feel as though rape culture on college campuses is something that they can change. This team up is reminiscent of the formation of the teen vigilante group, the Red Brigade in India. The Red Brigade is a group of girls who patrol the streets in their community of Lucknow in order to protect others from sexual harassment and violence. The "motivation is painfully clear. Every single girl in the so-called 'Red Brigade' has been a victim of sexual assault—some have even been raped by their own family members" (Armstrong 2013). Furthermore, most women in India have a story about harassment on public transit, an issue which garnered worldwide attention in 2012 when a twenty-three-year-old woman was gang raped and beaten to death by a gang of men on a public bus. The self-defense group was started by Usha Vishwakarma, a teacher, who learned that all of her students had experienced "some form of abuse—from lewd comments and cat-calls, to molestation and rape. Many of the girls said they were afraid to go out alone for fear of being groped or worse. It was then that Vishwakarma decided the girls had to protect themselves amid the deafening silence from within their own community (Armstrong 2013). They learn Kung Fu, and then they patrol in groups of four or five in order to approach perpetrators and demand that they stop harassing. If they refuse to heed their warning, they first use public humiliation, and then if necessary, utilize physical violence such as slapping. They note that this is a form of self-defense, and that since police do nothing to protect them, they must protect themselves. In most cases, the crimes have gone unpunished and the victim left to suffer the trauma in silent shame. These girls have been forced to act, they say, because no one else will (Armstrong 2013).

Jules regularly attends a survivor support group, and this is where she first heard the stories of other victims that inspired her to become a vigilante. That is where Beth told the story that inspired Jules' initial plan to attack rapists, and it was her attacker that Jules first went after as the vigilante. Beth explained that she felt helpless: "I wish I could strip away his sense of safety. I wish I could make him feel like I do. Like fear is running through his entire body." That is what gives Jules the idea to do what she does as the vigilante, to make them feel what it feels like to not have control, to be at someone else's mercy, to ask someone to stop and find they are not listening, to feel that fear. At the support group, Jules hears a girl named Jesse talking more about her assault, and Jules and Ophelia make him one of their targets. Jesse explains: "Living in the aftermath of that night is somehow worse than what happened. How am I supposed to go to class if I can't even walk across the campus without having a panic attack? But the thing that really kills me is thinking how unfair it is. My rapist isn't having any trouble sleeping. He gets to go to class, and hang out with his friends, and just live his life. But me? I'm failing out of school, I'm a mess, and I'm probably going to have to drop out and go home." Jules listens to this, understanding and frustrated. She goes to Ophelia's house and says, "What's the point, if Jesse doesn't know? Aren't we doing this so she can feel safe? We're doing this to make Darlington safer." The whole point of their vigilantism is a quest for justice, and it seems like the whole thing has less meaning if those who have been victimized do not know that they can rest a little easier. They devise a plan for Jesse to be walking across the quad right as her rapist is passing through, limping heavily, and badly bruised. They also tell her what his real name is, so that she can appropriately file charges if she wants to (*Sweet/Vicious*, season 1, episode 3, "Sucker").

Jules and Jesse have had similar post-trauma experiences. Jules does not sleep, and when she does, she has nightmares. She can barely be touched without jumping out of her skin, and the only time she feels like herself is when she is wearing the black suit, acting the part of the vigilante. She tells Ophelia that she can barely remember the girl that she was before she was raped, and that she misses that girl. Debra Jackson notes, in "Answering the Call: Crisis Intervention and Rape Survivor Advocacy as Witnessing Trauma," that survivors of trauma share the same feelings that Jules is describing, such as "the trauma . . . splitting them into two distinct selves. . . . Many other survivors describe their experience as a kind of death, not only in terms of facing a life-threatening event, but also in the annihilation of their sense of personhood" (Jackson 2016, 208). The fact that Jules cannot access her former self is as though that person has died, and she is trying to resurrect her by acting as a vigilante. Furthermore, the flashbacks and nightmares that Jules is experiencing is a normal part of the process of working through trauma's aftermath: "Through involuntary repetitions such as nightmares, flashbacks, and/or hallucinations, the survivor's re-experiencing of the traumatic event generates a voice that is released from the wound, which bears witness to the trauma" (Jackson 2016, 207). This may be why when Jules is dressed in her vigilante gear, experiencing the adrenaline rush of a mission, working actively to control her environment and making a difference for others, she says she feels "like herself." In fact, Jules even views this work as healing, when she tells Ophelia that being the vigilante is "the only way I can get better."

White and Rastogi, in writing about the Gulabi Gang in India, describe vigilantism by women as healing for the community, as well. They articulate that this "feminist strategy[y] for correcting existing power imbalances," comes from "a wish to vindicate the value of the victim and the community as a whole, drawing on feminist theories of punishment that some scholars have examined in criminal cases" (White and Rastogi 2009, 316–317). They explain that "ethical forms of violence against wrongdoers reflects a retributive model of justice. Retributive justice models emphasize 'proportionate' punishment (retribution) as a morally acceptable response to crime, with the satisfaction of the victim as its priority" (White and Rastogi 2009, 316). Jules' whole reason for being a vigilante is sparked not only by her own experience as a survivor, but as a person who believes she can achieve a sort of "proportionate punishment" of rapists on behalf of fellow college women at Darlington University.

During sorority rush week, a video goes viral showing a pledge being tormented by being stipped down to her underwear, and having the words "slut," and "whore" written on her stomach in blacklight ink. In the video you can hear a sorority sister taunting her: "Are you going to cry little pledgie? Look up and smile" (*Sweet/Vicious*, season 1, episode 4, "Tragic Kingdom"). Jules sends the video to Ophelia, raging, "This is sexual assault, no question! Stripping somebody down and then writing on their body, it's awful." The sorority is well known on campus to be a house that tortures their pledges, but they wear masks in their videos so that there is no incriminating evidence, and the video signatures Ophelia finds "have been scrubbed clean." Kappa's bad behavior is yet another example of something that happens at Darlington University in plain sight, but which goes unchecked. Jules and Ophelia decide to take them down. They do not want to just bring down the Kappa Executive Board, because then another one will just step in to replace them. They want to find a way to disband Kappa entirely. To do a mission of that magnitude, they need undeniable evidence in order to take down a powerful institution, and so they devise a plan for Ophelia to pledge. It turns out that she is a Kappa legacy—her mother was Kappa and is on the national board. The reality inside pledging is grotesque: the pledges are forced to hold themselves up by their arms in a pike position with a plate of human feces under their faces; and they are locked in the basement, without access to a bathroom, with piles of cigars and several kegs of beer which they must smoke and drink in three hours or less. When one of the pledges passes out from drinking so much, the sorority president sends her to the hospital with the instructions that they need to ask for a specific doctor, who will keep quiet about the incident (*Sweet/Vicious*, season 1, episode 4, "Tragic Kingdom").

While locked in the basement, Ophelia finds a secret room that is jam packed with high tech equipment, including a "CIA-level" server. She taps into it, and finds that the entire Kappa house is bugged, and that they record themselves twenty-four hours a day. The Kappa president has been running a highly lucrative pay-for-access hazing site (hazegirls.com—"Watch the hottest undergrad pledges get hardcore hazed!"). When Jules and Ophelia arrive at Kappa, they find that the three sisters of the Kappa Executive Board are well-trained in physical combat, and they find the fight more challenging than they anticipated. However, when the Kappas are subdued and tied up, Jules and Ophelia, in black gear and using voice scramblers, tell them that they know about the website and the recordings. Jules tells them that what they are doing is illegal pornography, which is a felony. Ophelia directs them to turn themselves in to the school for hazing, disband Kappa, and shut down hazegirls.com. If they do not, they will turn their evidence over to the police. As well, Ophelia re-routes all the money they made with their website to a battered women's shelter (*Sweet/Vicious*, season 1, episode 4, "Tragic Kingdom").

Their next case involves a ride-share service, called "Get In" (*Sweet/ Vicious*, season 1, episode 5, "All Eyez on Me"). A girl named Rachel who was raped after getting into a ride-share car hands out flyers on campus that say "Women of Darlington: STAY OUT of Get In." Rachel is in Jules' Economics class, and Ophelia also knows her because they had been lab partners in experimental chemistry. "What kind of idiot assaults someone while they're driving a Get In?" Jules asks, to which Ophelia replies: "I get the allure, drunk girls getting into your car by themselves, on purpose." Ophelia hacks into Rachel's Get In account and finds that she had actually reported the assault the previous Tuesday, with no response from the company. According to the details of the report, Ophelia can identify when and where Rachel got into the car, and that she reported that she woke up at home with no recollection of what had happened. Her underwear was ripped, and she was afraid she had been assaulted. There is an address on the Get In driver's account, which is in a Darlington University residence hall. The RA tells Ophelia that the driver's name is Landon Mays, who is the son of Darlington University's President Mays. Ophelia hacks into the car's GPS system, and traces its location. Using herself as bait, Ophelia leaves the same bar appearing to be a drunk girl ordering the same Get In car that she knows the rapist drives. However, he does not end up taking her to the same spot where he had taken Rachel, and where Jules is waiting for her. She frantically texts Jules letting her know that she has no idea where he is taking her. It turns out to be an abandoned parking lot in what appears to be an industrial area. Ophelia has a taser, and is ready to attack the driver, but she is taken by surprise when she is dragged out the door from behind by a second man. She tases one and fights the other off and runs just as Jules makes it around the corner on her bike (*Sweet/Vicious*, season 1, episode 5, "All Eyez on Me").

After this incident goes awry, Ophelia becomes one of the countless women who has been assaulted at Darlington University. She was able to fight them off, and because Jules arrived shortly after she was ultimately physically safe. But she knows that their intent was to rape her, and she recognizes how close she was to being harmed. She is extremely shaken but assures Jules "Your training worked. I had a taser, I was never in any real danger." As they discuss the information that they now have, which is that there are two attackers involved with the Get In driver assaults, Ophelia shares, "There was something about Rachel's story that always bugged me. She has a window of, what, twelve hours where she can't remember anything? I know it's different for everyone, but when have you ever heard of alcohol causing that kind of blackout?" Jules asks, "You think there was something else in her system?" And Ophelia replies, "I think she was roofied. The last thing she remembers is talking to a guy at the bar." They break it down, and determine that it is a "two-man relay system," where one guy's job is to scout the bar and slip the drug into a drink, and the one in the car's job is to abduct and restrain (*Sweet/Vicious*, season 1, episode 5, "All Eyez on Me").

A sub-theme throughout the show is the fact that Jules' rapist is Nate Griffin, who is not only the star quarterback, but also her best friend Kennedy's boyfriend. Jules has been depressed and has not been able to talk to her friends about what Nate did. After her rape, she spent weeks in bed. As such, Jules is on academic probation. Her sorority sisters ultimately find out about it by secretly reading a letter in Jules' mailbox, and Kennedy remarks that it is really unlike Jules to be in trouble academically since her scholarship is dependent on it. It is also uncharacteristic of Jules not to tell her friends about being in that kind of trouble. Kennedy confronts Jules who admits that things are not going well, but Jules has chosen not to tell Kennedy that she was raped by Kennedy's boyfriend. Adding to Jules' anxiety is the fact that Nate has been treating the rape as a "secret between friends," spinning it as him and Jules "cheating" together. One night while Jules is home at the sorority house getting a late-night snack at the refrigerator, Nate surprises her in the kitchen to tell her that he is glad to have heard that Jules and Kennedy have been having a good week. He tells her he hopes "they can all be friends, maybe all hang out together sometime, like we used to." Jules freezes, and cannot respond. Then she breaks down, slumping to the floor when he leaves (*Sweet/Vicious*, season 1, episode 5, "All Eyez on Me").

Jules' reaction is a normal trauma response. Debra Jackson explains that survivors of trauma experience a variety of cognitive, affective, and physical symptoms, which are indicative of PTSD, and which cause significant disruption to their lives. Some of these are feelings of "helplessness, loss of control, anger, dissociation, numbing, denial, insomnia, nausea, heightened startle response, and hypervigilance, as well as revisiting the experience through nightmares, flashbacks, and/or hallucinations" (Jackson 2016, 207). The stakes are high for students who experience sexual violence on their college campuses. According to the American Association of Universities 2019 report about sexual assault on college campuses, for incidents of penetration, 92.2 percent of women and transgender, genderqueer, and non-binary (TGQN) students reported at least one type of behavioral or emotional consequence compared to 79.6 percent of men. Common reactions include avoiding or trying to avoid the person (77.4 percent of women, 76.1 percent of TGQN, 20.4 percent of men), and fearfulness and concern for their safety (40.6 percent of women, 59.4 percent of TGQN, 20.4 percent of men). It also affected their well-being, such as loss of interest in daily activities (40.9 percent of women, 60.1 percent of TGQN, 29.2 percent of men), withdrawal from interactions with friends (46.4 percent of women, 60.1 percent of TGQN, 29.2 percent of men), nightmares or trouble sleeping (42.2 percent of women, 55.8 percent of TGQN, 21.5 percent of men) and feeling numb or detached (60.2 percent of women, 72.9 percent of TGQN, 38.5 percent of men). Other reactions include feelings of helplessness or hopelessness, not participating in extracurricular activities, headaches or stomach aches, eating problems or disorders, and increased drug and alcohol use (Cantor, et al. 2020, 25–26). Also, academic and professional consequences were very prevalent, including decreased class attendance (36.3 percent of women, 54.1 percent of TGQN, 28 percent of men); difficulty concentrating on studies, assignments, and exams (55.5 percent of women, 68.7 percent of TGQN, 38.2 percent of men); and difficulty going to work (23.2 percent of women, 39 percent of TGQN, 17.7 percent of men) (Cantor, et al. 2020, 26). Research, like the study by Kokesh and Sternadori, demonstrates that viewers closely identify with the characters they love, and so having a character who experiences the realistic after-effects of rape is brave and potentially life-changing for audiences.

Jules and Ophelia make a plan to bring down Landon Mays and his partner in crime. Ophelia locates Landon Mays' car in a garage on campus, and the girls put on their gear. They know the two guys are together, because Ophelia has put tracking software on their phones. They place spikes behind the tires, so that when the driver goes to reverse the car the tires blow. When that happens, they both get out of the car to see what happened and Jules and Ophelia attack them. They are incredibly skilled opponents, however. One grabs the spike used to blow the back tire, and slashes Jules across the leg. Landon manages to run away. Ophelia chases him down to the quad, where she throws her knife with precision and hits him in the back of the thigh, knocking him to the ground. She kneels on his back and delivers her message: "These things that you are doing with your friend are going to stop, now, and you are never going to raise your hand again against another woman as long as you live. If you do, I'll know, and there will be a world of trouble for you and your sick sidekick." Instead of looking terrified, like most of their subjects do, he begins laughing. It turns out that several people witnessed Ophelia throwing a knife and holding him to the ground with it. The cameras do not pick up what she says, though, so it looks like she has attacked without provocation. "I think you're the one in trouble now," Landon taunts her, as she flees the scene (*Sweet/Vicious*, season 1, episode 5, "All Eyez on Me").

Their actions provoke a campus-wide lockdown, as the video goes viral and the police swarm campus looking for the armed suspect. During the lockdown, Nate arrives at the location where Jules and Ophelia are sheltering in place, "to make sure Jules feels safe." Nate keeps trying to talk to Jules, until she eventually cracks. She shoves him up against a wall, covering his mouth with her hand, and says:

> You shut it! You're going to listen to me. Let me get one thing straight. I told you to stop, and I told you no, and you did this, you put your hand over my mouth, and then you raped me. What you took from me wasn't yours to take, and the fact that you thought it was sex for just one second is disgusting. You

came here today to make me feel safe, I don't think I'll ever feel safe again because of you, all I feel is just empty inside. And I've tried everything I can to get rid of it, I've lied to myself, I've lied to my friends, and I've smiled and pretended that I was going to run away, I've done everything I could except this, which is tell you how alone and broken I feel watching you with my best friend like nothing ever happened, because you don't carry this like I do. And I hate you for that. And I envy you for that. And I just, I thought you should finally know. (*Sweet/Vicious*, season 1, episode 6, "Fearless")

Nate leaves without saying anything but goes to Kennedy to spin the story. He tells Kennedy that he cheated with Jules, and that Jules is going to say she he raped her to cover it up. When Jules goes to finally tell Kennedy about Nate raping her, Kennedy does not believe Jules, and so Jules moves out of the sorority and in with Ophelia. (*Sweet/Vicious*, season 1, episode 6, "Fearless")

What Kennedy feels for Nate is what Kate Manne terms "himpathy," which was described in chapter 3 and is the "excessive sympathy" that is sometimes shown toward male perpetrators of sexual violence. In contemporary America, these are often men "who are white, nondisabled, and otherwise privileged 'golden boys'" (Manne 2018, 187), just like Nate. Manne argues that himpathy is often accompanied by a reluctance to believe the women who testify against these men or punish the perpetrators even if their guilt has been firmly established. As the star quarterback at Darlington University, Nate is accustomed to getting what he wants. As Manne writes "When men are privileged, or long have been, they may proceed with a sense of not only legal impunity but also moral entitlement—secure in the idea that what they seize is theirs for the taking, and sometimes trying to wreak revenge on women who fail to uphold their end of history's bad gendered bargain" (Manne 2018, 217). When Jules tells Kennedy that Nate raped her, she is breaking the misogynist code of behavior that is assigned to her as a result of getting wrapped up in Nate's story. Once Jules claims victimhood, she places herself at the center of the story, which makes her seem "self-dramatizing and self-important," and she is expected to move on. When Jules cannot simply move on, and she decides instead to challenge the dominant position of her attacker, she risks: not being believed in the first place, and being suspected of being duplicitous or "crazy," hysterical; being blamed for what happened; having the crime not investigated properly; having the charges minimized or treated dismissively; being subject to counteraccusations of selfishness, aggression, mendacity, and manipulativeness; being belittled, being harassed, threatened, and possibly (re-)injured by the accused fans and defenders (Manne 2018, 236–238). This is the way that misogyny operates to discredit and dissuade women from speaking out against their attackers, especially when they are powerful men.

Jules stays in bed for days. She is deeply depressed. A flashback during episode 7, "Heartbreaker," takes viewers through the night that Nate raped Jules. Jules is at the fraternity house, at a "Hos and CEOs" party without Kennedy who is home sick. Jules is drinking and having a good time with Nate, because she sees him as her friend. She gets very drunk, so much so that she can barely stand. Nate asks her if she is okay, and Jules tells him that she needs to lie down and asks him if she can go lay down in his bed. He says of course. After telling one of his friends that he is going to "get that," Nate follows her upstairs, and when he opens the door Jules is sound asleep on his bed. When she wakes up, he is on top of her. She tells him no, that she does not want to do this, and to "please stop" multiple times. She is clear with both her verbal and physical cues that she does not want to have sex with Nate. But he covers her mouth, and holds her down, and tells her "Shhhh. This is going to be our little secret." When he is finished, he rolls over and falls asleep, and Jules puts on her underwear and finds her shoes, and stumbles home distraught. She researches rape on her laptop and finds out what she is supposed to do. She does not bathe, she puts her clothes in a plastic bag, and she goes to the health clinic to request a rape kit. The woman who does her rape kit is kind, and tells her what her options are, in terms of reporting to her school and the police. Jules' father is a police officer, so she does not want to file a police report since he would find out. The nurse recommends that Jules talk to someone and notifies her of a counselor at Darlington in the Title IX Office (*Sweet/Vicious*, season 1, episode 7, "Heartbreaker").

In the weeks after, Jules stays in bed a lot. Her grades slip. She grows distant from her friends. Kennedy is worried that she is sick, "It's been weeks, maybe you should go to the doctor." When Jules finally decides to report her assault to the Title IX office, she learns that the counselor is new. She tells the counselor what happened. The counselor's response to Jules' story is: "I need to make sure this is about assault and not regret. . . . You know, you slept with your best friend's boyfriend. I'm not belittling what happened, but I do need to find out the facts." Jules pushes back: "I am telling you the facts. I was asleep and then he assaulted me." The counselor asks if she was drinking, if she was intoxicated. Jules tells her that she did not feel well and asked to go lie down in his bed, and the counselor says: "Wait—you asked to go in his bed?" Jules replies "It's not like that. We were friends." Then the counselor asks the name of the student, and when Jules tells her that it is Nate Griffin, the counselor replies: "I am worried that you don't understand what will happen if we move forward opening a case like this. Nate is one of our most high-profile students. So, the Administration, the media, they are all going to rip into your life, overturning every indiscretion that you have ever had. Every Facebook comment, every picture, every Tweet. I don't want to see you go through that over something that sounds like it was just a mistake between yourself and Nathan. Do you understand?"

Jules says she does, and she leaves. She does not file a report (*Sweet/Vicious*, season 1, episode 7, "Heartbreaker").

The American Association of University Women explains that both sexual harassment and sexual violence are forms of sex discrimination covered under Title IX, which "protects students from sexual harassment and violence that occur in the course of a school's education programs and activities. Once a school knows of or reasonably should have known about sexual harassment or sexual assault on campus, Title IX requires the school to promptly investigate the complaint and take steps to protect its students." In fact, schools are obligated under Title IX "to stop sex discrimination, prevent its recurrence, and address its effects. In order to do so, schools must have a policy in place that prohibits sex discrimination, including sexual harassment and sexual violence, and grievance procedures that provide for a prompt and equitable resolution when incidents occur" (American Association of University Women, Where We Stand: Sexual Harassment and Sexual Violence in School 2020). Schools must make accommodations and interim measures available to victims of sexual violence, including things like changing class schedules to avoid contact between students to providing campus escort services, and also may include taking disciplinary measures against the perpetrator. At the heart of these accommodations must be an official, often called a Title IX Coordinator, who monitors and arranges responses to complaints. However, the reality on many college campuses since this policy was enacted by the Department of Education in 2011 with the "Dear Colleague" letter has often been far less hospitable.

The American Association of Universities 2019 report indicates that reporting rates are extremely low: 29.5 percent of undergraduate women reported incidents involving penetration; this proportion is lower by half for incidents of sexual touching (Cantor, et al. 2020, 28). The most common reasons for non-reporting included thinking they could handle it themselves (48.8 percent of women); not thinking it was serious enough to merit help (41.7 percent of women); embarrassed, ashamed, or believed it would be emotionally difficult (41.7 percent of women); did not think that resources could help them (21.9 percent of women); and not wanting to get the perpetrator in trouble (24.5 percent of women) (Cantor, et al. 2020, 30). Other reasons include: I did not think anyone would believe me; I feared negative academic, social, or professional consequences; I was not injured or hurt; the event happened in a context that began consensually; alcohol and/or drugs were present; and events like this seem common (Cantor, et al. 2020, 32). Victims are significantly less likely than the overall student population to have confidence in campus official reactions. Overall, only 45 percent of those who reported nonconsensual sexual contact by force or inability to consent thought it was "very" or "extremely" likely campus officials would take a report seriously. This is 20 percentage points below the overall total for students. Similarly, only 29.6 percent of victims thought it was "very" or "extremely" likely campus officials would conduct fair investigations into the report. This is also 20 percentage points below the total for the entire student body (Cantor, et al. 2020, 60). However, 81.8 percent of women, 73.2 percent of men, and 76.2 percent of transgender, genderqueer, and non-binary students told a friend what happened (Cantor, et al. 2020, 32).

Breanne Fahs affirms these norms of perception in "Naming Sexual Trauma: On the Political Nuance in Rape and Sex Offender Discourses." Women often feel "shame, guilt, embarrassment, concerns about confidentiality, and fear of not being believed," and the range of reactions women experience vary from "highly supportive and nurturing to complete disbelief." Incidentally, Fahs notes that "women had more positive mental health outcomes if they reported rape within one month of its occurrence." However, even timely reporting does not protect women from intense scrutiny, because when women do report rape their relationship with the perpetrator, whether or not alcohol was consumed, "and the victim's demeanor and dress affected legal outcomes of rape trails, perhaps indicating that 'blaming the victim' ideologies are enhanced by the perception that women drank too much or otherwise 'asked for it.' This may help in part to explain women's hesitation to name and report rape" (Fahs 2016, 67). And no matter what, "research consistently shows that women who describe coercive sexual encounters experience a range of mental health consequences, including PTSD, depression, anxiety, mood disorders, sexual disorders, and borderline personality disorder" (Fahs 2016, 68).

Officer Barton informs the Dean of Darlington University that he believes the Darlington Vigilante is targeting students who have been accused of sexual assault, and whose cases were found to be without merit. He is then fired by President Mays, who indicates that Barton's services are no longer needed by the University. They do not want the negative press about the motivation of the vigilante to mar their public image, and they do not want to provoke fear on campus that there is a serial vigilante on the loose. So, in order to set a trap to catch the vigilante on their own, Barton and Harris add a new name to the wall of rapists—Brady Teller. Barton knows from the files he had access to as a campus police officer that Brady was accused of sexual assault, and that the investigation was dropped. Barton believes that if they add Brady to the wall, the Darlington Vigilante will make him their next target, and he is right; when Jules and Ophelia see the new name, they start reconnaissance and begin to plan a mission. Barton comes up with a plan to protect Brady from the vigilante, in hopes of being able to draw out the vigilantes and identify them. When Jules does recon in Brady's room, she finds a box filled with underwear, and photos of his victims, including of the girl who accused him of sexual assault and reported it to campus police (*Sweet/Vicious*, season 1, episode 8, "Back to Black").

Jules develops a plan to entice Brady up to a bedroom at a frat party. When Jules and Ophelia get Brady into the room, they beat him severely. In fact, this time Jules loses control a bit, and beats him up much worse than usual. When Ophelia pulls Jules off an extremely bloody Brady, she demands, "What are you doing?" "Getting justice!" Jules replies, "This is what he deserves. This is what we do. . . . This is the only way that I feel alive," Jules exclaims. "This is the only way to stop him from turning girls into me" (*Sweet/Vicious*, season 1, episode 8, "Back to Black"). Not only are "hypersensitivity, unprovoked violent outbursts," and "irrational anger" all symptoms of the effects of trauma on the body (Earle 2017, 31), but this scene also demonstrates how enacting violence makes Jules feel. She notes that it makes her feel alive, and her motivation is the protection of others, so they do not have to experience what she has experienced.

Jules' violent outburst leads Kennedy to realize that Jules is struggling and suffering, and she realizes that she believes what Jules told her about Nate. She believed her all along, she just had a difficult time coming to terms with the fact that her boyfriend was a rapist. With Kennedy supporting her, Jules decides to report her sexual assault to the Title IX Office. The telling of the story is critically important for Jules' healing. Jackson explains that one important step toward reestablishing embodied agency in the wake of trauma is to be able to tell ones' own story: "Constructing a self-narrative, particularly after experiencing traumatic events, is an essential component of resubjectification, and it is an intersubjective process involving dialogue with an empathetic other, a witness to trauma" (Jackson 2016, 211). During the hearing, the Title IX counselor and the Dean of Students listen to the stories of Jules, Nate, and several witnesses. Jules tells them that she was passed out when Nate raped her. Nate says that Jules was waiting for him, and enthusiastically consented. Jules recounts struggling with Nate but being unable to free herself, and of telling him no, that she did not want to do this. Nate claims that once they started having sex, Jules got worried that Kennedy would find out, and so he told her it would be a secret. Nate tells the hearing committee: "I feel sick that she thinks that what happened between us was anything but sex between two friends." After investigating, the Title IX committee finds Nate guilty of sexually assaulting Jules, and he is expelled. Jules and Ophelia have a moment of disbelief where they question their motives, since they had been working as vigilantes for justice based on the assumption that the school was not punishing perpetrators. When Jules is believed and Nate is expelled, they realize that, while the Title IX office had most certainly tried to convince Jules not to go forward, Jules had never made a formal report. Once the formal report was made, she was believed. Momentarily, at least (*Sweet/Vicious*, season 1, episode 9, "An Innocent Man").

What ultimately happens, however, is another example of this power system gone awry. Nate's family hires an attorney, they appeal the decision, and the president of the University overturns the school's finding. Nate's case is not unique. As a football player, he is less scrutinized and more protected than the average student. His behavior demonstrates the "overwhelming links between hegemonic masculinity and sexual violence that occur in multiple spheres of men's lives. 'Normal' masculinity dictates men's control of, and access to, women's bodies and blames women for sexual violence (teaching women to hold tightly to their keys when walking through deserted parking lots or entering buildings late at night)" (Fahs 2016, 74–75). This scenario is reminiscent of what happened during *The People v. Brock Turner*, where his "defenders exhibited forgiving tendencies, and spun exonerating narratives" (Manne 2018, 200). Oftentimes people disbelieve victims and support attackers because in their imagination a rapist must be a monster. But as Manne notes, "misogynist violence and sexual assault are generally perpetrated by unremarkable, non-monstrous-seeming people. . . . We must accept the *banality* of misogyny" (Manne 2018, 211). Nate manages to control the story by spreading it around and painting Jules as a jealous liar. His fraternity brothers come to his defense, and it looks like it could be business as usual at Darlington University.

However, this time, when the University overturns the verdict against Nate Griffin students start to feel supportive of the work of the vigilantes, and angry about the University's handling of the case. Social media dubs the vigilante #sweetvicious, and a groundswell of support among students shows that people believe that things need to change, and that the vigilantes are part of that reckoning. Ophelia tells Jules that she could appeal her case, but Jules says she wants them to handle it themselves. Even Kennedy and the sorority sisters try to contact #sweetvicious on social media, to let them know about Jules' case (and the injustice that Nate got away with), hoping that the vigilantes will give "justice for Jules." For Kennedy, vigilante justice could be closure. Ophelia shows Jules Kennedy's tweet which says, "Darlington Vigilante: I have a target for you. #sweetvicious" and Jules asks Ophelia what #sweetvicious is. "Us, I guess. . . . It's really crazy. A lot of people love it. Some hate it. A lot of people hate us. But, some love us." Using this as a formal starting point, Sweet Vicious begins taking on cases (*Sweet/Vicious*, season 1, episode 10, "Pure Heroine").

Ophelia tells Jules that the Nate-take-down has to be special; they need to take away everything that is important to him, just like he did to her. They come up with a name "Mission IntimiNate," and they deliver hand-made invitations to Jules' friends to help, making it into a full-scale operation of cooperation, teamwork, and trickery. After sending a campus Emergency Alert that says, "We're coming for you Nate," and sneaking into his bedroom to take Polaroids of him sleeping, Nate gets his fraternity brothers to walk with him everywhere. When the seven fraternity brothers arrive to back him up when Jules and Ophelia jump him at a pizza shop, Jules and Ophelia fight off all seven of them with tasers, night sticks, and ninja skills. Harris walks in on them taking down the entire fraternity and tells them that was the coolest thing he had ever seen. Harris helps them come up with a plan to convince one sympathetic frat brother, Myles, who went to high school with Nate and knows he is lying, to help them get a taped confession. Myles gets the next hand-made invitation from #sweetvicious. Myles gets Nate to talk, and he records it. Nate tells Myles that he is a god on campus; that the president probably did not even read the file before overturning his verdict. "He knows what it means if I'm not on the field on Saturday." Nate explains to Myles that nine times out of ten the girls really want it, even if they say they do not, and that the one time someone really did not it was his word against hers. He recounts that something similar happened in high school with a girl named Shelby, "the biggest slut in our grade. Nobody was going to believe her." He says he would go on stage tomorrow, to the MVP ceremony, and let every-body know "I am Nate Griffin. And if I want it, I'm going to take it." Ophelia breaks into the main video feed during Nate's MVP celebration and plays this recording, where he claims "they're never going to kick me out" while doing lines of cocaine.

As Lisa Wade writes in "Rape on Campus: Athletes, Status, and the Sexual Assault Crisis," college "athletes are more likely than other students on campus to identify with hypermasculinity and to accept 'rape myths' to justify sexual assaults. Evidence also suggests they're more likely to be confused about consent and admit to having committed acts of sexual aggres-sion" (Wade 2017). Furthermore, high-status athletes are able to act on those beliefs with greater impunity than their peers. Wade's research found that "Since their star status gives athletes plentiful opportunities to hook up, athletes sometimes find themselves following a hookup script that bears a queasy resemblance to sexual assault . . . it's expected in hookup culture that students will get people drunk with the aim of having sex with them; be sexually persistent, even forceful; pull peers into secluded parts of a party; and proceed quickly to sexual intercourse, even when their partners are near incapacitation" (Wade 2017). She also noted that athletes are far less likely to be interrupted when they are crossing the line. Perhaps unsurprisingly, when victims report these assaults by beloved athletes, their institutions are often inclined to protect the perpetrator. A number of cases at nineteen different colleges and universities between 2012 and 2017 demonstrated that adminis-trative responses to sexual assault, especially involving athletes, were insuffi-cient (Wade 2017). This scenario is very much in line with Jules' experience, up until she is believed at her hearing. Ultimately, though, the University still sides with Nate, overturning his expulsion and reinstating him to the football team.

Despite being shown video footage of Nate saying all of this, Nate still calls Jules a liar, and stands up on stage saying "I didn't say any of this. This isn't real." The video feed continues, as his voice continues on: "These girls walk around in these tight skirts, asking for it, and then you screw them and they get mad. I tried to tell Jules, nobody was going to believe her." The video cuts out with a flash of pink lips and the silhouettes of two black clad figures, a voicebox-voice saying, "We believe you," and ending with their logo: S/V. The video is followed by an immediate all-campus e-mail from "Sweet Vicious," with a website to "REPORT INJUSTICE" at www.sweetvicious.com. Nate is escorted off stage by his coach, while the president tells everyone to return to their dorms or their homes, saying "My deepest apologies to anyone who was offended by this content. This is over" (*Sweet/Vicious*, season 1, episode 10, "Pure Heroine").

Season 1 ends with Harris telling Ophelia that he found out that there were twenty-six cases of sexual misconduct taken to the District Attorney's office in the past year that were either "completely mishandled, dismissed, or flat-out unattended to." He tells her that he wants to help, and so he joins the DA's office as an intern, so that he can gain internal intel and help Sweet/ Vicious find targets. The show closes with a Take Back the Night Rally organized by Kennedy and the sisters, "Almost everyone we invited RSVPd." The Sweet/Vicious website reporting system is inundated with reports when it goes live. "Looks like we're going to be busy," Ophelia exclaims in both relief, because people took it seriously, and anger that the problem is an epidemic (*Sweet/Vicious*, season 1, episode 10, "Pure Heroine"). Though the show was not renewed for a second season, it was supposed to live on in the form of a comic with Black Mask Studies in 2019. As of October 2019, Black Mask did not have a release date, and noted that they hoped to be able to announce one soon. It seems the perfect home for *Sweet/ Vicious*, which takes so many of its conceptual cues from vigilante superheroines. To date, it has not been published.

In 2013, End Rape on Campus was founded by Sofie Karasek, Andrea Pino, and Annie Clark, after their successful filing of grievances with the Office of Civil Rights related to the cover-ups and mismanagement they faced when they reported their sexual assault cases to their institutions. They felt there was a national need to "formalize and centralize work around campus sexual assault," and since its founding, survivors across the country have connected through social media, spoken out about deliberate indifference and betrayal, and held institutions accountable to federal laws" (End Rape on Campus n.d.). Their website's Campus Accountability Map shows that "survivors have begun to break the silence about institutional cover-ups and hold their institutions accountable under Title IX, spurring institutions to change their ways or risk scrutiny in the public eye" (End Rape on Campus, "The Campus Accountability Map" n.d.). The map is intended to show how seriously schools take this issue (which is generally "not very") and identify institutions that need to make changes faster. The founders of End Rape on Campus join Emma Sulkowicz, also known as Mattress Girl, in finding ways to publicly call out their institutions after they failed to take their allegations seriously. As Kelly Oliver, author of *Hunting Girls*, writes, "[t]hese real-life heroines are not afraid to tell their stories, even if it means facing retaliation and death threats in order to bring sexual violence out of the shadows and into the spotlight . . . their use of Title IX has changed the terms of discussions over sexual assault on campus" (Oliver 2013, 149). Oliver notes that "anti-rape activism is on the vanguard of shifting blame and responsibility from individuals to social systems and institutions," but that the "solution must also address the culture of sexual violence that perpetuates sexual assault" (Oliver 2013, 150). She argues that despite evidence indicating "that sexual assault is a problem on campuses across the country, over 40 percent of colleges and universities report no sexual assaults. If colleges have become 'hunting grounds' for sexual predators who prey on young women, and if they are effectively safe havens for serial rapists who face little to no consequences for their sexual violence, then it seems reasonable to hold colleges and universities responsible for allowing rape to continue unchecked, even if schools are not themselves to blame for rape" (Oliver 2013, 161).

Jules is a survivor, and her actions as a vigilante help her work through her trauma. She feels alive when she is wearing her vigilante gear and getting justice for other survivors whose stories have been ignored. Not only is her vigilantism important as a mechanism for Jules to find herself, and to reclaim her body and her story after her rape, but it is important for others in the Darlington University community. What Jules and Ophelia uncover is an epidemic of sexual violence on campus that is brushed under the carpet at all levels; from the initial visit to the Title IX counselor, through the campus police, up to the District Attorney's office. As the DA states to Harris, the DA's office is tax-payer funded, and Darlington is the biggest show in town, and it looks bad for them if they receive the publicity that rape accusations bring. Jules begins to formulate her plan while she is at a support group, as she feels the need to find a way to enact the vengeance that the other girls say they wish they could have, but it ends up being significantly bigger than her as her actions lead to a genuine growth of awareness and a campus culture shift around survivor advocacy.

Jules is a lot like a comic book superheroine, with her seemingly superhuman capacity to train and develop unique physical skill, and defensive and offensive capacity over the span of one summer. She is not magical or traditionally superpowered. She develops her skill in the way that superheroines like Kate Bishop/Hawkeye, Natasha Romanoff/Black Widow, and Kate Kane/Batwoman do, through practice, dedication, and hard work. Jules' father is a police officer, and so there is an innate knowledge and practical skill that she possesses just from being raised as his kid. But when she puts her mind to it to become the best that she can be, she hones her body into a weapon that takes on a sort of mythical quality. No one on campus suspects Jules because she is small, and the men she takes on are athletic and strong. But she is more highly skilled in self-defense than logic would dictate she would be able to gain over just one summer of focus and study.

Critically important is the way that this show mimics the "real world." Darlington is a small city with a public university. It is highly recognizable. And as such, it is easier to directly compare and contrast this show to "real life" than it is for the other subjects explored in this book. *Sweet/Vicious* symbolically brings together the stories about real life vigilante women with the tradition of vigilante heroines in fiction. Jules and Ophelia are reminiscent of the Red Brigade in India, for example, as a group of teenage girls who come together to publicly shame rapists, and sometimes to beat them up physically as well (Armstrong 2013). Jules' training of Ophelia in self-defense mimics the training videos released by the Red Brigade, showing them practicing Kung Fu and self-defense techniques (CNN 2013). And *Sweet/Vicious* represents a palpable wish-fulfillment for the It's on Us era, for all of the things that bystander awareness programs on college campuses cannot say about the potential roles of bystanders in the (sometimes necessarily violent) interruption of violence on campus, but that Jules and Ophelia—under the guise of an MTV show—can bring out into the open.

In their article "The Good, the Bad, and the Ugly: A Qualitative Study of How Young Adult Fiction Affects Identity Construction," Jessica Kokesh and Miglena Sternadori study the ways in which young adult fiction affects teen readers' gender identity construction and social attitudes. Though the article examines novels, their theoretical framework is drawn from media studies. Here, they articulate that gender identity construction is impacted by identification with heroines in film, television, and fiction. In interviews, they found that "All of the participants said they did identify with certain characters to a great degree. They usually 'saw' themselves in characters experiencing situations, thoughts, and feelings highly similar to their own" (Kokesh and Sternadori 2015, 151). Futhermore, audiences feel strong emotional attachments to characters, and feel as though they are active participants in the characters' lives. Importantly, the "more readers felt that they shared experiences with a specific character, the higher their degree of perceived realism seemed to be" (Kokesh and Sternadori 2015, 153). Because of the ways in which young adult audiences are impacted and influenced by the texts that they consume, it is crucially important that they have opportunities to interact with characters who are agents in their own lives. *Sweet/Vicious* depicts Darlington University as a recognizable college campus where sexual assault is an epidemic, but Jules and Ophelia have the opportunity to fight back against it by taking on the role of vigilantes. This is vicariously satisfying for girls and women who feel powerless in a society that normalizes violence against girls and women.

NOTES

1. The quote in the title is from *Sweet/Vicious* season 1, episode 1, "The Blueprint," when Jules explains to Ophelia how she has trained herself in vigilante fighting tactics. It is evocative of the chapter because Jules is doing what most people will not, or cannot, do on behalf of justice for the victims of sexual assault at Darlington University.

Conclusion

As I finish writing this book, the United States is once again wracked by violence. Just weeks ago, police killed George Floyd in Minneapolis and Breonna Taylor in Louisville, and two white men shot and killed Ahmaud Arbury in Georgia in their supposed capacity as a neighborhood watch conducting a citizen's arrest. Protests erupted across the country to demand the end of unjustifiable use of force upon black bodies by police, as well as to bring attention to the core issues of the Black Lives Matter movement, that black and brown bodies have always been devalued in the United States, creating the conditions in which a man who is out for a jog in Georgia (echoing too closely Trayvon Martin's quiet walk through a neighborhood in Florida in 2015) can end up harassed and then killed by white men who allege themselves to be keeping people safe. Anger, frustration, sadness, and rage have poured out in rallies, petitions, and social media campaigns, as people come together to demand immediate and systemic changes that will bring true equity and justice to America. Many peaceful protests are being met with extreme force by police and the National Guard, as curfews are established and authorities order crowds to disperse; reports of rubber bullets, tear gas, batons, and shields being used on citizens exercising their first amendment right to assembly have people feeling frazzled and exhausted (Stone and Feibel 2020). Some protestors are responding by rioting, looting, burning police cars, destroying property, and returning the volley of tear gas grenades back to police and militia. When this kind of action of the oppressed against the oppressor is taken in fiction, we tend to call it heroic; when it happens in our real world streets, it is often critiqued as meeting violence with violence—an unjustified loss of composure under pressure.

Martin Luther King, Jr. wrote in a speech titled "The Other America" in 1953, that "America must see that riots do not develop out of thin air. In the final analysis, the riot is the language of the unheard. What is it that America has failed to hear? . . . As long as America postpones justice, we stand in the position of having these occurrences of riots and violence over and over again. Social justice and progress are the absolute guarantors of riot prevention." In 2020, Jesse Jackson explained that "Rioting is the voice of those who truly have no way to express themselves." And Shonda Craft notes that rioting can feel like a tangible solution when people "don't know what else to do with their fear, the anger and their sadness" (W. N. Staff 2020). Ibram X. Kendi writes about the ways in which political confrontation has been essential to change in the United States:

> Political confrontation and harassment is as civil as it is American. Evading confrontation as the children cry, as their oppressors cry for more cries, is as uncivil as it is un-American. Instead of encircling political confrontation and harassment in incivility, we should be recognizing the dividing line in American politics—a line that has continuously changed American history for better or worse, always to the chagrin of the gradual or do-nothing moderate Americans. The dividing line in American politics is constructive or destructive political confrontation and harassment. . . . Harassing political opponents is fully American and American history is full of it. If my ideological ancestors did not harass their political opponents, I would still be enslaved. I would still be segregated by law. I would still be one traffic stop away from death without any sustained movement insisting that my black life matters. (Kendi 2018)

The history of social change in America is punctuated by moments in which people, fed up with the status quo and tired of being silenced of erased, stood up—sometimes aggressively, sometimes violently—until their cries of pain were heard.

The forces that coalesce in the United States to marginalize and oppress black and brown bodies stem from the same position of dominance as the misogyny that allows violence against girls and women to thrive. It is the same force of dominance that enables corrupt officials and ineffective judiciaries to stand by when violence is done against people of color and women. White supremacy is a colonial legacy of oppression that has centered white men, legitimized the needs and desires of white men, and set up institutions that work primarily for white men. Historically, when others have asked for an equal place at the table they have been met with resistance, and then force. This is playing out now simultaneously as institutionalized violence against black and brown bodies, and as violence against girls and women. For those who are both black or brown and girls or women, the oppressions are even more compounded by these intersections.

The rhetoric of the President of the United States during this moment is eerily similar to that of the corrupt governments and judiciaries in the countries that have seen a rise in vigilante women's groups. On June 1, 2020,

Donald Trump declared that "Mayors and governors must establish an over-whelming law enforcement presence until the violence has been quelled. If a city or state refuses to take the actions that are necessary to defend the life and property of their residents, then I will deploy the United States military and quickly solve the problem for them" (Bowman 2020). His demand that governors and local officials take a harder line with protests in their individu-al states was coupled with calling them out as weak, and as fools, if they did not take him up on his recommendation that they call upon military force in regaining law and order in their cities: "Trump told governors that if they don't take back the streets and use force to confront protesters they would look like 'fools,' alarming several governors on the call as they communicat-ed privately. . . . 'You have to dominate. If you don't dominate, you're wasting your time,' he said. 'They're going to run over you. You're going to look like a bunch of jerks'" (Costa, Kim and Dawsey 2020). His calls have been so divisive that even representatives of various branches of the military are talking back, reminding him that the military is not designed to handle domestic concerns, with the Secretary of Defense publicly rejecting Trump's threat to deploy combat troops (Pengelly, et al. 2020).

In India, Nigeria, and Mexico volatile, violent, and divisive leaders have enabled a vacuum of power that has created pervasive corruption, such that many citizens do not even expect to find justice in those places. Those are the spaces where real life vigilantes have taken a hold, committed to justice for the oppressed even when they must break the so-called "law" to do it. What we are seeing right now in the United States is a group of people who are looking at their government and judiciary and accusing them of corruption and injustice. Wide ranging calls to defund the police and reform the criminal justice system are gaining traction, and some school districts, colleges, and universities have already broken agreements with police departments to pro-vide security and advisement (Beckett 2020). It has been made clear that there are entire groups of people in the United States, such as black and trans people, who have never expected to be treated fairly or justly by authority, and these changes echo the success of their outcry.

I am releasing a book into the world which asks readers to consider the possibility of the righteousness of vigilante violence in spaces where people are left unprotected. I have argued that it serves a particular function in real life in some parts of the world, and that it is a vehicle for empowerment in young adult fiction and comics in the United States. It is a vicarious escape and a space to explore the ways that girls and young women have worked through trauma in order to reclaim their sense of agency. This book is about fantasy violence that can be healing or constructive for the identity develop-ment of young adult readers and derives part of its theoretical frame from the experiences of real life vigilante women. This book does not posit violence as preferable to peace; rather, it starts from the position that we are not living in a peaceful world to begin with. The violence is always already there, and this book is about how girls and young women in young adult fiction and comics survive it.

The four chapters of this book serve as an exploration of characters who use violence in ways that are empowering for them, and which offer them the tools through which to protect others from harm.[1] This book resists the categorization of violence as an inherently negative act, considering the ways that it is used by girls and young women to make the world around them a better place. This book is about fiction subjects, but as cultural productions they are artifacts of their twenty-first century cultural moment, and as such they serve as mirrors that reflect back real-world problems like sexism, misogyny, and violence against women. Part of this reality is the statistics about sexual violence in the United States, that one in four girls experiences sexual abuse or sexual assault by the age of eighteen; that seven in ten girls are sexually harassed at some point in high school (Girls, Inc. 2020); that around forty percent of women and transgender, genderqueer, or gender non-conforming fourth year students report experiencing nonconsensual sexual contact involving force, incapacitation, coercion, absence of affirmative consent, and lack of ongoing voluntary agreement since first enrolling at school (Cantor, et al. 2020, 42). This book also considers the global context of violence against women as an epidemic, reaching unprecedented levels in the modern day. Using the actions of real vigilante women in India, Nigeria, and Mexico against the backdrop of massive atrocities, corrupt governments, and ineffective judiciaries as context for ways in which vigilante violence can be theorized as feminist, this book also provides an important analysis of the way that we read the representation of violence in fiction consumed by girls and women. The development of the teenage vigilante feminist super/heroine provides a character type found across young adult literature and media, providing an opportunity to think critically about the role of violence in the fantasy lives of girls and young women who are healing from trauma.

Investigating the teenage vigilante super/heroine, I used trauma, empowerment, violence, and agency as a trajectory of character development. The characters I wrote about all experience trauma as children or teens, which was a defining characteristic of their development into the heroines they became. In the cases I wrote about in this book, the traumas were all violent; Feyre is tortured and imprisoned in darkness by an evil Fae Queen, forcibly turned to Fae after she is murdered, and she is coerced into an intimate partner relationship that is volatile and manipulative; Scarlett and Gretchen were attacked by the Fenris as children, and have since been hunted by them their entire lives; X-23 was raised in a lab and forced to be a child assassin with a trigger scent developed to overcome her resistance, and was also forced into child prostitution to survive on the streets after she accidentally killed her mother; Jules is a rape survivor, and Ophelia experienced attempted rape, which fuels their pathway to vigilante justice on their college campus. Each trauma was a turning point, a moment of realization that they are vulnerable, and that no one is coming to their rescue. It is a trauma from which the characters must heal in order to reclaim the sense of agency that has been taken by the violence. Thinking about the ways that these characters experience and work through trauma puts this book in conversation with the interdisciplinary field of critical trauma studies, by thinking about the representation of trauma in cultural productions like literature and popular culture, and identifying the ways that trauma is treated as a personal, clinical, and collective cultural phenomenon. Young readers reading about trauma have the opportunity to both see their own experiences reflected in these stories, for those who have experienced it themselves, or to vicariously work through the trauma that permeates readers' consciousness simply by being raised as a girl in a world that tactily accepts violence against women. Since young adult readers use stories to work through their own identities and build familiarity and confidence about social issues, what they are consuming matters.

Each character develops a sense of agency that emerges as they find ways to cope with the pain of their trauma. The trauma is a loss of agency, because it is a negative bodily experience that leaves them feeling unsafe and unprotected in their own bodies. Each character searches for a way to reclaim that sense of agency. The process of their reclamation of agency begins when they have come to terms with their own vulnerability and recognized the ways in which they have been disempowered in their lives by factors beyond their control. They also realize that there is no one protecting others from the harms they experienced; those who have been tasked with their protection are corrupt, silent, or ineffective, and therefore lack the capacity to create change. In Feyre's case, this comes when she moves to the Night Court, and has the space to reflect on the coercive nature of her relationship with Tamlin, and all of the things that led her to think and do. After she is turned to Fae, which is also a mechanism by which agency is taken from her since she does not consent to the change, she realizes that she has the power and the capacity to change the world for those she loves. For X-23, agency begins when she recognizes that she can resist the full force of the trigger scent, and when she realizes that she can use her superpowers to protect and save— rather than only destroy and kill. Choice becomes her superpower, as she can choose to use her power as she wishes. In the stories of Scarlett and Gretchen, agency begins when they choose to hone their bodies and develop their skill with weaponry to feel some sense of control over their own lives and bodies, and so that they can hunt the Fenris who kill girls and young women with impunity. Lastly, for Jules agency also arrives when she decides to turn the tables on attackers by forging her own body into a weapon that can cause pain to those who have caused pain for so many others. Each character embraces their capacity for violence during this stage, and in so doing, shifts the meaning of that violence. Rather than a weapon of the patriarchy used against them, it becomes a toolkit in their own arsenal of defense and protection.

I argue that this movement from trauma to agency is one that empowers the characters within the stories, as well as the people around them. It is also important to think about the ways that a sense of belonging and empowerment is experienced by readers who witness this transformation. For empowerment to be feminist, it should be used toward collective changes, societal transformations, or the benefit of the community. In each of the cases I have written about in this book, the characters experience an empowerment that allows them to make the world safer for others. Feyre uses her power stop sexual assault, to create a more equal society for people of all genders, sexualities, and classes. X-23 uses her power, among other things, to save her family, stop sex trafficking, rescue mutants from experimentation by the Facility, and end other cloning experiments. Scarlett and Gretchen hunt the hunters, identifying themselves with a destiny to protect and defend all people against the Fenris. And Jules and Ophelia's vigilantism at Darlington University starts a conversation about changing campus rape culture and forces a push toward a more transparent and responsive community, administration, and judiciary. Their empowerment is not of the "girl power" variety, it is not about individual choice. It is about making the world a better place, especially for girls and young women.

This book reads violence for its utility as a mechanism of survival in a world that is already violent toward girls and women. The violence explored in this analysis is not violent for the sake of power or domination and does not read violence as preferable to peace. Rather, as identified in the introduction and throughout several of the chapters, violence against women is a global epidemic, and it is worsening. Reports of violence against girls and women are rising, while the arrest and prosecution rates for attackers is declining. Readers who may still feel as though violence is never the answer might ponder the challenge of survival in a violent world; if you, or your child, will die if you do not use violence against those who wish you harm, what would you do? This is a story of bad options. Were there no violence against girls and women, girls and women would not need to be violent in defense of themselves or their communities. But that is not anyone's reality, and that is reflected in the fiction worlds created in the texts explored in this book.

The teenage vigilante feminist super/heroine is a fictitious representation of a vicarious fantasy that so many girls and women have, to be physically capable of not only defending oneself from harm, but to also be able to protect others from harm as well and forge better worlds in the process. It is important for audiences to have these stories, in order to work through and process the realities of their own lives. It is also healthy for them to be able to see heroines who can overcome the odds and be agents of their own lives and destinies. Scholars such as Alison Graham-Bertolini, Aaronette White and Shagun Rastogi, Amana Fontanella-Khan, Jayne Gackenbach, Megan Seely, Anastasia Higginbotham, and Jocelyn A. Hollander have begun to theorize ways that violence can be used for feminist ends. Reading novels and comics and watching television shows with empowering superheroines who kick ass feels good, it feels cathartic, and it opens up our ideas of what is possible for girls and young women to accomplish. This book delves deeper into what is at stake when fiction violence feels empowering.

What makes this story uplifting is the ultimate endgame presented by each of the texts explored in this book. In offering stories in which the heroines are not violent for the sake of violence, but who are, in fact, working for the collective betterment of others, they offer a sense of hope. Despite the trauma and coercion that Feyre endures, her new world is one of healing, where consent and choice are prioritized, and people's right to wellness and happiness are celebrated. X-23 is offered a way to psychically heal from the pain of her past, and to escape the power of the trigger scent—which is a symbol of her inability to give consent for her entire childhood and teen years. She takes in the youngest of her clones, Gabby, and becomes, in a sense, the mother she never had. She has the power to save others from her own fate. Scarlett and Gretchen find allies in their work, and a sense of direction and purpose—destiny—in the path they choose. And Jules and Ophelia are celebrated and appreciated for the work they do; the vigilantes are welcomed with open arms by their peers, and their bystander reporting site is an instant success. At its core, this book is about violence. But it is also about the way that violence empowers the super/heroines to forge better endings for their own stories, and the stories of their communities.

NOTES

1. There are other super/heroines that could be added to this list. For example, Eleven from *Stranger Things* has an eerily similar trajectory to X-23/Laura Kinney, in terms of her growth in a lab for the sole purpose of becoming a weapon. She suffers from the same integration challenges that Laura does when she finally escapes the lab (Eleven at age twelve, Laura at age thirteen), and she comes into an understanding of her violent capacity as a necessary weapon against alien invasion and the end of the world. Also, Celaena Sardothien/Aelin Galathynius from Sarah J. Maas' *Throne of Glass* series, which begins as a (very loose) retelling of Cinderella. Aelin's parents are killed when she is a young child, and she is found by the King of Assassins nearly frozen to death in a riverbed. He offers her a choice to stay with him and be trained as an assassin, or to be cast-off in the streets; she chooses to be trained, changes her name to Celaena, and kills her first target at the age of nine. She is raised as a child prodigy assassin, treated brutally by the league's leader, and forced to excel at unspeakable violence in order to survive. She is framed for a crime and sent to prison in a labor camp so brutal that most people do not survive a year there. At her lowest moment she is released from prison to serve as the King's champion in a contest to the death, at the end of which lies her freedom. She spends the rest of her life, after freedom, to create the conditions in which others—especially chil-

dren—do not have to experience the trauma, torture, and torment that she did. As well, Kate Bishop/Hawkeye, from Marvel Comics' *Young Avengers* and her own comic title *Hawkeye*, has an origin story that begins with her rape in a New York City park on her way home from school. She never felt safe again after that night, and so she learned how to fight. As she recalls to Jessica Jones, "It doesn't matter how good your grades are—or how many hours you put in at the soup kitchen—you're not safe. Bad things happen. Things you can't control. Things that have nothing to do with you. And they will destroy you if you let them. Or you can try to learn from them . . . so that next time, you'll be prepared. So that—even if you never feel safe again—you can do your best to make sure that what happens to you never happens to anyone else" (*Young Avengers Special*, 2006, pp. 23–24, *Young Avengers Vol. 2; Family Matters*). She takes up kickboxing and self-defense classes, learns archery, hones her skills at making herself physically strong, eventually earning her place as a superheroine and private investigator (Stone and Feibel 2020).

Bibliography

Adichie, Chimimanda Ngozi. 2014. "I Decided to Call Myself a Happy Feminist." *The Guardian*. October 17, 2014. Accessed July 29, 2015. https://www.theguardian.com/books/2014/oct/17/chimamanda-ngozi-adichie-extract-we-should-all-be-feminists.
———. 2015. *We Should All Be Feminists*. Norwell, MA: Anchor Press.
American Association of University Women. 2020. *Know Your Rights: Sexual Harassment and Assault on Campus*. May 25, 2020. Accessed May 25, 2020. https://www.aauw.org/resources/legal/laf/title-ix/.
———. 2020. *Where We Stand: Sexual Harassment and Sexual Violence in School*. May 25, 2020. Accessed May 25, 2020. https://www.aauw.org/resources/policy/position-school-harassment/.
Anderson, Greta. 2020. "U.S. Publishes New Regulations on Campus Sexual Assault." *Inside Higher Ed*, May 7, 2020. Accessed May 20,2020. https://www.insidehighered.com/news/2020/05/07/education-department-releases-final-title-ix-regulations.
Armstrong, Paul. 2013. "Meet India's Red Brigade: The teens fighting back against rape." *CNN.com*, August 14, 2013. Accessed October 28, 2020. https://www.cnn.com/2013/08/13/world/asia/india-red-brigade/index.html.
Baldrich, Roxana. 2014. "Master's Thesis." *Taking the Law into Our Own Hands: Female Vigilantism in India and Mexico*. Paris: Sciences PO.
Ballard, Celeste, writer. *Sweet/Vicious*, Season 1, episode 4, "Tragic Kingdom." Directed by Brian Dannelly, featuring Eliza Bennett and Taylor Dearden. Aired December 6, 2016. Viacom Media Network, https://www.amazon.com/gp/video/detail/B01M3W4U4C/ref=atv_yv_hom_c_unkc_1_1
Beckett, Lois. 2020. "Minneapolis public school board votes to terminate its contract with police." *The Guardian*, June 2, 2020. Accessed August 15, 2020. https://www.theguardian.com/us-news/2020/jun/01/minneapolis-public-school-end-police-contract.
Biermann, Todd, writer. *Sweet/Vicious*, Season 1, episode 6, "Fearless." Directed by Todd Biermann, featuring Eliza Bennett and Taylor Dearden. Aired January 3, 2017. Viacom Media Network, https://www.amazon.com/gp/video/detail/B01M3W4U4C/ref=atv_yv_hom_c_unkc_1_1.
Black, M. C., K. C. Basile, M. J. Breiding, S. G. Smith, J. Chen, M. R. Stevens, M. L. Walters, and M. T. Merrick. 2011. *The National Intimate Partner and Sexual Violence Survey (NISVS): 2010 Summary Report*. Atlanta, GA: Center for Disease Control.
Bote, Joshua. 2019. "Two NYPD Detectives accused of raping teen in their custody won't get jail time." *USA Today*, August 30, 2019. Accessed August 15, 2020. https://

www.usatoday.com/story/news/nation/2019/08/30/nypd-detectives-accused-raping-teen-wont-get-jail-time/2166015001/.

Bowman, Tom. 2020. "Trump Threatens to Send U.S. Military to States to End Violent Protests." *NPR.org*, June 2, 2020. Accessed August 15, 2020. https://www.npr.org/2020/06/02/867578071/trump-threatens-to-send-u-s-military-to-states-to-end-violent-protests.

Brown, Jeffrey A. 2015. *Beyond Bombshells: The New Action Heroine in Popular Culture*. Jackson: University Press of Mississippi.

Brown, Sarah. 2020. "What Colleges Need to Know About the New Title IX Rules." *Chronicle of Higher Education*, May 6, 2020. Accessed August 15, 2020. https://www.chronicle.com/article/what-colleges-need-to-know-about-the-new-title-ix-rules/.

Burr, Ty. 2015. "'*Hunting Ground*' maps out atrocity of campus rape." *The Boston Globe*. March 13, 2015. G6.

Cantor, David, Bonnie Fisher, Susan Chibnall, Shauna Harps, Reanne Townsend, Gail Thomas, Hyunshik Lee, Vanessa Kranz, Randy Herbison, and Kristen Madden. 2020. *Report on the AAU Campus Climate Survey on Sexual Assault and Misconduct*. Rockville, MD: Westat.

Casper, Monica J., and Eric Wertheimer, eds. 2016. *Critical Trauma Studies: Understanding Violence, Conflict and Memory in Everyday Life*. New York: NYU Press.

Castro, Ingrid E., and Jessica Clark, eds. 2019. *Child and Youth Agency in Science Fiction: Travel, Technology, Time*. Lanham, MD: Lexington Books.

CNN. 2013. "Meet Indias Red Brigade: The teens fighting back against rape." *CNN.com*, August 17, 2013.Accessed October 30, 2020. https://www.youtube.com/watch?v=frK5EVXVgFU.

Cocca, Carolyn. 2016. *Superwomen: Gender, Power, and Representation*. London: Bloomsbury.

Cockburn, Cynthia, and Cynthia Enloe. 2012. "Militarism, Patriarchy, and Peace Movements." *International Feminist Journal of Politics*, 550–557.

Costa, Robert, Seung Min Kim, and Josh Dawsey. 2020. "Trump calls governors 'weak,' urges them to use force against unruly protests." *The Washington Post*, June 1, 2020. Accessed November 5, 2020. https://www.washingtonpost.com/politics/trump-governors-george-floyd-protests/2020/06/01/430a6226-a421-11ea-b619-3f9133bbb482_story.html.

Coulthard, Lisa. 2007. "Killing Bill: Rethinking Feminism and Film Violence." In *Interrogating Post-Feminism: Gender and the Politics of Pop Culture*, by Yvonne Tasker and Diane Negra. Durham, NC: Duke University Press. 153–175.

Cruger, Katherine. 2017. "Men are Stronger; Women Endure: A Critical Analysis of the Throne of Glass and The Mortal Instruments YA Fantasy Series." *Journal of Media Critiques*, 115–132.

D'Amore, Laura Mattoon. 2017. "Vigilante Feminism: Revising Trauma, Abduction, and Assault in American Fairy-Tale Revisions." *Marvels and Tales*, 386–405.

de Beaumont, Jeanne-Marie LePrince. 1783. "Beauty and the Beast." In *The Young Misses Magazine, Containing Dialogues between a Governess and Several Young Ladies of Quality Her Scholars*, by Madam Prince de Beaumont, 45–67. London: C. Nourse.

de Lauretis, Teresa. 1993. "Upping the Anti (sic) in Feminist Theory." In *The Cultural Studies Reader*, by ed. Simon During, 307–319. New York: Routledge.

Deffenbacher, Kristina. 2014. "Rape Myths' Twilight and Women's Paranormal Revenge in Romantic and Urban Fantasy Fiction." *The Journal of Popular Culture*.

Del Negro, Janice M. 2017. "Telling Stories to Young Adults." In *Engaging Teens with Story: How to Inspire and Educate Youth with Storytelling*, by Janice M. Del Negro and Melanie A., eds. Kimball. Santa Barbara, CA: ABC-CLIO.

Del Negro, Janice M., Kimball, Melanie A., eds. 2017. *Engaging Teens with Story: How to Inspire and Educate Youth with Storytelling*. Santa Barbara, CA: ABC-CLIO.

Earle, Harriet E. H. 2017. *Comics, Trauma, and the New Art of War*. Jackson: University Press of Mississippi.

End Rape on Campus. n.d. *Frequently Asked Questions*. Accessed May 25, 2020. https://endrapeoncampus.org/faq.

———. n.d. *The Campus Accountability Map*. Accessed May 25, 2020. https://endrapeoncampus.org/map-about#maplearnmore.

Fahs, Breanne. 2016. "Naming Sexual Trauma: On the Political Necessity of Nuance in Rape and Sex Offender Discourses." In *Critical Trauma Studies: Understanding Violence, Conflict, and Memory in Everyday Life*, by Monica J. Casper and Eric, eds. Wertheimer. New York: NYU Press.

Feinman, Ilene Rose. 2000. *Citizenship Rites: Feminist Soldiers and Feminist Antimilitarists*. New York: NYU Press.

Fernandez, Manny. 2019. "You Have to Pay With Your Body: The Hidden Nightmare of Sexual Violence on the Border." *The New York Times*, March 3, 2019. Accessed August 15, 2020. https://www.nytimes.com/2019/03/03/us/border-rapes-migrant-women.html.

Ferre-Sadurny, Luis. 2019. "Teenager Accused of rape Deserves Leniency Because He's From a Good Family, Judge Says." *The New York Times*, July 2, 2019. Accessed August 15, 2020. https://www.nytimes.com/2019/07/02/nyregion/judge-james-troiano-rape.html.

Fontanella-Khan, Amana. 2013. *Pink Sari Revolution: A Tale of Women and Power in India*. New York: W. W. Norton & Company, Inc.

Frankel, Valerie Estelle. 2017. *Superheroines and the Epic Journey: Mythic Themes in Comics, Film and Television*. Jefferson, NC: McFarland.

Frieder, Jared and Celeste Ballard, writers. *Sweet/Vicious*, Season 1, episode 8, "Back to Black." Directed by Elodie Keene, featuring Eliza Bennett and Taylor Dearden. Aired January 17, 2017. Viacom Media Network, https://www.amazon.com/gp/video/detail/B01M3W4U4C/ref=atv_yv_hom_c_unkc_1_1

Gackenbach, Jayne, Arielle Boyes, Ann Sinyard, Carson Flockhart, and Caterina Snyder. 2016. "The Impact of Digital Technology on Children's Dreams." In *Sleep Monsters and Superheroes: Empowering Children Through Creative Dreamplay*, by Clare R. Johnson and Jean M., eds. Campbell, 92–93. Santa Barbara, CA: Praeger.

Girls, Inc. January 2020 Accessed May 25, 2020. https://girlsinc.org/girls-too/.

Goodenberger, Jayne. 2015. *Then and Now: A Look at the Messages Young Adult Fiction Sends Teenage Girls in the 1970s and the 2000s*. Master's Thesis. Columbus: Ohio Dominican University.

Graham-Bertolini, Alison. 2011. *Vigilante Women in Contemporary American Fiction*. New York: Palgrave MacMillan.

Hare, Breanna. 2014. "Beyonce opens up on feminism, fame and marriage." *CNN Enternatinment*. December 12, 2014. Accessed May 25, 2020. http://www.cnn.com/2014/12/12/showbiz/music/beyonce-feminism-yours-and-mine-video/index.html.

HeForShe.org. 2014. Accessed May 27, 2015. http://www.heforshe.org/.

Hentges, Sarah. 2018. *Girls on Fire: Heroines in Young Adult Dystopian Literature*. Jefferson, NC: McFarland.

Herman, Emma. 2014. "Emma Watson's UN gender equality campaign is an invitation to men, too." *The Guardian*. October 3, 2014. Accessed May 25, 2020. https://www.theguardian.com/global-development/poverty-matters/2014/oct/03/emma-watsons-un-gender-equality-campaign-is-an-invitation-to-men-too.

Higginbotham, Anastasia. 2019. "Sex Worth Fighting For." In *Yes Means Yes: Visions of Female Sexual Power and a World Without Rape*, by Jacklyn Friedman and Jessica, eds. Valenti. San Francisco: Seal Press.

Hollander, Jocelyn A. 2016. "The Importance of self-defense training for sexual violence prevention." *Feminism & Psychology*, 207–226.

hooks, bell. 1984. *Feminist Theory: From Margin to Center*. Boston: South End Press.

———. 2000. *Feminism is for Everybody*. Boston: South End Press.

———. 2013. *Writing Beyond Race: Living Theory and Practice*. New York: Taylor and Francis.

———. 2015. *Are You Still a Slave?* The New School, New York. May 6.

———. 2016. "Moving Beyond Pain." *The bell hooks Institute*. May 9. Accessed May 25, 2020. http://www.bellhooksinstitute.com/blog/2016/5/9/moving-beyond-pain.

Huggins, Sujin. 2017. "Storytelling and Young Adults: An Overview of Contemporary Practices." In *Engaging Teens with Story: How to Inspire and Educate Youth with Storytelling*, by Janice M. Del Negro and Melanie A. Kimball. Santa Barbara: ABC-CLIO.

The Hunting Ground. 2015. Directed by Amy Ziering and Kirby Dick.

Interesting, All That's. 2015. "I Am Revenge: The Unheard Stories Of Female Vigilantes." *All That's Interesting*, September 11, 2015. Accessed August 15, 2020. https://allthatsinterest ing.com/female-vigilantes.

Jackson, Debra. 2016. "Answering the Call: Crisis Intervention and Rape Survivor Advocacy as Witnessing Trauma." In *Critical Trauma Studies: Violence, Conflict, and Memory in Everyday Life*, by Monica J. Casper and Eric, eds. Wertheimer. New York: NYU Press.

Johnson, Clare R., and Jean M., eds. Campbell. 2016. *Sleep Monsters and Superheroes: Empowering Children Through Creative Dreamplay*. Santa Barbara, CA: Praeger.

Kaur, Harmeet. 2019. "Black kids go missing at a higher rate than white kids. Here's why we don't hear about them." *CNN.com*, November 3, 2019. Accessed October 16, 2020. https://www.cnn.com/2019/11/03/us/missing-children-of-color-trnd/index.html.

Kendi, Ibram X. 2018. "More Devoted to Order Than to Justice." *The Atlantic*, June 28, 2018. Accessed August 15, 2020. https://www.theatlantic.com/ideas/archive/2018/06/incivility/563963/.

Kimball, Melanie A. 2017. "Folk and Fairy Tales and Popular Media: Strong Females, Rehabilitated Witches, and Villains We Love to Hate." In *Engaging Teens with Story: How to Inspire and Educate Youth with Storytelling*, by Janice M. Del Negro and Melanie A. Kimball, eds. Santa Barbara, CA: Praeger.

Kokesh, Jessica and Miglena Sternadori. 2015. "The Good, the Bad, and the Ugly: A Qualitative Study of How Young Adult Fiction Affects Identity Construction." *Atlantic Journal of Communication*.

Kyle, Craig, and Christopher Yost (w), Billy Tan (p), Jon Sibal (i). 2006. "*X-23: Innocence Lost.*" Collects *X-23* (2005) #1–#6. New York: Marvel Comics.

Kyle, Craig and Christopher Yost (w), Clayton Crain (a). 2011. "*X-Force Vol. 1: Angels and Demons.*" Collects *X-Force* (2008) #1–#6. New York: Marvel Comics.

Kyle, Craig and Christopher Yost (w), Clayton Crain, Mike Choi, and Sonia Oback (a). 2010. "*X-Force Vol. 3: Not Forgotten.*" Collects *X-Force* (2009) #12–#13, and #17–#20. New York: Marvel Comics.

Kyle, Craig and Christopher Yost (w), Mark Brooks and Paul Pelletier (p), Jaime Mendoza, Jay Leisten, and Dave Meikis (i). 2006. "*New X-Men: Childhood's End Vol. 1.*" Collects *New X-Men* (2004) #20–#23. New York: Marvel Comics.

Kyle, Craig, and Christopher Yost (w), Mike Choi and Sonia Oback (a). 2007. "*X-23: Target X.*" Collects *X-23: Target X* (2006) #1–#6. New York: Marvel Comics.

Kyle, Craig and Christopher Yost (w), Paco Medina (p), Juan Vlasco (i). 2006. "*New X-Men: Childhood's End Vol. 4.*" Collects *New X-Men* (2004) #33–#36. New York: Marvel Comics.

Lasher, Amanda, writer. *Sweet/Vicious*, Season 1, episode 3, "Sucker." Directed by Brian Dannelly, featuring Eliza Bennett and Taylor Dearden. Aired November 29, 2016, Viacom Media Network, https://www.amazon.com/gp/video/detail/B01M3W4U4C/ref=atv_yv_hom_c_unkc_1_1.

———. *Sweet/Vicious*, Season 1, episode 9, "An Innocent Man." Directed by Leslie Libman, featuring Eliza Bennett and Taylor Dearden. Aired January 24, 2017. Viacom Media Network, https://www.amazon.com/gp/video/detail/B01M3W4U4C/ref=atv_yv_hom_c_unkc_1_1.

Lavin, Maud. 2012. *Push Comes to Shove: New Images of Aggressive Women*. Cambridge: MIT Press.

Lindsey, Treva. 2020. "The urgent crisis of missing Black women and girls." *Women's Media Center News & Features*, February 20, 2020. Accessed October 16, 2020. https://womensmediacenter.com/news-features/the-urgent-crisis-of-missing-black-women-and-girls.

Liu, Marjorie (w), Sana Takeda and Phil Noto (a). 2012. "*X-23 Vol. 3: Don't Look Back.*" Collects *X-23* (2011) #17–#21. New York: Marvel Comics.

Liu, Marjorie (w), Will Conrad (a). 2011. "*X-23 Vol. 1: The Killing Dream.*" Collects *X-23* (2010–2011) #1–#6. New York: Marvel Comics.

Lorde, Audre. 2007. "The Master's Tools Will Never Dismantle the Master's House (1979)." In *The Essential Feminist Reader*, by Estelle Freedman, 331–335. New York: The Modern Library.

Maas, Sarah J. 2016. *A Court of Thorns and Roses*. New York: Bloomsbury USA.

————. 2017. *A Court of Mist and Fury*. New York: Bloomsbury USA.

————. 2018. *A Court of Wings and Ruin*. New York: Bloomsbury USA.

Manne, Kate. 2018. *Down Girl: The Logic of Misogyny*. New York: Oxford University Press.

Maxwell, Claire, and Peter Aggleton. 2012. "Bodies and Agentic Practice in Young Women's Sexual and Intimate Relationships." *Sociology*, 306–321.

McDonough, Megan. 2019. "From Tribute to Mockingjay: Representations of Katniss Everdeen's Agency in the Hunger Games Series." In *Child and Youth Agency in Science Fiction: Travel, Technology, Time*, by Ingrid E. Castro and Jessica Clark, eds. Lanham, MD: Lexington Books.

McLaughlin, Eliott C. and Sara Sidner. 2016. "Oklahoma City cop convicted of rape sentenced to 263 years in prison." *CNN.com*, January 22, 2016. Accessed October 16, 2020. https://www.cnn.com/2016/01/21/us/oklahoma-city-officer-daniel-holtzclaw-rape-sentencing/index.html.

Miller, Chanel. 2019. *Know My Name: A Memoir*. New York: Viking.

Miller, Joshua Rhett. 2019. "Ohio parole officer Keith Cooper charged with sexually assaulting female parolees." *New York Post*, July 25, 2019. Accessed August 15, 2020. https://nypost.com/2019/07/25/ohio-parole-officer-keith-cooper-charged-with-sexually-assaulting-female-parolees/.

Nikolajeva, Maria. 2005. *Aesthetic Approaches to Children's Literature: An Introduction*. Lanham, MD: Scarecrow Press.

Office, Press. 2020. "Secretary DeVos Takes Historic Action to Strengthen Title IX Protections for All Students." *U.S. Department of Education*. May 6. Accessed May 9, 2020. https://www.ed.gov/news/press-releases/secretary-devos-takes-historic-action-strengthen-title-ix-protections-all-students.

————. 2020. "Secretary DeVos Takes Historic Action to Strengthen Title IX Protections for All Students." *ed.gov*. May 6. Accessed May 25, 2020. https://www.ed.gov/news/press-releases/secretary-devos-takes-historic-action-strengthen-title-ix-protections-all-students.

Okeowo, Alexis. 2015. "The Women Fighting Boko Haram." *The New Yorker*, December 22, 2015. Accessed August 15, 2020. https://www.newyorker.com/news/news-desk/the-women-fighting-boko-haram.

Oliver, Kelly. 2013. *Hunting Girls: Sexual Violence from The Hunger Games to Campus Rape*. New York: Columbia University Press.

Pearce, Jackson. 2010. *Sisters Red*. New York: Little, Brown Books for Young Readers.

————. 2011. *Sweetly*. New York: Little, Brown Books for Young Readers.

Pengelly, Martin, Vivian Ho, Maanvi Singh, and Julia Carrie Wong. 2020. "Protests continue as US defense secretary rejects Trump's demand for troops." *The Guardian*, June 3, 2020. Accessed November 5, 2020. https://www.theguardian.com/us-news/2020/jun/03/george-floyd-protests-trump-troops-esper.

Phillips, Leah Beth. 2016. "Myth (Un)Making: The Adolescent Female Body in Mythopeic YA Fantasy." *PhD Thesis*. 2016: University of Warwick, April.

Pipher, Mary, and Sara Pipher Gilliam. 2019. *Reviving Ophelia: Saving the Selves of Adolescent Girls*. New York: Riverhead Books.

Quesada, Joe (w), Joshua Middleton and Robert Teranishi (a), "*NYX: Wannabe*." 2011. Collects *NYX* #1–#7. New York: Marvel Comics.

Rahim, M. 2014. "Developmental trauma disorder: an attachment-based perspective." *Clinical Child Psychiatry*, 548–560.

Robinson, Jennifer Kaytin, writer. *Sweet/Vicious*, Season 1, episode 1, "The Blueprint." Directed by Joseph Kahn and Rebecca Thomas, featuring Eliza Bennett and Taylor Dearden. Aired November 15, 2016. Viacom Media Network, https://www.amazon.com/gp/video/detail/B01M3W4U4C/ref=atv_yv_hom_c_unkc_1_1.

————. *Sweet/Vicious*, Season 1, episode 2, "The Writing's On the Wall." Directed by Joseph Kahn, featuring Eliza Bennett and Taylor Dearden. Aired November 22, 2016. Viacom Media Network, https://www.amazon.com/gp/video/detail/B01M3W4U4C/ref=atv_yv_hom_c_unkc_1_1.

———. *Sweet/Vicious*, Season 1, episode 7, "Heartbreaker." Directed by Elodie Keene, featuring Eliza Bennett and Taylor Dearden. Aired January 10, 2017. Viacom Media Network, https://www.amazon.com/gp/video/detail/B01M3W4U4C/ref=atv_yv_hom_c_unkc_1_1.

———. *Sweet/Vicious*, Season 1, episode 10, "Pure Heroine." Directed by Leslie Libman, featuring Eliza Bennett and Taylor Dearden. Aired January 31, 2017. Viacom Media Network, https://www.amazon.com/gp/video/detail/B01M3W4U4C/ref=atv_yv_hom_c_unkc_1_1.

Seely, Megan. 2007. *Fight Like a Girl: How to be a Fearless Feminist*. New York: NYU Press.

Sibielski, Rosalind. 2019. "Reviving Cinderella: Contested Feminism and Conflicting Models of Female Empowement in 21st Century Film and Video Adaptations of Cinderella." *Quarterly Review of Film and Video*. 584–610.

Smith, Emily E. 2014. "Rape Survivors Tweets Answer the question." *Oregon Live*, March 21, 2014.

Staff, Mayo Clinic. 2011. *Self-Injury/cutting*. June 9, 2011. Accessed May 25, 2020. https://www.mayoclinic.org/diseases-conditions/self-injury/symptoms-causes/syc-20350950.

Staff, NPR. 2016. "What's Being Done to Address the Country's Backlog of Untested Rape Kits." *NPR.org*. January 17, 2016. Accessed May 25, 2020. http://www.npr.org/2016/01/17/463358406/whats-being-done-to-address-the-countrys-backlog-of-untested-rape-kits.

Stevens, Heidi. 2017. "What Were You Wearing?" *The Chicago Tribune*, September 14, 2017. Accessed August 15, 2020. https://www.chicagotribune.com/columns/heidi-stevens/ct-life-stevens-thursday-ku-what-were-you-wearing-0914-story.html.

Stone, Will and Carrie Feibel. 2020. "From 'Flash Bangs' To 'Rubber' Bullets: The Very Real Risks of 'Riot Control Agents.' *NPR.org*, May 6, 2020. Accessed August 15, 2020. https://www.kunc.org/npr-news/2020-06-06/from-flash-bangs-to-rubber-bullets-the-very-real-risks-of-riot-control-agents.

Suico, Terri. 2019. "Fractured Friendships and Finding Oneself: Adolescent Girls Losing Friends but Finding Their Voices in Recent Young Adult Literature." In *Representing Agency in Popular Culture: Children and Youth on Page, Screen, and In Between*, by Jessica Clark and Ingrid E. Castro. Lanham, MD: Lexington Books.

Sweet/Vicious. Directed by Stacy Sher, Jennifer Kaytin Robinson and Amanda Lasher. 2016–2017. Performed by Viacom Media Networks.

Taylor, Tom. 2016–2018. "All-New Wolverine." New York: Marvel Comics.

Taylor, Tom (w), David Lopez and David Navarrot (a). *"All-New Wolverine Vol. 1: The Four Sisters."* Collects *All-New Wolverine* (2015) #1–#6. 2016. New York: Marvel Comics.

Taylor, Tom (w), Nic Virella, Scott Hanna, and Djibril Morrisette-Phan (a). *"All-New Wolverine Vol. 3: Enemy of the State."* Collects *All-New Wolverine* (2015) #13–#18. 2017. New York: Marvel Comics.

Tembo, Kwasu David, and Muireann B. Crowley. 2019. "In the Shadow of the Claw: Jubilee, X-23, and the Mutated Possibilities of Youth Agency across Generations in the World of the X-Men." In *Child and Youth Agency in Science Fiction: Travel, Technology, Time*, by Ingrid E. Castro and Jessica Clark, eds. Lanham, MD: Lexington Books.

Turner, Kay, and Pauline Greenhill. 2012. "Introduction: Once Upon a Queer Time." In *Transgressive Tales: Queering the Grimms*, by Kay Turner and Pauline, eds. Greenhill, 1–24. Detroit, MI: Wayne State University Press.

Valenti, Jessica. 2007. *Full Frontal Feminism: A Young Woman's Guide to Why Feminism Matters*. San Francisco: Seal Press.

———. 2011. "SlutWalks and the Future of Feminism." The Washington Post, June 1, 2011.

van der Kolk, Bessel A. 2005. "Developmental Trauma Disorder: Toward a rational diagnosis for children with complex trauma histories." *Psychiatric Annals*, 401–408.

Vares, Tiina. 2001. "Action Heroines and Female Viewers: What Women Have to Say." In *Reel Knockouts: Violent Women in the Movies*, by Martha McCaughey and Neal King. Austin: University of Texas Press.

Veach, M. Scott, writer. *Sweet/Vicious*, Season 1, episode 5, "All Eyez on Me." Directed by Todd Biermann, featuring Eliza Bennett and Taylor Dearden. Aired December 13, 2016. Viacom Media Network, https://www.amazon.com/gp/video/detail/B01M3W4U4C/ref=atv_yv_hom_c_unkc_1_1.

Wade, Lisa. 2017. "Rape on campus: Athletes, status, and the sexual assault crisis." *The Conversation*, March 6, 2017. Accessed on October 30, 2020. https://theconversation.com/rape-on-campus-athletes-status-and-the-sexual-assault-crisis-72255.

Walker, Whitney. 2001. "Why I Fight Back." In *Listen Up: Voices from the Next Feminist Generation*, by ed. Barbara Findlen, 126–132. Berkeley, CA: Seal Press.

WHAS11 News Staff. 2020. "Why do protests escalate into riots? Martin L. King, Jr. explained it 53 years ago." *WHAS11.com*, June 3, 2020. Accessed August 15, 2020. https://www.whas11.com/article/news/local/why-riot-louisville-minneapolis-breonna-taylor-george-floyd-police/417-51a9bf89-c9be-4c53-8462-05215094f86a.

White, Aaronette, and Shagun Rastogi. 2009. "Justice by Any Means Necessary: Vigilantism among Indian Women." *Feminism and Psychology*, 313–327.

Williams, Christy. 2010. "The Shoe Still Fits: Ever After and the Pursuit of a Feminist Cinderella." In *Fairy Tale Films: Visions of Ambiguity*, by Pauline Greenhill and Sidney Eve, eds. Matrix, 99–115. Logan: Utah State University Press.

———. 2018. "Ambiguous Villains and Fairy-Tale Monsters in Kelly Link's 'The Cinderella Game.'" *Journal of the Fantastic in the Arts*.

Index

About the Author

Laura Mattoon D'Amore, PhD, is associate professor of cultural studies at Roger Williams University. Her research interests coalesce around feminist analysis of popular literature and media, with particular focus on the representation of girls and women. She has published extensively on comics and fairy tale retellings and was a featured expert on women in comics for the History Channel documentary series *Superheroes Decoded* (2017). Her previous books include *Smart Chicks on Screen* (2014), *We Are What We Remember* (2012), and *Bound by Love* (2011).